'An inspirational and accessible synthesis of business and organization management, psychology and brain science, brought to life with vivid and engaging anecdotes.'

Trevor Robbins, Professor of Cognitive Neuroscience,
University of Cambridge

'Highly practical yet deeply substantive, *The Performance Curve* is a masterful synthesis of the best of what we know about how to become the better version of ourselves we were meant to be.'

Robert Kegan, Harvard University, co-author of
Immunity to Change *and* An Everyone Culture

'Carries an important message for boards and executive teams seeking practical ways to build the social capital of their organizations.'

Paul Coombes, Chairman, Centre for Corporate Governance,
London Business School

'You couldn't ask for a better, more credible guide to raising your professional game and getting more from your life.'

David Morley, MD and Head of Europe at CDPQ.
Former CEO and Executive Chairman of Allen & Overy

'A very engaging and thought-provoking read.'

Elona Mortimer-Zhika, CEO, IRIS Software Group

'I can't think of a more timely and valuable book to help us navigate the changes in mindset we need to perform and thrive, today and in the future.'

Mark Joseph, CEO, Mobitas Advisors

'These methods help individuals to develop their leadership muscles and sustainable performance, and businesses to build an effective pipeline for talent and a growth-oriented culture.'

Janet Dekker, EVP Human Resources, Safran Aircraft Engines

'Compelling and full of new insights for unleashing individual and organizational performance.'

Heather Bock PhD., Global Chief Learning Officer, Hogan Lovells

'This is an important book. It goes beyond the platitudes of "look after yourself to be your best" and provides evidence-based tools for maximizing your potential and driving sustained organizational performance.'

Colin Price, Former Global Managing Partner,
Organization Practice, McKinsey & Co.

'A comprehensive guide to being your best in today's uncertain world and to building winning teams that get breakthrough results.'

Chris de Lapuente, Chairman and CEO,
LVMH Selective Retailing, Perfumes & Cosmetics

'Practically distils a wide variety of highly effective approaches to enable leadership success in a post-conventional world. Read it and be better.'

Nicolas Ceasar, Head of Leadership Development and Coaching,
NatWest Group

'A manifesto for aiming higher, individually and collectively.'

Sharon Toye, Founder of Leadership Mindset Partners
and author of Accelerating Performance

'Highlights the importance of lifelong learning for developing and maintaining our best cognitive function and wellbeing.'

Barbara J Sahakian, Professor of Clinical Neuropsychology,
University of Cambridge

'Offers an insightful map for development which has breadth and depth, and provides solid handholds for the climb to performance.'

David Rooke, Founder, Harthill Consulting

'*The Performance Curve* goes deep into the catalysts that drive effectiveness and well-being. Highly recommended.'

Tsun-yan Hsieh, Chairman, LinHart Group and
Senior Partner Emeritus, McKinsey & Co.

'Everyone will learn something from this excellent book on development and performance. The clear frameworks, relatable personal anecdotes and practical suggestions make *The Performance Curve* an indispensable read for anyone looking to achieve both effectiveness and well-being.'

Dena McCallum, Co-Founder, Eden McCallum

Laura Watkins and **Vanessa Dietzel**

THE PERFORMANCE CURVE

Maximize

your potential at work

while strengthening your well-being

BLOOMSBURY BUSINESS

LONDON · OXFORD · NEW YORK · NEW DELHI · SYDNEY

Laura: To Mark and Maria – always inspiring, never forgotten.
Vanessa: To KB, my biggest catalyst.

BLOOMSBURY BUSINESS
Bloomsbury Publishing Plc
50 Bedford Square, London, WC1B 3DP, UK
29 Earlsfort Terrace, Dublin 2, Ireland

BLOOMSBURY, BLOOMSBURY BUSINESS and the Diana logo are trademarks
of Bloomsbury Publishing Plc

First published in Great Britain 2021

A catalogue record for this book is available from the British Library

Library of Congress Cataloguing-in-Publication data has been applied for

ISBN: 978-1-4729-8554-5; eBook: 978-1-4729-8552-1

2 4 6 8 10 9 7 5 3 1

Typeset by Deanta Global Publishing Services, Chennai, India
Printed and bound in Great Britain by CPI Group (UK) Ltd, Croydon CR0 4YY

To find out more about our authors and books visit www.bloomsbury.com
and sign up for our newsletters

Contents

Translate your purpose into reality
Build 'habits of purpose'

Defining paradoxical thinking
Why does paradoxical thinking provide fuel?
A beautiful paradox
Practising paradoxical thinking: five steps

PART THREE: The Connection Catalyst
How to Build Developmental Relationships

The connection catalyst of the performance curve
What to find in the chapters of Part 3: connection catalyst
How emotional bond helps us move on the performance curve
The source of emotional bond: vulnerability and empathy
The basis for vulnerability and empathy: socio-emotional cognition
How to build more emotional bond

The essence of developmental relationships: emotional bond
    and stretch
What happens when we lack emotional bond or stretch?
How to build developmental relationships: developmental
    conversations

The three mindsets of performance curve cultures
Building habits of a performance curve culture
Role-modelling a performance curve culture
Using training to cultivate a performance curve culture

Redefining performance: the virtuous circle of effectiveness and well-being

We only have one life. What would make yours a life well lived?

Our guess is that you want to maximize your potential in some way and reach certain goals, such as through your work, studies or community involvement. No doubt you also want to be healthy (mentally and physically), enjoy fulfilling relationships, and generally feel happy. In essence, you want to be *effective* and have *well-being*.

The performance curve is the path to achieve exactly that. The very first step is to stop seeing performance in its narrow sense of getting results, and instead broaden its definition to match what most of us want out of life. In *The Performance Curve, 'performance' means being effective and having well-being*.

The good news is that effectiveness and well-being can be synergistic: when combined, they can lead to higher overall performance. Doing our best is easier when we feel our best, and vice versa.

The bad news is that, in reality, most people are caught in a battle between effectiveness and well-being. Take our client Nick, for example, an executive in a large organization and single dad. Ambitious about wanting to leave a mark on the world and fiercely protective of his relationship with his daughter, the hours in the day just did not seem enough. Smart and self-aware, he tried mindfulness and various productivity tools. They helped him keep the balls in the air, but nothing stopped him experiencing each day as a tense and draining juggling act. As a last resort, he signed up to a gym with childcare, hoping regular exercise would help him feel more energized and balanced. But, instead of getting on the treadmill, he started putting his daughter into the gym's childcare on weekends to catch up on work and personal admin. In order to be effective, he traded-off his well-being further. Your situation may look very different to Nick's, but do you also find yourself making painful compromises, or would you like better results for the efforts you put in?

This struggle between effectiveness and well-being is also visible at the collective level. Even before the COVID-19 pandemic, we were facing economic and environmental issues, with many countries seeing declining health and social well-being trends, including growing concerns about well-being in the workplace. Our world is increasingly VUCA (Volatile, Uncertain, Complex, Ambiguous) and the pandemic has not only highlighted how interrelated economic, social and environmental issues are, but also our difficulties in dealing with them. The need to find effective solutions, whilst taking care of well-being, is greater than ever.

So, individually and collectively, how can we build a virtuous circle of effectiveness and well-being, for a life well lived and to better meet the complex challenges of our time? In the past 25 years of helping people and organizations be their best, and being personal development junkies ourselves, we have developed and tested many approaches. We have discovered that the best results do not come from surface-level 'hacks', but rather from methods that evolve our *inner operating system*: the deep wiring in our brain that guides how we function in the world. Often outside of our awareness, it determines how we make sense of situations, prioritize what matters, react emotionally, and take action. Like a computer's operating system, our inner operating system can be adapted to be stronger, especially when facing new demands. These adaptations help us dissolve the trade-off between effectiveness and well-being and unlock higher performance with greater ease.

Developing our inner operating system to be on this virtuous circle of effectiveness and well-being is what we call *being on the performance curve*. On the performance curve, we can harness the gifts that challenges contain, and find fulfilment in life's ups and downs, to maximize our potential and strengthen our well-being. By contrast, we refer to the path Nick was on as the *boom-and-bust curve*, characterized by struggle and unused potential.

This book lays out the *three catalysts* that help us be on the performance curve: *wisdom, fuel and connection*. Part 1 (the wisdom catalyst) lays out the core components of our inner operating system – mindsets, emotions and habits – and how to work with them. In Part 2 (the fuel catalyst), we share how to sustain the continuous development of our inner operating system day-to-day and over the long-haul. And in Part 3 (the connection catalyst), we cover how to build relationships and environments that bring the best out in ourselves and others.

What you will get from this book

The Performance Curve offers you a path for developing your inner operating system to help you work and live better. As a consolidation of our combined work and life experience, it is underpinned by cutting-edge neuroscience and adult development psychology, as well as more practical knowledge from experience-based traditions and therapies. We have also conducted two dozen in-depth research interviews with remarkable individuals who we observe have made strides towards this broader vision of performance. Their lives and ways of maintaining high performance are quite different, but they share a focus on developing their inner operating system to fuel their activities and accomplishments. We have selected 10 of these individuals from different walks of life and corners of the globe to bring alive the ideas in this book.

You will hear from renowned cellist Yo-Yo Ma, who has spent almost six decades seeking to bring his best to connect with and inspire others through his music. We also feature Margareth (Maggie) Henriquez, CEO of the Krug Champagne house, whose authenticity and learning spirit have helped her forge an adventurous career in challenging markets. Tom Rippin, the founder and CEO of On Purpose, is growing a community of leaders who seek to build an economy that works for all. You will also encounter economics professor Eric Beinhocker, media executive Luke Bradley-Jones, CEO of a medical devices manufacturer Juan Jose Gonzalez, round-the-world pilot Gaby Kennard, CEO of Teach For All Wendy Kopp, international development and humanitarian leader Lorina McAdam, and education institution builder Pramath Sinha. We have described each of them in the summary at the end of Chapter 1. We are grateful for their courage and generosity in giving us a peek into how they evolve their operating systems. We hope you enjoy meeting them and take inspiration from them as much as we have done, without perceiving that we put them on a pedestal and deny them their human flaws or room for further growth.

We base the book on academic research, but keep it practical without straying into oversimplification or popularization of the science. We also build on the ideas of others who have focused on specific aspects of the performance curve. Some of what we cover in a page has had several entire books written about it. Instead of having to buy, digest and integrate these multiple books, we want *The Performance Curve* to be a one-stop-shop on performance. We provide references so you can delve further into topics if desired.

There is no single silver bullet for developing our inner operating system. Our modern world is too complex, uncertain and diverse, and so are we as human beings. Our diversity can take many forms, including quite significant differences in our brain machinery. Furthermore, human growth is a messy process. All this means that what works for some people will not work for others. This book therefore provides a structure (through the three catalysts) for you to create your own developmental route map; so that you can take charge of your unique brain and life, to make them work for you.

You might query what is not covered by this approach. What about factors such as sleep, eating or exercise, or learning new skills (such as techniques for creative thinking)? These factors can also help us feel better and make good use of our brains. But we do not believe they get to the core of what it takes to raise our effectiveness and well-being significantly and sustainably. We want you to maximize your potential, not simply feel on good form because you happen to have slept well. Focusing on those other factors without doing the inner work on your operating system is like pouring high-octane racing car fuel into a regular car: it will make the car drive faster to a point, but no faster than the engine can cope with. Upgrade the engine, and it will be able to get the full benefits of the increased power.

In addition, we have seen (in clients and ourselves) how working with our inner operating system yields improvements to these other factors, because they are impacted by how we manage ourselves and interact with others. For example, one of our Jumpstart Development programmes, which focuses on the inner operating system, does not even mention sleep or exercise, yet participants report an average 37 per cent improvement in sleep after taking part. They also report feeling more effective, and mentally and emotionally stronger; we believe this is what helps them switch off at night and make clearer choices about their well-being, including sleep and exercise. We also find that feeling more content and in control of life reduces our impulse for unhealthy snacks, which we might have otherwise picked up when we were feeling down or low on inner batteries.

Finally, we all know that to have a strong, healthy body we need to exercise and move ('use it or lose it'). Muscles need to be exposed to a certain degree of strain to make them stronger. Though the brain's functioning is highly complex and there is still much we do not understand about it, it seems the same holds true for our 'brain muscle'.

'Exercising' our brain more seems to boost its resilience[1]. Developing our inner operating system gives our brain a good workout, which may help it stay stronger longer-term.

About the authors

Drawing from her PhD in cognitive neuroscience, Laura has been working for two decades to help people and organizations be at their best. She co-founded the European leadership practice at management consultancy McKinsey & Co and has since co-founded two leadership development firms: The Cognitas Group and Jumpstart Development. Introduced by a common acquaintance who had spotted kindred spirits, Vanessa knocked on Laura's door one wintry afternoon some years ago. Having also started her career in management consulting (at Boston Consulting Group), Vanessa spent several years working in emotional health and well-being as a breathwork therapist and teaching yoga and meditation – which in those days was a lot less mainstream than it is today.

We quickly discovered our mutual passion for adult development, and how complementary our different experiences and perspectives were. The turning point came when Vanessa took Laura and her partner Olivier through a programme based on her methods. Despite their different backgrounds and contexts (Olivier trained as an engineer and was running a FTSE-listed investment firm at the time), Laura and Olivier felt more balanced and effective afterwards. Since then, we have been collaborating to bring the best of modern science and experience-based wisdom traditions together to help our clients achieve high performance. The book you are reading now is the consolidation of this work.

We authors are committed life-long learners, with our fair share of struggles, so you will also come across elements from our own developmental journeys in *The Performance Curve*. We hope this inspires you to share your own successes and vulnerabilities with others and thereby help make developing your inner operating system a natural part of a life well lived, not a remedy for something broken or a sign of weakness. We feel honoured that you are reading *The Performance Curve*. And we would be even more thrilled if you put into practice some of these ideas to help you achieve more than you thought possible, tap into the inherent sense of fun and reward that spreading your wings brings, and live the life you want. We cannot wait to hear how you get on, and to learn with you too.

Ready to explore the performance curve?

CHAPTER ONE

Which curve are you on?

It is no wonder that many of us try to adapt to an increasingly fast-paced and complex world by running faster, working longer hours or being on red alert most of the time. This is the fight for survival in the jungle of modern times: we are trying to secure our income, attain status or prove our worth. In doing so, we often engage with the world in the reactive, fear-fuelled way our brains developed to respond to a tiger suddenly showing up outside our cave (often called a fight-flight-or-freeze response)[1]. In the face of danger, when we need to act quickly for survival, there is no time to think. This threat- or crisis-triggered response can lead to an uplift in performance as shown following Crisis 1 on the boom-and-bust curve in Figure 1.1. But we call it the *boom-and-bust curve* because we have observed that there is an upper ceiling to this kind of performance and that it is time-limited, leading to the oscillation of performance over time. By contrast, when we are on the *performance curve*, we more steadily grow our performance by increasing both effectiveness and well-being (as shown by the upper curve in Figure 1.1). These two curves are the two performance trajectories we typically see in our clients, ourselves and those around us. Let's look at them in more detail.

The boom-and-bust curve

Many of the automatic, survival-based coping mechanisms we bring to modern-day challenges do not actually use our brain's full potential. When we feel under threat, what we call *protect mode*, there is reduced

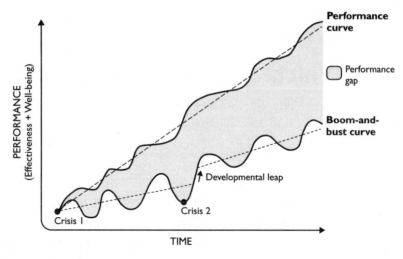

Figure 1.1 Which curve are you on?

activity in parts of the executive centre of the brain, located in the prefrontal cortex (PFC)[2]. That means our brain's capacity to carry out higher-level executive functions involving creativity, problem solving and self-regulation is reduced. As a result, we become more reactive, less able to make plans, and at risk of being less collaborative. This caps our performance and limits the results we can achieve, individually and collectively, in tackling the more complex challenges we face.

Putting in extra hours to resolve a true crisis might work in the short-term, but any uplift in performance will not be sustainable. When the tiger is gone (for example, we hit our quarterly sales target), the crisis-fuelled performance boost will disappear with it. In caveman days, this would have been a time for our bodies and brains to recover from the exertion. But, in a VUCA world, the next tiger is already in front of us or just around the corner (or, if it is not, we may be so addicted to the adrenaline that we seek it out). If we do not feel, or we ignore, the signals that we need rest, we might think we are high performing because we are constantly busy and reacting.

It is also likely that we are compromising our effectiveness and our ability to reach our potential longer-term. Consistently pushing beyond our reserves will likely reduce our executive functioning[2]. We will then further compound the problem by allocating our attention and energy less effectively[3]. Many successful people we come across operate in this way, unaware of the toll this is taking or at a loss as to how to break out of this cycle. Unfortunately, missing out on recovery time comes back to bite us: the underlying damage that causes burnout and other stress-related diseases will likely be accumulating over time before we experience the symptoms we associate with these illnesses. Brain scans show that chronic stress weakens not only the functioning but also the structure of our brains, particularly in areas that are important for memory, emotional regulation and self-control[2,4].

This then sets up a vicious circle, in which being less effective dampens our sense of well-being and increases time or resources needed to replenish ourselves. Furthermore, there is plenty of research to indicate the benefits of well-being to our effectiveness. For example, one study showed that people who report feeling happy are up to 30 per cent more productive and achieve 40 per cent better results[5]. When our well-being suffers, we will likely be less effective, especially in challenging situations. This also has a collective impact: not only does treating illness cost money, but society and the economy miss out on our full contribution of ideas, expertise and energy.

In summary, crisis-triggered effectiveness will not help us reach challenging goals over longer periods of time without paying a heavy price in terms of well-being. Making too many sacrifices then further undermines our effectiveness and well-being. Performance on the boom-and-bust curve declines after a crisis-fuelled high, either because we realize we have to take rest, or because our bodies and brains try to recover by taking energy away from our effectiveness. Then the next crisis fuels another uplift in performance and we repeat the boom-and-bust cycle, as with the large oscillations you see on the lower curve in Figure 1.1. As a result, we fail to maximize our potential.

Nick, the overwhelmed executive who had put his daughter in the crèche at his gym to catch up on his work, was on the boom-and-bust curve when he came to us. He realized he needed to break out of this vicious circle to advance his career and create a better life for himself and his family. He just did not know how.

Uncovering the workings of his inner operating system opened Nick's mind to doing things differently to get different results. For example, he took an honest look at how he had contributed to his overload at work. He realized how important it was to him to be liked, and that had led him to say 'yes' to extra work and unnecessary meetings, or avoid tackling conflicting views head on. His automatic drive to feel liked by others had helped him get to where he was today, but it was also a major reason why his life was such a whirlwind and it was a barrier to advancing his career. Nick's predicament as a victim of his own success resembles that of many clients we meet, and is often the starting point for greater change.

Nick realized that his fear of not being liked made him stressed and hampered his brain's capacity for complex problem solving, creativity and collaboration. He started to rewire his inner operating system to respond differently to his boss and colleagues and get different results. He realized he could set and live by his own goals and rules, and still be liked by people who were important to him. He became more flexible in how he interpreted situations, and stopped taking on every one of his boss's ideas. As he felt less in protect mode, his brain seemed to work better. He became more confident to express his points of view and able to bring clarity to complex situations. This helped him and his colleagues move forwards, and freed up time to spend with his daughter and look after his health.

Six months later, Nick had lost the extra weight he had been carrying, and he walked with a spring in his step. He talked excitedly about his work, which was benefiting from his new sense of clarity. He was smiling, evidently happy, and with an infectious lightness and sense of positivity.

Nick was able to use the adversity of his situation to make a developmental leap in his inner operating system and lift his performance to a new level, as shown by the incline after Crisis 2 in Figure 1.1. Had Nick left it at that, his higher level of both effectiveness and well-being would have become his 'new normal'. His performance would still have fluctuated, but not as much, as shown by the continuation of the boom-and-bust curve after the developmental leap. However, after seeing the benefits he gained from developing as a result of this crisis, Nick chose to keep working on his inner operating system, so his future performance could follow the trajectory of the performance curve.

The performance curve

The performance curve, the upper curve in Figure 1.1, represents a different performance trajectory, in which we maximize our potential while strengthening our well-being. On the performance curve, well-being is not just the icing on the performance cake; it is a key ingredient of it. Therefore, the *first core principle* of the performance curve is: dissolving the trade-off between effectiveness and well-being is the key to unlocking the higher performance levels of a life well lived. On the performance curve, the rises in performance come from increasing our inner capacity to deal with challenges and complexity, so there is less strain on our brains and bodies compared to the crisis-fuelled uplifts of the boom-and-bust curve. Being able to take bigger steps on shorter routes to our goals demands fewer sacrifices and frees us up to take better care of our well-being.

In addition, the growth we pursue on the performance curve is fuelled by a deeper sense of purpose, passion to shape our life, and joy from spreading our wings and having more fulfilling connections with others, all of which also increase our well-being. That is why on the performance curve, we see plateaus rather than the bigger dips in performance of the boom-and-bust curve. Neither of the two curves is a continuously upward sloping line because, after each developmental shift into a new performance realm, our brains need to consolidate and embed the changes. But overall, the gradient of the performance curve will be steeper. The shaded area in Figure 1.1 shows how much cumulative performance we gain by proactively working to be on the performance curve. Regardless of our starting point, at any point we can choose to take this steeper trajectory.

Luke Bradley-Jones, the British executive who has overseen several high-pressure media launches for the BBC, Sky and Disney, told us about how he strives to have his effectiveness and well-being work in a virtuous (rather than vicious) cycle. 'I love that feeling of having accountability and being at the outer level of my capability, where the challenge and my performance are perfectly matched. Feeling a bit outside my comfort zone brings out the best of me, but it can feel stressful, and I can't do it all of the time, otherwise I start to feel anxious and I focus too much on myself. So, if I'm off track, I take time to reset, by reflecting, learning and getting perspective on what will really matter in five years. The drive for high performance can come from dissatisfaction and restlessness, so we have to take time to notice the good stuff. And happiness helps performance.'

As Luke implies, it is not to say that crises don't happen on the performance curve or we won't feel challenged or overwhelmed at times. We cannot develop our way out of being human. Given the ups and downs that life brings, we can't expect to be perfectly effective, healthy and happy all the time. Sometimes we need to put our feet up and rest. But we can learn to face our limits and move beyond them, and to embrace light and shadow as inseparable and equally important aspects of life. When we are used to doing this, we succumb less to protect mode under pressure so the executive functions in our brain's prefrontal cortex will work unimpeded. This gives us greater ability to make deliberate choices in how we act. We are more effective, so we can achieve results with greater ease and reach higher levels of potential.

Cellist Yo-Yo Ma also knows how much his state of mind affects his performance, 'it's amazing how, in a few seconds, the physical self can go into emergency mode'. He therefore pays close attention to his state of mind in order to bring his best, which for him is about 'conveying content [usually music, but could be words] so that it is not just received by the audience, but lives within them and they can recreate that state afterwards'. Yo-Yo's deeper sense of purpose fuels the development of his inner operating system. He has cultivated ways to deal with adversity, and keep his attention on listening and the audience. For example, he has developed his inner operating system to focus on the opportunity of something going wrong, rather than the downside. 'If a string breaks at the start of a concert, it's perfect; because it is unexpected and then it's a sure-fire thing the audience is on your side. The bad thing has happened and I become much more relaxed. I feel free.'

So how do we reach the higher trajectory of the performance curve? By deliberately developing our inner operating system and becoming masters at evolving how we think and feel, and what we do. Despite the many differences between computers and the living systems of our brains and bodies, we find it helpful to extend this analogy. Much like the operating system in a computer that connects hardware with software and allocates resources, our inner operating system is the central 'software' we run as humans. It contains the many rules that govern how we manage ourselves and interact with the world around us. These rules guide our default ways of interpreting situations (our mindsets, such as what we think about set-backs); how we respond emotionally in particular situations (such as the emotions we tend to feel when someone disagrees with us); when to go into protect mode and which behaviours to adopt in it. They also drive our habits: which may be routines (such as how we start our working day) or default responses in a given situation (such as whom we pay more attention to in a tense meeting). All these rules develop and embed in our brains from early childhood, as experience teaches us what is threatening or rewarding and how to behave to get the results we want. Sometimes we might be aware of the whole chain of rules, from mindsets to emotions and behaviours and hence results we create but, at other times, we may have little awareness of it.

The good news is that we can adapt our inner operating system. You heard examples of how Nick, Luke and Yo-Yo have developed their inner operating systems to serve them better. Neuroscientific research over the past 30 years has clearly indicated that the adult brain has the capacity to reorganize and remould itself[6]. This capacity enables us to evolve our inner operating system, i.e. to change our thought, emotional and behaviour patterns to better suit our current circumstances and help us deal more easily with greater complexity and change. This is particularly important given that so much of our inner operating system is laid down when we are young.

You might have already experienced a change in your inner operating system or seen it in others. Such changes are often set in motion by significant life events or experiences, such as a new role or promotion, having children, getting divorced, a major setback or a loss. Even if the cause is positive, this is a form of crisis or upheaval: the world as we knew it has gone, or our old ways of going about life do not work any longer. Sometimes smaller challenges of daily life (such as a disagreement at home or at work, or a demanding project or meeting) can also bring out in us a sense of crisis or upheaval, even if quite modest. Though Nick was not facing a major life event or setback, he felt at a point of crisis when he realized his ways of operating were no longer working.

A sense of crisis or upheaval helps us realize that our inner operating system is not serving us optimally, and this creates an opening for adapting our ways of thinking and behaving. We will feel some level of discomfort, depending on how much our inner operating system is under strain. And here we have a choice: if the discomfort leads us to bury our head in the sand and avoid confronting how we operate, we will miss out on the opportunity to grow. But if we can find the gifts that these challenges contain (however painfully they may present themselves), they will lead to a strengthening of our inner operating system and of our performance.

If you have faced a situation that rattled your inner operating system, and taken the plunge to adapt how you think, feel and act, you might have noticed an uplift in your effectiveness and/or your well-being. Perhaps you had a new sense of your potential, were clearer on what mattered to you and made bolder decisions to prioritize accordingly. Maybe you became more flexible in how you interpreted situations or other people's behaviours and felt more able to choose how you responded (ah, the magic when things or people that previously annoyed us don't anymore!). Perhaps you felt more confident about grabbing opportunities or dealing with obstacles, having survived a crisis. Changes like these come from a transformation in our inner operating system.

On the boom-and-bust curve, the development of our inner operating system – if it occurs – is triggered by a sense of crisis or upheaval. But why wait for a crisis? We can each proactively evolve our inner operating system with the right structure and support. This is the *second core principle* of the performance curve: that sustained, and even higher, performance is possible through the ongoing, proactive development of our inner operating system. If we are proactive about developing our inner operating system, we will more quickly identify when it is hitting challenges and needs to evolve. We will also be more able and prepared to question and evolve it. This is why the ups and downs in performance will be less marked (the reduced amplitude of the waves you see in the performance curve in Figure 1.1).

Many of our interviewees mentioned the importance of this second principle and have developed practices that support this ongoing development. For example, media executive Luke Bradley-Jones maintains his effectiveness and well-being in high-pressure roles by working on his inner operating system all the time. He has a set of practices to support this, including daily mindfulness, systematically reflecting on his purpose and connecting it to his priorities, and sending appreciative notes to colleagues (we will look at many practices like this in Chapter 7).

Developing our inner operating systems is more powerful when done collectively (in teams, networks, organizations and at home) and benefits ourselves, our organizations, our families and society more broadly. That's because our inner operating systems bump up against one another all the time, which means that we can support or disrupt growth for other people. Furthermore, brilliant strategies and slick processes only get organizations so far: the human element – how we think, feel, make decisions and behave – is crucial for making any initiative successful. This means how people grow at a deeper, personal level is fundamental to collective success. The *third core principle* of the performance curve is that we can interact with each other in ways that develop our inner operating system to reach even higher levels of performance.

International development and humanitarian leader Lorina McAdam talked about how field teams are often thrown together in very tough circumstances. This can create the conditions for tight teams, but it can also be challenging; for example when there are incoming suspicions between different team members or parts of the team. Lorina has learned to build team cultures in which people can share their mistakes and vulnerabilities, learn from one another, and celebrate each other's successes. To achieve this, she herself tries to be extremely attuned to what each individual needs and to meet that, so she role-models empathy and helps her colleagues bring their best.

Collective development is also powerful with family and friends. Luke told us how he has cultivated a weekend ritual with his wife and three young girls where they talk about what they have most enjoyed during the week, to build everyone's muscles of 'paying attention to the good stuff'.

Based on the three core principles of the performance curve we have laid out, this book describes three catalysts for being on the performance curve. We call these catalysts because we can use them to propel ourselves towards maximizing our potential whilst strengthening our well-being, regardless of our starting point. They are mechanisms to support our growth, not psychometrics to measure ourselves against. You will see that they are also interdependent: they complement and reinforce one another.

The three performance curve catalysts: wisdom, fuel and connection

The first catalyst is *wisdom*, which we define as seeing and continually adapting our inner operating system as the world changes, particularly so that we can deal with complex or challenging situations with breadth and depth of perspective. The first part of this book is focused on the wisdom catalyst, and covers the core components of our inner operating system of our brain, what affects our brain's functioning, and how to evolve to higher effectiveness and well-being.

The second catalyst is *fuel*, which we define as sustaining the continuous development of our inner operating system day-to-day and over the long haul. In the second part of the book, the fuel catalyst, we offer practical ways for you to sustain your journey on the performance curve. These include strengthening helpful habits, tools for self-awareness and self-management, purpose, and the power of paradoxical thinking.

The third catalyst is *connection*, which we define as forming developmental relationships that enable us to develop our inner operating systems together. The third part of the book, the connection catalyst, is dedicated to building such relationships at or beyond your workplace. Whilst this third part specifically addresses connection, the earlier two parts do contain ideas for interacting with others to bring and grow your best and help them do the same.

We arranged the catalysts in this order because there are many foundational concepts covered in wisdom, and many aspects of both wisdom and fuel are important for forming the developmental relationships we talk about in connection. So we recommend you read *The Performance Curve* systematically front to back, but you may prefer to focus your reading on the catalysts that you think will bring you the most benefit at the moment. To help you navigate, the first chapter of every catalyst describes the contents of the chapters within it.

Before we dive into the detail of the three catalysts, let us introduce the interviewees featured in this book (ordered by surname):

- Eric Beinhocker – University of Oxford professor, author and Executive Director of Oxford's Institute for New Economic Thinking, which seeks to challenge conventional economic approaches to the big financial, economic and environmental issues of our times. Eric is known as a big thinker, skilled communicator and coalition-builder who encourages fresh perspectives on complex topics. Originally from Boston, Massachusetts.
- Luke Bradley-Jones – British media executive who loves leading teams to launch disruptive products. After long stints at the BBC and Sky, his most recent mission has been to launch Disney+ in Europe. To thrive under this pressure, Luke deliberately works hard to bring his best. He manages to be measured, genuine and balanced, which includes finding time for charitable work.
- Juan Jose Gonzalez – Peruvian CEO of Danish global medical devices firm Ambu, which seeks to disrupt established markets through rapid innovation. He previously ran several Johnson & Johnson businesses in Europe and the Americas. Determined to win whilst acting with integrity, Juan Jose draws on the perseverance, courage and composure he built in his youth during a long quest to excel at karate.
- Margareth (Maggie) Henriquez – Venezuelan-born President and CEO of Krug Champagne. She has a track record of transforming consumer businesses in challenging markets, including in Venezuela, Mexico,

Argentina and France. A life-long learner who trained originally as a systems engineer and recently completed a PhD in Business Administration, Maggie inspires others with her unique cocktail of authenticity, care, courage and thoughtfulness.

- Gabrielle (Gaby) Kennard – First Australian woman to fly solo around the globe in a single-engined airplane in 1989. Proving that it is possible for an 'ordinary' single mother of two to fulfil her dream, she became an inspirational speaker and raised funds for the Royal Flying Doctor Service of Australia. Lives in Byron Bay, Australia, and Switzerland.

- Wendy Kopp – Texan dedicated to helping children get the education they need to fulfil their potential. She founded Teach For America as a fresh graduate and now leads Teach For All, the global network that nurtures similar organizations in close to 60 countries. Wendy reflects deeply on how she shapes her organizations and leads them, in order to create a ripple effect of empowerment that benefits young people. Lives in New York City with her family.

- Yo-Yo Ma – Chinese-American cellist, born in Paris. Musician who has spent close to six decades performing under pressure on the world's stages. But, alongside his technical skill, Yo-Yo has an infectious zest for life and deep commitment to building human connections and inspiring others through his work.

- Lorina McAdam – International development and humanitarian leader with over 20 years of experience leading field teams in civil society development and combating malaria and HIV/AIDS, in countries such as Iraq, South Sudan, Democratic Republic of Congo, and Myanmar. Lorina brings calm, care and presence of mind in challenging situations. She is Australian, living in France.

- Tom Rippin – PhD bio-physicist who founded and runs On Purpose, which develops leaders for an economy that works for all and operates in London, Berlin and Paris. He is passionate about building a healthy economy, and a deep thinker about societal systems and what purposeful business really means. Lives in London.

- Pramath Sinha – Veteran institution builder in India. Founded top Indian business school, ISB, and a liberal arts university, Ashoka, as well as numerous other education and media ventures. Behind his warm and humble persona lies a huge ambition: for the people he works with, the institutions they build, and the evolution of his country.

Clients also featuring in this book whose names, identifying details or personal characteristics have been changed to protect their privacy:

- Nick – Director of Operations and Project Management for new products in a large consumer goods organization. He is also a single dad with shared custody of his four-year-old daughter, Molly.
- Rachel – Californian entrepreneur who became CEO of her family's statewide media company. She quickly grew it to national scale through a series of acquisitions.

PART ONE

The Wisdom Catalyst

How to Bring and Grow your Best

CHAPTER TWO

Working with your inner operating system: mindsets, emotions and habits

This chapter introduces the first catalyst for being on the performance curve, the wisdom catalyst. It covers the different components of our inner operating system (i.e. the rules that determine how we manage ourselves and interact with the world) and how to develop it.

There would be little need for developing our inner operating system if our lives were stable, certain, simple and clear, because we could simply keep doing what we have always done. However, a VUCA world continually presents us with unfamiliar and challenging situations. Being able to see and adapt how we operate helps us to maintain effectiveness and well-being in these situations. This means we can notice when the path we are taking is not working and have the flexibility to create and take other routes. We are also able to find the gifts that challenges contain and use them to grow beyond our limits. In short, being able to evolve our inner operating system is the source for navigating life wisely.

Cellist Yo-Yo Ma described to us a metaphor for the wisdom catalyst: 'There are many ways to Rome. When you are 20, it is really great if you have found one path to Rome. If, later on, you can find 20 ways to Rome, and each way has its own delights and attractions, then you don't have to be a control freak. If you only know one way, that's it: if things don't go your way along the route, you're going to be upset.' As

Yo-Yo mentioned, there is an age factor here: more time means more opportunity to have seen that there are multiple paths. But age and experience alone do not necessarily make us wiser. So what does, and how can we become wiser more quickly?

The wisdom catalyst of the performance curve

We can become wiser by upgrading our inner operating system to build in greater perspective, choice and flexibility, which enables us to bring out the best in ourselves and in others, as well as grow our potential over time. This is different to acquiring more knowledge or specific skills, though it will help us make the most of knowledge or skills we have or attain. As Tom Rippin, founder and CEO of On Purpose, put it: 'This is about learning how to *be*.'

In *The Performance Curve* we therefore put aside the notion of wisdom as an endpoint of human development: a destination to arrive at or specific traits to attain. Instead, *the wisdom catalyst of the performance curve is our ability to see and continually adapt our inner operating system as the world changes.* In the first part of this book, we explore how to strengthen and use this ability, no matter what our starting point. There are two main aspects to the wisdom catalyst:

1) *Bringing our best as it is right now*, so we can make the most of our current knowledge, skills and experience;
2) *Growing our best over time*, particularly our ability to bring breadth and depth of perspective to deal with complex or challenging situations.

Bringing our best as it is right now means approaching situations, even challenging ones, with our brain at its best to take in and process information, make decisions and relate to others. As things will not always go smoothly, bringing our best also includes being able to bounce back after getting knocked off course.

Bringing our best requires self-awareness. We were struck by the sharp clarity and focus many of our interviewees had about their strengths and weaknesses and how to be at their best. Media executive Luke Bradley-Jones illustrated this when he talked about needing to feel under pressure to bring out his best. He is also aware how easily this can tip into anxiety and self-focus, and knows how to get himself back on track.

Growing our best over time is having a brain that is fast and proficient at continually developing itself. This means our brain keeps getting better every day, and can adapt to bring its best even as the world changes. Again, this is not about laying down memories such as facts or 'how to' skills. The emphasis is on the deep and complex brain wiring that underlies how we view ourselves, others and the world, and how we decide what we do.

We will focus particularly here on how to develop our inner operating system so we can thrive in a VUCA world, i.e. having more and different perspectives, and more freedom of choice in our behaviours. This has made a difference for many of our interviewees. For example, Oxford professor Eric Beinhocker needs to operate nimbly to navigate the economic and policy landscape and encourage creative thinking. He is careful to be open to new perspectives: 'I have points of view, but I try to be open to challenge, willing to be asked why, and open to being proved wrong. We cannot always be right, and I try to validate views, get new ideas, keep my aspirations grounded, learn, create empathy and link points/parts.' He has also built freedom of choice in his behaviours: 'That said, collaboration is nice, but I can also be authoritative when I need to be.'

What to find in the chapters of Part I: wisdom catalyst

The next few chapters cover different ways in which you can develop your inner operating system. They also contain many foundation notions about our brain and inner operating system that are relevant for the later parts of the book on the other two catalysts.

In the rest of this chapter, we explore three important building blocks of our inner operating system – *mindsets, emotions* and *habits* – and illustrate techniques for recognizing and adapting them. This gives you the core science and concepts that underpin the rest of *The Performance Curve.*

In Chapter 3, we dive more deeply into what (or who) is driving our brains. This gives us insight into how to get the best out of our brains, especially when under pressure (the first aspect of the wisdom catalyst). You will learn more about protect mode and how to cultivate an alternative mode – explore mode – to allow you to draw on your full brain capacity and give you more deliberate choice in how to act. We also show how the triggers for protect mode are clues for how to get back on track and to evolve our inner operating system longer term.

Chapter 4 focuses on the second aspect of the wisdom catalyst: how to deliberately grow our best over the course of our lives. We look at the longer-term path of development of our inner operating system and how we can accelerate our movement along this path to help us better rise to life's challenges and complexities. This type of development is often called 'vertical development' and, if you want to grow and better understand how others tick, it is at least as important as neuroscience, but much less well known. The chapter will offer ways we can get the immediate benefits of the later stages of vertical development and strengthen the neural pathways that support us to operate more fully from those later stages.

In the final chapter on wisdom, Chapter 5, we introduce three mindsets that unlock individual and collective performance: 1) accountability mindset, 2) growth mindset and 3) big picture mindset. Each of these mindsets propels us on to the performance curve and helps us maximize our potential, at work and elsewhere in life. By contrast, when we succumb to their nemeses (victim mindset, fixed mindset and silo mindset), we feed the dynamics of the boom-and-bust curve. You will learn practical ways to cultivate these mindsets in yourself and others.

Let's now take a look at how our inner operating system embeds in our brain, to prepare us for making changes to it.

Our brain and the inner operating system

The brain is truly miraculous in how it takes in and processes sensory information, makes decisions and relates to others, often within a fraction of a second and outside of our conscious awareness. How does it do that?

We each have about 80–90 billion nerve cells, called neurons, in our brains[1]. An average neuron has several thousand connections with other neurons.[2] That is potential for chaos, especially when you factor in that our brains are bombarded with millions of sensory stimuli per second. This means our brains need to carefully manage attention and energy and avoid being overwhelmed. We also need them to react quickly to protect us when a sudden threat emerges, instead of taking a long time to weigh up pros and cons of different options.

To cope with this potential overload, our brains develop automatic shortcuts for how we take in sensory information, manage ourselves and interact with the world. Our brains are particularly active in forming these automatic shortcuts before our teenage years, as we learn how to operate at home and in our early social environments, such as school (through a process called 'pruning')[3].

Given there is so much processing going on at any one time in our brain, it would be impossible for us to be aware of it all. It would also be unhelpful because it would slow us down and overload us. While it is difficult to measure what proportion of our cognitive processing is outside our conscious awareness, we have often heard estimates that it is higher than 90 per cent and we think this seems reasonable.

Our inner operating system is simply a huge network of these automatic shortcuts, which generate our default patterns of thinking, feeling and behaving (the rules we described in Chapter 1). In other words, behind every decision or action we are aware of, our inner operating system is doing a huge amount of automatic processing, of which we are largely unaware.

The physical structure of our brain embeds our inner operating system and each automatic shortcut will be underpinned by neural pathways. When these pathways are well used, the neurons within them will make stronger connections between themselves[4]. Some neurons will also build up more fatty insulation around themselves, which means they conduct signals faster[5]. The difference this 'hardware' change makes is astounding: it is estimated that our unconscious mind processes sensory information at a speed of at least a million bits of data per second vs. only ~3–60 bits per second for conscious processing[6].

But there is a price we pay for the gain in speed and reduced cognitive effort that these automated shortcuts afford us: they may have helped us stay safe and get desired results in the past, but they may not work well in novel situations that require a different approach. When our inner operating system does not match well to a situation or our goals, it can become an autopilot-gone-awry, which overrides our control of the steering wheel and can land us in a ditch.

If we want to bring and grow our best to move on the performance curve, it is therefore essential that we get to know the defaults that are embedded in our inner operating system, and learn how to adapt them when they are not leading to desired outcomes.

The wonderful news is that our brains are wired to grow and change as adults: they can change their structure and functioning through a mechanism called neuroplasticity. Advances in modern neuroscience, particularly through functional magnetic resonance imaging (fMRI), are allowing scientists to better observe the extent of neuroplasticity our brains undergo. We can now see more clearly that adult brains do continue to change during our entire lifetime, albeit at a slower pace and with more effort than in our early years[5].

We can also see how it is possible to deliberately intervene to change the function and structure of our brains. For example, there are clear changes in the brain activity and structure of regular meditators' brains, including an increase in size of some parts as the connections between nerve cells strengthen[7]. Even a single session of mindfulness can initiate shifts in brain activity patterns[8].

This means that even shortcuts that are well embedded in our inner operating system should be modifiable, with the right interventions. What is the right intervention for each of us will vary, given that our genetics and experiences make our brains diverse. But the mechanisms for changing our brains are ready and waiting for us. We now look at the different components of our inner operating system, and how we can take advantage of neuroplasticity to work with them.

Working with the building blocks of our inner operating system

To be on the performance curve, the aim is to become masters at evolving how we think and feel, and what we do. This helps us to adapt as situations unfold so that we can bring our best, and to grow our potential by upgrading our inner operating system. We therefore need to be able to identify and work with the three core building blocks of our inner operating system that drive our default responses:

1) Mindsets – our beliefs or assumptions;
2) Emotions – the blend of our physiological state and cognitive interpretations;
3) Habits – our automatic behaviours.

We first briefly describe each of these building blocks and then turn to strengthening our ability to see and adapt them.

Mindsets: beliefs that shape reality

Mindsets are our beliefs about ourselves, others and the world. They are lenses through which we see the world and interact with it. This means they influence how we think and feel and what we do. As a result, they powerfully shape the outcomes we get, as many of our interviewees told us. Gaby Kennard, our solo round-the-world pilot, said, 'I had a big belief that, if you can dream it, you can do it.' This mindset helped her overcome the many obstacles – external barriers and inner moments of doubt – to making her voyage possible. Margareth (Maggie) Henriquez, CEO of Krug Champagne, spoke to us about how 'crisis is always an opportunity'. You will hear more about how this, and related mindsets, have helped her to learn from challenges and failures to make them the breeding ground of her successes.

Luke Bradley-Jones described how important it has been for him to become aware of and shift his mindsets, so he can keep performing in different roles and companies. 'I spent the early part of my career setting goals and working with my colleagues to achieve them. I thought I was collaborative, but then I got feedback that it was not enough to be collaborative to achieve my goals; it was also essential for me to see the bigger picture and help my colleagues achieve their goals. That was an interesting personal development challenge. I have shifted my mindset about what defines success from achieving objectives I set for myself, to achieving objectives I share with others and helping them achieve their own. And that mindset drives me to put more time and effort into understanding what my colleagues are worrying about, then worrying about it myself and seeing how I can help them.'

The usefulness of a particular mindset depends on the situation and our goals. Luke got results with his first mindset but, with feedback, he realized that mindset had become outdated, and let go of it to allow the second one to emerge and shape his behaviours. The key is to A) recognize the mindsets we hold and see whether they help us in a given situation or get in the way, and B) build our capacity for embedding a different mindset in our brains that will serve us better. That said, there are some mindsets (namely the accountability, growth, and big picture mindsets) that are generally beneficial in most situations for moving on the performance curve and we introduce them in Chapter 5.

Emotions: the prompt and energy for action

Emotions animate our mindsets into behaviours: they prompt action and provide the energy for it, through their effects on our brain and our physiology. They mobilize our bodies into movement; a helpful way to think of this is 'emotion = energy-in-motion'. Emotions help us fully experience what it is to be human and are a crucial part of communicating and forming social bonds. They are usually felt as physical sensations in the body, with people commonly citing the chest area[9]. Hence the commonly used reference to the 'heart' when emotions are concerned, even though cognitive interpretation (the 'head') is involved in generating the physiological component of emotions and our experience of it.

Interestingly, although emotions are a fundamental part of human experience, there has been much debate about their classification into emotional families. As a result, you might have seen different ways to categorize emotions[10]. Likewise, whilst most researchers agree emotions have at least some universal elements across culture, some researchers argue that emotions are not tied to a single, objective state in the body, and how we interpret our physical feelings depends on where and how we are brought up.

We find a list of four core emotions – joy, fear, anger, sadness (see Figure 2.1) – the most practical way to help navigate this aspect of our inner world and have a language to talk about it[11].

JOY	HAPPY	GRATEFUL	PROUD
	EXCITED	CONTENT	CONFIDENT
	LOVING	INSPIRED	CURIOUS
FEAR	AFRAID	OVERWHELMED	UNCERTAIN
	ANXIOUS	WORRIED	CAUTIOUS
	SHOCKED	INSECURE	CONFUSED
ANGER	MAD	FRUSTRATED	IMPATIENT
	CROSS	IRRITATED	DISTANT
	ANNOYED	CRITICAL	DISGUSTED
SADNESS	DEPRESSED	GUILTY	BORED
	DISAPPOINTED	LONELY	EMPTY
	DISCOURAGED	ASHAMED	REGRETFUL

Figure 2.1 Four core emotions

These core emotions come in many flavours and levels of intensity. We show a few examples in Figure 2.1, but there are many more: a team of researchers has compiled an (English) emotion taxonomy of 412 discrete (mutually exclusive, semantically distinct) human emotions[12]. There is value to being able to describe what we feel: naming our emotions settles our brain's reactivity and reduces impediments to our prefrontal cortex functioning[13,14]. Furthermore, there is evidence that being able to recognize our precise emotions from moment-to-moment (such as distinguishing between feeling anxious or cautious) gives us better coping strategies when under pressure, and boosts our resilience and well-being (scientists call this ability 'emotional granularity')[15].

We often get asked why there are three 'negative' and only one 'positive' emotion in this framework. We love this question, because it opens up an important aspect of emotions: how we relate to them. Why do we judge some emotions as positive and some as negative?

And is this helpful, given that emotions are part of human experience and we cannot selectively switch some off and leave others on? In fact, studies have found that attempting to suppress emotions like fear or anger has the counter-productive effect of increasing the brain's protect mode. This is perhaps because suppressing emotions stops us from recognizing how we are feeling, so it gets in the way of us being able to identify why we are feeling that way and how to move forwards[16,17]. Many mindfulness practices involve training our minds to separate the physical sensation of an emotion from our judgement of it, i.e. whether we find it pleasant or not. This is because they recognize the importance of being able to feel emotions (rather than judge or suppress them). This creates more room for constructive reflection and deliberate choices, rather than acting on emotions impulsively.

If we drop the judgement about whether an emotion is positive or negative, we can more easily discover the valuable messages it contains for us. For example:

- joy alerts us to what brings purpose and meaning to us and fuels us to pursue these, and it can also draw in others to join us in our visions;
- fear alerts us to potential threats to our safety and enables us to react quickly;
- anger alerts us to a violation of our values or boundaries and gives us the energy to move against or away from the violation;
- sadness alerts us to loss, shows us what we value and love, and can prompt us to reach out for connection and support.

Furthermore, just because there are three 'negative' emotions and only one 'positive', it does not mean that we all spend three times as much time feeling 'negative' emotions. You might like to identify where your 'emotional home' or centre of gravity is and make a decision if that is serving you or is something you would like to change.

Habits: automatic behaviours

When we repeatedly do something and get rewarded for it, our brains will automate that behaviour to save energy. The more rewarding the behaviour is, the quicker and stronger this automation will be[18]. This process is how we form habits. Structures deep inside the brain, called the basal ganglia, are responsible for embedding these habits. They can trigger movement directly, without depending on the more constrained executive centre, and they are less sensitive to stress (from fatigue or otherwise).

Studies show that about half of what we do every day is based on habits. Habit scientist Wendy Wood and her colleagues have found that around 90 per cent of our self-care is based on habits, and more than half of what we do at work[19]. Picture your morning routine: getting dressed, making your breakfast or coffee, brushing your teeth, unlocking the front door ... think of all the habits you have followed before you even leave the house in the morning.

As well as the habit routines we follow, our brains also automate habits for how we respond in particular situations. For example, imagine someone has a tendency to go silent when others are arguing. Their brain might have embedded some mindsets, such as about the risks of conflict. Their brain will probably also have automated some behaviours, just by virtue of the behaviours having been repeated and associated in some way with reward. The result: as soon as the cue appears, say, in a heated team discussion, the habit kicks in. Their mouth will shut and they might physically sit back (this has characteristics of a 'freeze' protect mode response).

Habits are therefore important for upgrading our operating system. We should make sure we can flex our response according to the situation and our goals. We can also use this fantastic feature of our brains to build automatic habits that serve us well for reaching our potential and strengthening our well-being.

The interaction of mindsets, emotions and habits

The three building blocks of our inner operating system interact in different ways to drive what we do (i.e. our behaviours) and the results we get (including our effectiveness and our well-being). Sometimes our habits will largely drive our behaviour, with our mindset and emotional processing playing less of a role. For example, a habit such as 'shut mouth and sit back' might be so ingrained in our basal ganglia that, when we hear raised voices, we put the habit into action automatically with little or no complex mindset and emotion processing. At other times, our mindset and emotional processing is more involved, and then a habitual response kicks in. For example, we might hear someone in a meeting mention reorganizing the team, and we might have a mindset that 'team reorganizations lead to tension and upset' and start to feel in protect mode, and it thus might trigger the same 'shut mouth and sit back' response.

When we seek to create different results, it can be tempting to target change in our behaviours. For example, as we become more aware of our behaviours, we might immediately analyse which ones to change and try to behave differently. This would be short-changing ourselves, for three reasons. First, among all the behaviours we observe, we do not know yet which one will lead to the most impact. Second, since mindsets powerfully drive behaviours, working with the underlying mindset may help us change behaviour more easily. Third, as described above, habits are powerful because it takes the brain a lot of effort and energy to act in a way that is different to its habitual wiring. Our brain's executive centre has a finite capacity, so using it to override habits typically only produces a temporary shift in behaviour. As soon as our executive capacity comes under strain, for example when we are upset, overwhelmed or tired, we would then revert to the well-trodden, easier-to-follow neural pathways of the old behaviours.

Most change efforts therefore fail for one or both of the following reasons: 1) relying on willpower to change behaviour, rather than building sticky new habits and letting go of old ones; and 2) failing to tackle the underlying mindsets and emotions. We advocate addressing mindsets, emotions and habits to make change stick, i.e. to reprogramme our inner operating system to align our mindsets, emotions and our habits so that we default to our desired behaviours automatically.

We show how to work with habits in the second part of the book on the fuel catalyst, including how they can help us sustain the continuous development of our inner operating system. As part of the wisdom catalyst, we spend the rest of this chapter focusing on the other two building blocks of our inner operating system: our mindsets, and the emotions that help us track them down. A useful tool to help us uncover and adapt the mindsets and emotions that are at play in our inner operating system comes in the shape of an iceberg.

The iceberg: from mindsets and emotions to behaviours and results

We find it helpful to use an iceberg to illustrate how our mindsets and emotions lead to behaviours and then results (see Figure 2.2). As with a real iceberg, only a small part of it is visible above the waterline and the rest lies below it. What is above the waterline is more visible (to us and others), and what is below the waterline is less easily visible. Using the iceberg tool helps make the hidden parts visible.

At the top of the iceberg are the results we get, both for the short and longer term. Underneath are the behaviours that drive those results, i.e. what we do and say, and how we do it. They include how we choose to spend our time, how we approach and handle specific tasks or conversations, and how we react to situations. Habits sit at this level: they are the many behaviours we repeat. We will be aware

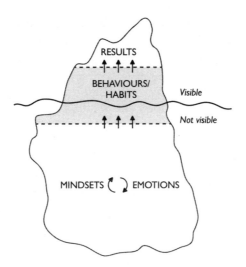

Figure 2.2 The iceberg

of most of our behaviours, but we may not be aware of all of them (for example, we may not realize we shut our mouth and sit back as soon as we experience conflict in a meeting). This is why the behaviours/habits sit above and below the waterline.

Our inner operating system is the large amount of default processing that drives our behaviours and includes mindsets, emotions and habits. Most of it sits deeper beneath the surface of the water and, while we do not see this portion of the iceberg straight away, it can help us climb to great heights or trip us up. These elements are not beneath the surface of our awareness because they are bad or need to be hidden. It is simply a function of how our brains are structured to be efficient by automating our interpretations of the world and ourselves, and building shortcuts for how to respond.

Let's see how to use the iceberg, with the help of Nick, the overwhelmed executive who had put his daughter in childcare at the gym on weekends so he could catch up on work. Nick wanted to get more out of his time at work. He started by looking at his calendar for the previous few weeks to see how much time he was actually spending on his priorities. He saw that he was spending most of his days in meetings that he felt he needed to attend, but which were not helping him make much direct progress with his objectives (unfortunately, not the first time we have heard this frustration in our work with leaders!). No immediate solution jumped out at Nick; he was convinced he had to attend those meetings. He therefore used the iceberg to step back and get some perspective (what is often called 'getting on the balcony'). It helped him identify his mindsets and emotions, and, through that process, come up with real options for getting more out of his time. Let's look at the steps for Nick. The summary is shown in Table 2.1.

Nick's iceberg today (his 'from' iceberg)

Results – The results we create are visible above the water's surface: in Nick's case, meetings that did not move his priorities forwards and (as a consequence of working late to catch up on his priorities) general exhaustion and insufficient quality time with his daughter.

Behaviours – Nick's first step was to identify his own behaviours relating to these unproductive meetings. Other people's behaviours may also have played a role, but the iceberg is to help us see our contribution to a situation and maximize the impact we can have on the results. Sometimes our behaviours are quite obvious to us or others, but other times we might not realize what we are doing (or not doing). Having been so caught up in his busy diary, Nick had not been paying attention to his behaviours, so he turned detective on himself for a few days and kept a log of what he was and was not doing. He noticed that, whenever the meetings seemed unproductive, his first tendency was to disengage and half-listen. He almost never tried to intervene to improve the productivity of the meeting. He also caught himself occasionally being abrupt or abrasive in his communication, particularly when he got frustrated and wanted his colleagues to stop talking about issues that were not relevant to him. And he saw that, in some meetings, he had been focused on the short-term actions just to finish the meeting rather than looking at the longer-term implications or opportunities.

Mindsets and emotions – How do we uncover mindsets given they cannot usually be seen from the surface? We dive. The mindsets that lead to a set of behaviours are often hidden behind what we are saying (to ourselves or others) about a situation. Emotions are our clues for where to dive and track down our mindsets. This is because the emotions we feel tell us about how our inner operating system is wired up, i.e. which mindsets are getting energy in our brain. As a result, we find it is more helpful to iterate between mindsets and emotions when laying out our iceberg, rather than trying to analyse them in sequence. Especially when new to working with mindsets, this diving process can take some time, but the more we do it, the easier it gets.

Nick started by asking himself, 'What assumptions or beliefs might I be holding about meetings that lead me to behave in this way?' Through writing down everything he was thinking and feeling about meetings (his stream of consciousness) and looking at this in a session with his coach, Nick found a few of his generalized assumptions, for example that 'meetings are all talk and no action'. Generalizations (making a universally applicable truth out of individual situations) are good examples of how mindsets filter what we see and narrow our options.

Next, Nick asked himself, 'What emotions do I feel when I behave this way?' Nick realized that, when he disengaged or only-half listened, rather than intervening, he was fearful of speaking up. Paying attention to this fear, he asked: what assumptions fuel that emotion? He uncovered an assumption that 'people will resent and dislike me if I try to influence how these meetings are run'. Ha! That was a particular light bulb moment for Nick, for he had not been aware of that assumption at all and would not have associated it with his generally hands-on, proactive self. Yet he understood how it was the key driver of him feeling unable to shape and take more charge of the meetings.

Nick then realized that when he was being occasionally abrupt or abrasive, it stemmed from anger, which was seeping through his usually friendly demeanour. This helped him uncover another assumption: that 'my colleagues are making me ineffective'.

That is how emotions really help us dive down the iceberg and identify the mindsets that are having the biggest effect on our behaviour in a given situation. It is a feeling, not a rational thinking, process. Once Nick got these 'juicy' mindsets, he could trace how they were impacting his behaviours, moving back up the iceberg. He could see how his three mindsets were driving him to be less present and less effective, and how he had contributed to making the meeting less productive for everyone else. Unknowingly, Nick had created a self-fulfilling prophecy. And that is what mindsets can do because, in a sense, they determine the drop-down menu of actions that are available to us.

Nick's new iceberg (his 'to' iceberg)

Nick picked one mindset that seemed quite fundamental to his iceberg and his issue: 'People will resent and dislike me if I try to influence how these meetings are run.' Nick then asked, 'What alternative mindsets would serve me better?' He first came up with: 'When I try to contribute to how we work together, people will like me because I show that I care.' But, when he thought about it more, he decided another mindset might be more helpful: 'We'll feel better together if we are more productive (even if someone resents me for trying).' Nick noticed that he felt more empowered with these mindsets. Which new behaviours might arise for Nick as a result of these mindsets and emotions? He might take more time beforehand to help prepare meetings with his colleagues. He might also suggest more efficient ways of running meetings in general, or speak up in meetings to get the discussion back on track. As a result, the meetings would be more beneficial, not just for Nick, but for everyone involved. He would

Table 2.1 Nick's icebergs

	From	To
Results	• Meetings that did not move his priorities forwards • Knock-on effects: general exhaustion and insufficient quality time with his daughter	• More effective meetings for everyone involved • Progress on his priorities • Better energy levels, quality time with his daughter
Behaviours	• Disengage or only half-listen • Use abrupt or abrasive tone • Focus on short-term actions rather than longer-term implications or opportunities	• Prepare more effectively to add value to the discussion • Suggest more efficient ways of running meetings • Speak up in meetings to get the discussion back on track
Emotions	• Fear • Anger	• Slightly uncomfortable, but more empowered
Mindsets	• Meetings are all talk and no action • People will resent and dislike me if I try to influence how these meetings are run • My colleagues are making me ineffective	• When I try to contribute to how we work together, people will like me because I show that I care • We'll feel better together if we are more productive (even if someone resents me for trying)

make more progress on his priorities, have more energy and be able to reclaim quality time with his daughter.

Identifying and shifting our mindsets is not only beneficial for changing our behaviours and creating different results, but it can also be used to help our brain move out of protect mode. Psychologists call this 'reappraisal'. It typically involves widening our focus to pay attention to mitigating or rewarding aspects of the situation, and then using those insights to take a broader, more constructive view. It sounds simple, but there is a lot of evidence that this is a powerful tool for regulating our emotions before we slip too far into protect mode[20]. Likewise, naming our emotions is well documented scientifically to help our brains move out of protect mode[14].

An exercise such as the iceberg is an important first step and it might well be enough to get to sustained change. But we might need to complement it with other techniques. In Nick's case, he might shirk away from behaviours such as taking charge of how he attends meetings and making them more productive. He might realize it feels uncomfortable or even somewhat risky, and that could be a sign he needs to dive further for deeper mindsets, or use techniques to help him move through those emotions. By contrast, if a mindset feels in some way rewarding to us, that naturally propels us to act in accordance with it. Nick failing to change his behaviour could also be a sign that his old behaviours are too heavily automated, which could make him cling on to them even if he shifts his mindsets. The rest of the book offers techniques to help with all these challenges.

Acknowledging the past to create a different present and future

Due to the way our inner operating system develops and embeds in the brain, we may leave childhood with more rigid notions of what is right or wrong, and how to behave to get the results we want; only to find that the world at large does not quite work the way our formative environments did, or that we actually hold different views. We might attribute how we feel to an external situation or the behaviour of others, while, in fact, this is significantly coloured by our own inner operating system. It is our individual past experiences that shape the emotions we initially feel about a particular mindset and that animate it into behaviours.

Sometimes, it can be helpful to revisit what happened in our earlier years to make changes to our inner operating system going forwards. However, we do not always need to know the background story to the emotions we are feeling today, as long as we are aware of what we are really feeling about a specific mindset. To make good choices in the present and create the futures we want, we need awareness of which mindsets and emotions are at play and to be able to work with them in case they are holding us back or no longer fit our sense of who we are.

How we wish to evolve our own inner operating system is very personal: there is no objectively right or wrong mindset, emotion or habit that applies to everyone or guarantees success in all situations in a VUCA world. You may face situations where you feel conflicted between different objectives that matter to you, or different mindsets about who you are or how to act. We encourage you to see these as opportunities for deliberately taking charge of crafting the building blocks of your inner operating system.

One such area of friction is when we engage with others. It means that our respective inner operating systems, or icebergs, bump up against those of people around us. When our icebergs interact – at home, work or in our community – our inner operating systems can limit or reinforce each other, in helpful or less helpful ways. There is much potential for misunderstandings and conflict. Therefore, addressing personal mindsets is important to help us collaborate better. Most of us know this, yet we so often, especially at work, take the personal out of the professional. That is why *The Performance Curve* combines working on individual and collective performance and we give you plenty of tools for doing this throughout the book and especially in the third part on the connection catalyst.

You now have the basic functioning of your inner operating system under your belt. We have covered the different components of our inner operating system and how they interact, as well as explored the iceberg as a tool for diving down into the parts of which we are not conscious.

Our next step, in Chapter 3, is to focus in on the first aspect of the wisdom catalyst: how to get the best out of our brains at any point in time and especially when under pressure. Through the story of another client, US entrepreneur Rachel, we will encounter a particular type of mindsets, called 'hidden drivers', which can keep us from drawing on our full brain capacity and also give important clues for how to get back on track and bring our best.

CHAPTER THREE

Taking charge of the hidden drivers of your brain

Our client Rachel grew up in a family of entrepreneurs in California, where her parents had been born as children of immigrants. Rachel's parents were masters at coming up with new business ideas and making them successful. Dinner table conversations built Rachel's competitive spirit and her ability to push through her position, for example on what pet to adopt or where to go on holiday. Whenever Rachel was struggling, notably with learning the clarinet, her dad would often say 'perseverance pays' and offer a pocket money bonus if she continued.

As an adult, accustomed to rivalry and hustle, Rachel flourished in the family business. When she took over as CEO, it was a statewide media business of 1,500 staff and she decided to take it national. She was brilliant at negotiating deals to acquire similar companies elsewhere in the country, and efficient at integrating them. Her tenacity, high energy and creative new ideas helped the company take market share from their competitors in a slow-growing market. She was liked by her staff for her low ego: she was not afraid to get involved in the detail and loved challenge and debate. Within five years, she was leading an organization of over 10,000 employees.

Then the market changed dramatically. A new player appeared with an aggressive expansion strategy. Under pressure, Rachel's brain followed the well-embedded neural pathways and behaviours that had made her successful in the past: to look for novel ideas and keep arguing them through. But her context – the market environment and needs of the organization – had changed. In stable times, when the overall direction had been clear, Rachel's creative ideas and her persistence in getting others to adopt them had brought an advantage. When a new strategy was needed to take the whole organization in a new direction, her default strengths became weaknesses.

Without a strategy to address the source of its competitiveness, the company's sales declined fast. Some executives tried to tell Rachel that they needed a new strategy, but Rachel focused on destroying 'the enemy', as she had come to call the new entrant. She was caught up in price wars and other tactics and lacked headspace to look to the future.

Rachel's team became frustrated and resentful of what they called her 'ideas of the day'. She felt let down and attacked by them, and responded by micromanaging their work. The more she was knocked off balance, a fierce temper started coming out. After a few bruising conversations involving some yelling and blaming, she lost two of her executives to the new entrant. Rachel felt deeply betrayed by her team and eventually agreed it was better for her to step aside. The family shareholders hired an external CEO.

What happened? Rachel was a highly capable and well-meaning executive, but she failed to bring her best to her precious family company at the time when it was most needed. Why was she not able to adapt her focus and behaviours to suit the new environment and demands on her as CEO? What made her hold on, and even intensify, her previous 'high-contact' way of leading, when she needed to refocus her energy on the bigger strategic questions?

Something else was driving Rachel's behaviour and affecting her performance: her brain's fluctuation between what we call *protect mode* and *explore mode*[1]. These modes are the focus of this chapter and we will see what drives us towards either of these modes, how they affect our behaviours, and how we can take charge of these modes by getting in the driving seat of our brain. Deliberately managing where we are on the spectrum between protect and explore modes helps us get the best out of our brain at any point in time – the first aspect of the wisdom catalyst. It also gives us important clues for how to grow our best longer term – the second aspect of the wisdom catalyst and focus for Chapter 4. All this helps us maximize our potential while strengthening our well-being, and minimize the chance of getting in our own way.

Protect–explore modes: who is that behind the steering wheel?

We humans can react very differently when facing challenge. We can fall prey to fear, overwhelm or rage. And we are also capable of extraordinary courage, growth and adaptability. Our brain activity reflects these different reactions, and it helps to think of this activity as along a spectrum between two alternative modes, protect mode and explore mode. Depending on where we are along this spectrum, the patterns of activity in our brain vary, as do the mindsets that gain energy in our inner operating system and the behaviours they give rise to. All this means that, at different times, we get drivers with different priorities and capabilities steering our course of action. The ability to identify and manage where we are on the protect–explore spectrum is therefore fundamental for moving on the performance curve.

Cellist Yo-Yo Ma illustrated these two modes when we were speaking to him about his 2015 BBC Proms performance at London's Royal Albert Hall. This was the first time Yo-Yo had sought to tell the full story of Bach's experimentation with the cello by playing the complete Bach solo cello suites in a single sitting without interval. One man and one cello, with an audience of more than 5,000 people, performing for over two and a half hours. Yo-Yo acknowledged he felt some level of fear and trepidation: 'Can I make it through? Is this mentally and physically possible? Might there be a breakdown and I won't be able to carry it through?' However, rather than dwell on the potential threats to what he sought to accomplish (protect mode), he shifted his focus to what would make this challenge rewarding (explore mode): 'It's such a special venue ... the audience are up for this, they're adventurous ... it's actually a very safe place ... there's a real purpose to showing what Bach sought to do with this one instrument.'

With Rachel and Yo-Yo's examples in mind, let's look at each brain mode more closely and their relevance to the performance curve.

Protect mode: fast, strong but limited

When we perceive any threat, whether physical, emotional or social, we will likely move towards protect mode. We focus our energy on ensuring survival, the most primal function of our brain, and the brain's survival circuits have elevated activity[2,3,4]. This is particularly true of the amygdala, a part of the limbic system (the brain's network for emotions and memories). It is thought that the amygdala signals the presence of a stressor and activates a variety of other brain regions to assess the nature of the stressor and cascade a defensive response to the rest of the body.

In life-threatening situations, the priority is to react quickly and stay focused on the danger. Therefore, this process relies on deeply embedded, fast, automatic responses, rather than deliberate, slower reflection and proactive choice about the best behaviours for a situation. It is like an autopilot with a limited range of emergency functions.

This protective, fight-flight-or-freeze response is a necessary and natural part of dealing with threats or challenges, which keeps us safe when facing a tiger in the jungle. In protect mode, we are more alert to dominating stimuli (noise, brightness, etc.). Our behaviours tend to be more fear-driven (flight or freeze) or aggressive (fight). Our bias is towards instinctive, pre-programmed defence and quick physical reactions (default motor reactions such as running or ducking or lashing out). We are stronger and faster, and we do not feel physical pain the same way as we normally would.

However, having all hands on deck to ensure our survival comes at a cost. The acute stress of protect mode reduces activity in many parts of the executive centre of the brain, located in the prefrontal cortex. As a result, cognitive flexibility, working memory and emotional regulation are likely impaired, affecting our problem solving, reasoning, self-management and how we relate with others[5,6].

Researchers have found that even mildly stressful situations (such as a small public speaking task), trigger changes in brain activity consistent with protect mode[6]. Furthermore, our brains typically respond more strongly to negative situations than to positive ones[7]. When we fight to get our way in a meeting as if our survival depends on it, our brain is likely in protect mode. We might not pay attention to positive avenues or other perspectives, even when they could be used to co-create a better solution. And who hasn't erupted like a volcano of anger with a deep sense of righteousness only to realize later, once the heat of the flare has subsided, that the reaction was disproportionate?

Sometimes, our reaction might not even be about the situation at all, but stem from our brain reacting to something else. While covering the topic of emotions at one of our programmes, one participant asked why he had 'blown a gasket' when his boyfriend couldn't find his house keys in the morning 'yet again!' After exploring his own thoughts and feelings more, he realized his anger actually stemmed from a message he had received from his boss the day before. Not having resolved the situation with his boss, it was still triggering protect mode the next morning. His partner helplessly searching for his keys lifted the lid on his simmering emotions about an entirely different situation.

Protect mode is so deeply tied to the evolution of our brains that we all experience it at times. Pioneering solo pilot Gaby Kennard told us how the prospect of a recent trip alone (on public transport!) in Europe activated mindsets that lowered her confidence and left her feeling anxious (in protect mode). Gaby told us this reaction was 'silly' compared with piloting herself in a single-engine plane around the world, but it is in fact perfectly human and unlikely to evolve out of our brain structure any time soon.

Explore mode: accessing our brain's full capacity

By contrast, when we are more focused on opportunities and rewards instead of averting a threat, our brains will be in explore mode. Once Gaby was in Berlin and Vienna, she was focused on discovering the delights the cities offered her: their parks, shops and art. 'I didn't worry about the fact that I was on my own anymore. It was really quite terrific.'

Unlike protect mode, in explore mode there is no increased activity in any specific brain areas at the expense of other areas. It is simply that we can access our brain's full and varied capacities to pursue reward, including the executive functions in the prefrontal cortex[8]. Other areas that also help us pursue rewards (e.g. the striatum in the basal ganglia) will also be guiding our brain's activity, stimulated particularly by the neurochemical dopamine. We can do the complex work of manipulating information in our heads, creating options, exploring perspectives, empathizing and thinking through decisions. We are focused on what matters and able to shift our attention accordingly. We can think objectively and bring more creativity and intuition to tackle difficult issues[9]. Our self-awareness and emotional regulation will work well, so that we can manage ourselves and our relationships with others.

The emotions and mindsets that accompany explore mode support us to bring our best to achieve the rewards we seek. In explore mode, we typically feel curiosity, openness, even playfulness, relate well with others and enjoy being stretched by challenges. We are also better able to notice and shift our own mindsets, emotions and behaviours. Explore mode is therefore most supportive of growth and change, and a powerful way to lift both effectiveness and well-being over sustained periods of time. Multiple studies also indicate that our ability to move towards explore mode is fundamental for psychological well-being and its related physical benefits[10].

Explore mode is not about sugar coating a bad situation. It is about putting ourselves in the best shape to tackle difficulties and collaborate well with others. It helps us bounce back after setbacks and move forward more strongly. Explore mode also does not mean we become overconfident or overly risk seeking: by contrast, there is evidence it makes us more accurate[9].

Why are brain modes so important for the performance curve?

A degree of protect mode might raise performance for a while, but not for long periods or above a certain level (protect mode is a driving force of the boom-and-bust curve we described in Chapter 1). There are two major pitfalls from being regularly in protect mode in our modern-day VUCA world.

First, when in protect mode, we are not able to harness the full capacity of our individual and collective brains to address the challenges of today's world, which require complex problem solving and collaboration. Explore mode, on the other hand, helps us identify and take advantage of the opportunities that complexity and change contain, and helps us grow our potential. In protect mode, the reduced openness and flexibility of our brain means it is also harder for us to grow and to adapt.

Second, the natural 'off button' for protect mode does not get activated in a constantly changing world with an unending stream of potential threats, and this negatively impacts our effectiveness and well-being. Our protect responses were primed to switch off when the threat subsided, which gave our brains and bodies time to recover, and space to perform more rewarding activities, such as social interaction. Unlike the tiger who might lose interest and go off to hunt other prey, stressors rarely disappear in our modern world. Customers will change their tastes; competitors will innovate; we will have ups and downs with our work colleagues, friends and family; we or our family might face ill health; and the negative news cycle is with us 24 hours a day.

If protect becomes our more habitual mode of operating instead of an occasional emergency response, we can no longer balance out the fear-fuelled alertness with periods of rest and recovery, and we actually erode the functioning of our bodies and minds. And, the more time we spend in protect mode, the more we will likely be strengthening its associated neural pathways and our inclination to respond to future threats in the same way. In other words, we risk getting trapped in a downward spiral of increasingly fear-based reactions and their consequences.

The consequences of living often in protect mode are not very appealing. There are well-documented effects of chronic stress (akin to ongoing protect mode) on physical health, in particular damages to cardiovascular and gastrointestinal health and immune system functioning[11,12,13]. There is also a wealth of research showing long-lasting changes in the structure and functioning of the brain. Chronic stress leads to a decline in cells in the prefrontal cortex (important for executive functioning) and the hippocampus (important for memory), and greater reactivity in the amygdala (important for detecting and regulating our emotional responses)[11,12].

Even putting aside brain functioning and physical consequences, accepting protect mode as normal can also mean we live so cautiously that we risk not living at all. We risk becoming more socially disconnected and missing out on opportunities, fun and joy.

So how do we get out of protect mode and shift to explore mode, to improve our effectiveness and well-being today and develop our inner operating system over time? In a VUCA world, the 'tiger' is unlikely to wander off, so we need to take charge of what we can control; to shape the part of our inner operating system that drives how we interpret and react to potential threats. Let's look now inside Rachel's inner operating system to understand what was driving her during the challenging period she faced.

Protect and explore mode in action: who was behind Rachel's steering wheel?

When the industry was stable, Rachel thrived on the challenge of making acquisitions. The qualities she had embedded in the neural pathways of her brain since childhood – looking for new ideas, negotiating, rolling up her sleeves, persistence – served her well. Being in explore mode helped her bring the best of these qualities and develop them further, she kept strengthening what we call her 'forehand'. There was no need for Rachel to even identify her 'backhand', let alone strengthen it.

When Rachel's company was threatened by a new entrant, her brain engaged in protect mode. She became reactive in her business decisions as well as with her colleagues, instead of proactively shaping a new strategy. Not only was her forehand no longer suitable in the new context, but protect mode was reducing the functioning of her brain's executive centre and leading her to be rigid, so it became a liability.

For example, let's look at Rachel's strongly held mindset of *perseverance pays*. When on form, her executive centre would be more able to take in data objectively, evaluate costs and benefits, and switch approaches. This would help her decide when to persevere and when to do something different. However, in protect mode, Rachel's executive centre functioning would have been sub-optimal, leading her to default more to automatic responses. She rigidly stuck to *perseverance pays* every time she encountered resistance. This amplified her forehand, which led her to micromanage her team. Rachel's self-regulation also suffered as her whole body was caught in fighting-for-survival, causing emotional eruptions that antagonized the very people who could have helped her: her own team.

What was it in Rachel's inner operating system that kept her going in the same direction, even though it was obviously not working? The answer is her *hidden drivers*, which are particularly deeply embedded mindsets and, in our experience, the key mechanism for moving us between protect and explore modes.

The 'hidden drivers' of protect and explore modes

Hidden drivers are the elemental human goals, surfacing as needs and fears, that govern our behaviours and habits to keep us safe and confirm our self-worth. They are core to our personality and sense of identity and will be deeply worn into brain areas that store and process memories (e.g. the hippocampus) and generate emotions (e.g. the amygdala). As with other mindsets, these hidden drivers are not beneath the surface of our awareness because they are bad or need to be hidden. It is because automating important beliefs about what matters to us and how the world works helps our brains respond efficiently.

Regardless of how aware we are of them, hidden drivers matter. They can have strong influence over whether we are in protect or explore mode and how we respond to situations. This is why many psychologists will help their clients uncover their 'core beliefs', which usually incorporate their hidden drivers. Table 3.1 shows a list of common hidden drivers.

Rachel later realized that she had been in the powerful grip of a hidden driver: she needed to feel strong and in control, and feared feeling powerless or weak. (This is the penultimate hidden driver

Table 3.1 Common hidden drivers

Hidden driver	Common needs	Common fears
Virtue	Doing the right or good thing, being perfect or beyond criticism	Feeling or being seen as bad, defective, hypocritical or imperfect
Closeness	Feeling liked, getting and giving care and affection	Not being wanted or liked, being rejected, or feeling disconnected from others
Value	Feeling valuable or recognized, impressing others	Not being needed or valuable, being overlooked
Authenticity	Being and expressing oneself, being seen as unique or special	Not being true to oneself, feeling or being seen as ordinary
Mastery	Understanding and knowing things, being seen as capable and competent	Not having things figured out, being seen as incompetent or uninformed
Security	Feeling supported, having certainty, clear direction or guidance	Not having support or direction, feeling rudderless or without structure
Freedom	Feeling free or stimulated, having options	Being held back, feeling bored or trapped, missing out
Strength	Being strong, being in control, seen as coping	Being controlled by someone or something else, feeling or showing weakness
Harmony	Feeling at peace, having a harmonious environment	Experiencing upset, confrontation or tension

This list is adapted from The Wisdom of the Enneagram *by Don Riso and Russ Hudson,* © *1999. All rights reserved. Used with permission.*

shown in Table 3.1). This driver stoked Rachel's success in leading the company's expansion spree (what better way to feel strong and in control than buying up other companies?) and gave her a sense of purpose and fulfilment. But it also contributed to her fall, as feeling weak led her to micromanage and be aggressive. Rachel came to understand how changing direction and asking for help seemed like signs of weakness to her. She also realized that she felt out of control when she was not in the detail. It was wired deeply into her brain to avoid feeling weak or out of control, at all costs.

It is common to have a couple of hidden drivers, usually a main and a secondary, that are deeply embedded and stay with us throughout our lives. Rachel's secondary hidden driver was freedom, with a fear of getting bored, hence her love of new ideas. (Of us authors, Laura has feeling valuable as her main hidden driver, with feeling closeness as a secondary one. Vanessa's main hidden driver is feeling virtuous, and she also has feeling closeness as a secondary one.) Each of us may have hints of the other hidden drivers too, but they will drive us much less strongly.

Over our lifetimes, as we develop our inner operating system, how we experience our hidden drivers often changes. First, our deeply embedded hidden drivers start to feel less strong: we may experience that our sense of safety or self-worth can exist whether we meet our hidden drivers or not, and therefore have more choice over when or how they drive us. Second, we start to embrace other hidden drivers more, finding fulfilment and balance from exploring them alongside our original stronger hidden drivers.

Without getting lost in the age-old debate between nature and nurture, it is likely that both interact to shape our hidden drivers. Many people will recount how their early life experiences shaped their hidden drivers. We can see a link between Rachel's main hidden driver of being strong and the ethos of her family as immigrants and entrepreneurs. However, children from the same family can have very different hidden drivers, and parents often comment on how these needs and fears were evident in their children from very young, so it is likely that nature is also important.

That said, we should not take hidden drivers as deterministic: we have more choice than we often think to shape how they influence us. It might be near impossible to let go of them completely, given how deeply wired they are in our inner operating system. It is also not necessarily desirable: they are a core part of us and have helped us get to where we are today. But we can change how we relate to them, i.e. the direction and strength of how they drive us, so that they aren't monkeys on our backs. Let's now look at how.

Figure 3.1 shows how our hidden drivers sit at the very bottom of our iceberg. We can think of them as deep, general mindsets about ourselves and what matters. Because they are so fundamental, they feed into other mindsets, which are shown by the first row of empty shaded mindset bubbles layered over the hidden drivers. These mindsets are less general and more situational, but usually contain the hidden driver embedded within them. For example, Rachel summarised her mindsets at this level as *asking for help is a sign of weakness* and *I have more control when I get into the detail*. Those mindsets might then spawn or be connected to other mindsets, which are further away from the hidden driver but nevertheless get energy from it (the upper row of tiny bubbles). In Rachel's case, this might be *strong leaders don't ask for help* or *I can only get into*

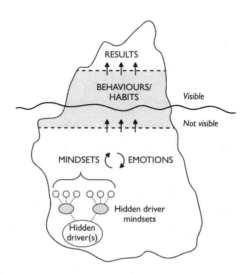

Figure 3.1 Hidden drivers

the heart of issues by going into the detail. All the mindsets closely connected to a hidden driver can be called *hidden driver mindsets*. Whilst the drawing just shows a few for simplicity, in reality this network of mindsets will be quite extensive and interlinked for each of us, which explains why our hidden drivers manifest in our lives as uniquely as our fingerprint.

The good news is that hidden driver mindsets are less deeply wired and core to who we are than the hidden drivers themselves, so they are easier to change. Furthermore, because they get their power from being connected to our hidden drivers, working with these mindsets will also help us get more perspective on our hidden drivers and feel less in the grip of them. This means, if you want to sustainably change deeply engrained behaviours linked to hidden drivers, shifting hidden driver mindsets can be powerful. The rest of this chapter explains how to shift our hidden driver mindsets, so we can relate differently to our hidden drivers and have them support us in reaching our potential, rather than getting in our way.

Have a say in who gets to be in the driving seat

We now cover how to take control of the steering wheel so you can deliberately move on the protect–explore spectrum. There are four steps: knowing where you are on that spectrum; diving to identify your hidden driver; shifting your hidden driver mindsets and loosening the grip of your hidden drivers; and helping others bring their best in challenging situations. You do not need to do these steps in sequence every time; see which one is most helpful to you in each situation. Though we primarily focus below on shifting from protect to explore mode, it is also beneficial to do these exercises when already in explore mode. It will raise your awareness about how your inner operating system works in explore mode, and give you clues about your strengths and sources of energy.

1. Put yourself on the protect–explore map

Sometimes we are so deeply on autopilot that we only notice that we were in protect mode retrospectively. If we can sharpen our in-the-moment awareness of where we are on the protect–explore spectrum, we get a chance to reset and pave the way for learning more about our hidden drivers.

What are the thoughts, emotions, behaviours and physical clues as to what brain mode we are in? In protect mode, our thoughts may be racing, and we may be quite narrowly focused on certain negative aspects of a situation. We might be speaking or moving quickly, not pausing to breathe. We may feel frustrated, anxious or defensive. We may feel stuck, or experience tension in our bodies. In explore mode, we may be thinking through situations more thoroughly, considering wider issues, or paying attention to opportunities or things we enjoy. We might be listening, smiling or leaning forwards, breathing deeper and more slowly. We may be excited, curious or hopeful. We will probably feel open and relaxed, alert and energized, but not tense or overexcited.

Some people find it easy to spot when they are in these different modes and some find it harder, especially given some of the signs of explore and protect mode can seem similar. If you find it harder, just keep observing yourself and it will become easier.

However, when in protect mode, resist the temptation to avoid or suppress these symptoms, even if they are unpleasant. Protect mode is there to help you when you need it. Just be mindful of reacting or making decisions when you are in its grip. Take a deep breath and use these symptoms to learn about your hidden drivers, as described in the next step.

2. Identify your hidden drivers

Awareness of the personal hidden drivers that send us towards protect or explore mode is an essential part of taking charge of our brains and bringing our best. Knowing what is triggering a brain mode can help us feel more willing and able to do something about it. Had Rachel known about her hidden drivers at the time, she would have had a much better chance of unhooking herself. How might we find out what our hidden drivers are, especially if they are outside, or at the edge of, our conscious awareness?

First, look again at Table 3.1: Common hidden drivers. Look down the middle column. Do you spot any needs that feel particularly important to you? They might feel very good when they are met, or motivate you to work towards them. Then look down the right-hand column. Do you recognize any of those fears in yourself? Which fears would you most dislike to come true for you? When we first show people this list, they will often see several of the drivers in themselves. This is not surprising because we all have seeds of all these drivers within us, to a greater or lesser extent, and may be influenced by the drivers of others around us. But, over time, it should be possible to zoom in on one or two drivers that are particularly strong for you, often a main and a secondary one.

Next, spot when you are in protect or explore mode, and dive to find out what is driving that. In protect mode, keep asking yourself questions such as 'What am I most afraid of?', 'What would be so awful about that?' and 'What am I really trying to avoid feeling, or being seen as?' In explore mode, ask yourself questions, such as 'What am I most drawn to or excited by?', 'What would I find so rewarding about that?' and 'How would I most like to feel, or be seen?' You might need to ask these questions a few times to get to your hidden driver(s).

The key is to focus on personal consequences: either for how you feel, or how others see you. For example, you might find yourself in protect mode because a colleague judged you inaccurately. You might realize that you dislike unfairness. What is so awful about unfairness for you? You might discover it is a fear of feeling weak, but it could equally be a fear of feeling unsupported, or a fear of not being valued (or something else entirely). Each would point towards a different driver in Table 3.1. You might find that some of the language describing a hidden driver in Table 3.1 really works for you, but some does not. What matters is that you have your own words to understand your hidden drivers. It might take time to get there.

Table 3.1 is based on the nine types from the Riso-Hudson version of the Enneagram, which we have found tremendously helpful. You could use this or other routes to learn more about your hidden drivers. Hidden drivers are built into various psychometrics, and Kegan and Lahey's Immunity to Change process also helps uncover them.

3. Shift your hidden driver mindsets and loosen the grip of your hidden drivers

As mentioned, we are not suggesting you try to change your hidden drivers. This step is about identifying and shifting the mindsets that are connected to them, to loosen the automatic grip of your hidden drivers. A by-product of this process is that you will gain more awareness and a different relationship to your hidden drivers, which will also lessen their grip. For this step, you need to work with a specific situation in which you suspect your hidden driver(s) are holding you back.

First, complete your 'from' iceberg, being sure to get to your hidden driver mindsets. Keep asking, 'What am I trying to avoid?' and 'Why am I worried about that happening?' to identify the mindsets closest to your hidden driver. Keep going until you have mindsets with a hidden driver embedded in them. As a reminder, we summarize Rachel's hidden driver mindsets in the 'from' mindsets in Table 3.2.

Next, get on the balcony to scrutinize those mindsets. Are the fears realistic? Look at what is really at stake, to calibrate the actual level of threat. What is the worst thing that could happen, how likely would this be and how could you respond if this happened? Even if your mindsets feel true, could you imagine seeing things differently?

Table 3.2 Rachel's hidden driver mindsets

'From' mindset	'To' mindset (after the pivot technique)
Asking for help is a sign of weakness	Getting help will reinforce and make me stronger
Strong leaders don't ask for help	Strong leaders pick when to ask for help
I have more control when I get into the detail	Balancing the big picture and the detail gives me more control
I can only get into the heart of issues by going into the detail	We can get into the heart of issues faster if we look at both the big picture and the detail

Finally, identify some alternative 'to' mindsets. As well as following the guidance to do this in Chapter 2, try what we call the *mindset pivot technique*, to turn the hidden driver that is holding you back into a source of momentum. You take the energy inside the mindset (the hidden driver) and pivot it towards the direction you want to go. It is a yin-yang technique, because it recognizes that, inside the protect mode reaction, there is a seed of something strong you can redirect towards explore mode.

In Table 3.2, Rachel's 'to' mindsets strike a balance between sending her towards explore mode and feeling realistic to her. An observer might challenge Rachel's 'to' mindsets even further (for example, you might argue that a CEO should spend little or no time in the detail). But these 'to' mindsets are a first realistic step for Rachel, which will help her enormously as she builds back her career, and she can evolve them further over time. If you look back to Table 2.1 for Nick's 'from' and 'to' mindsets, this is also a mindset pivot; both sides refer to his hidden drivers, but he gains more flexibility and choice from the 'to' mindsets.

To shift mindsets, it is essential to be aware of our emotions and how to disengage from the force they exert that turns our current mindsets into behaviours. The more a mindset is part of our identity, the more compelling its emotional force and physiological effect.

It is also difficult to adopt a new mindset when in protect mode, which will affect our brain's ability to get perspective or regulate our emotions. Since suppressing or working against emotions simply increases protect mode, it is more effective to pay attention to emotions and their physical sensations by labelling them, which sets up our brain for mindset shifting work[14]. Many people have told us how expressing their emotions safely frees up their thinking, for example channelling their anger into digging up the garden, a fast-paced run, or simply letting themselves cry[15].

To shift more deeply engrained hidden driver mindsets, we are also big fans of working with them in situations where they get triggered but less is at stake. This is like going to a big, empty car park to learn to drive instead of a busy, multiple-lane road. For example, one of us (Vanessa) is driven by wanting to do things perfectly straight away (her main hidden driver being virtue). She can default to protect mode when that is not the case, which then gets in the way of her learning and improving. She used the arduous (for her) process of learning to do a headstand, to help her embed new mindsets about persevering when not being able to do something immediately. She reminded herself of the new mindsets she wanted to strengthen (e.g. *practice makes perfect*, or *I can enjoy learning and making progress when I can't do something perfectly yet*) each time she got on the yoga mat and whenever she toppled over and felt protect mode coming on.

4. Helping others bring their best by being in explore mode

The most important way of helping others be in explore mode and bring their best is to be in explore mode yourself. Being in protect mode may drag someone else into it as well, especially if they have not yet built strong muscles for managing their own brain modes and/or if you are in a more senior or authoritative position. In addition, you can do the following to help them strengthen explore mode:

- plan how to approach difficult conversations to minimize others' sense of threat and maximize their sense of opportunity;
- notice when others are feeling threatened and give them a chance to reset;
- help others gain insight into their own triggers of protect–explore modes, for example when giving feedback, and create a safe space for doing so by sharing your own;
- work together to calibrate and manage threats and find opportunities.

We all spend time in protect mode as well as explore mode. If you feel at the mercy of, or frustrated by, your hidden drivers, remember they have helped you get to where you are today. We can move ourselves towards explore mode by compassionately learning about ourselves in protect mode and our hidden drivers. They contain important pointers for our direction of growth when we can meet them with curiosity, openness and acceptance.

Our longer-term growth as adults is the focus of the next chapter: how we can develop our brains longer term to see and manage the complexities we face in our lives and the world around us. This is the second aspect of the wisdom catalyst for being on the performance curve.

CHAPTER FOUR

The secret of vertical development

The previous chapters covered how we can proactively develop different aspects of our inner operating system, such as the mindsets that are closely connected to our hidden drivers and nudge us towards protect–explore modes. This chapter takes the longer view, looking at the path of development of our inner operating systems over our lifetime. We lay out this path of development and explain how we can accelerate our movement along it to help us better rise to life's challenges and complexities and, ultimately, maximize our potential and well-being.

This path of development over our lifetimes involves us gradually folding our current perspectives into new, expanded ones (what Harvard professor Robert Kegan describes as 'transcend but include'). It is often called *vertical development,* because it is as though we elevate our perspective[1]. From this more elevated viewpoint, we see more parts of the situation, more of the connections between the parts, and (importantly) more of our inner operating system and how it is impacting us in that situation *(i.e. we see more of the complexity in the situation).* This greater perspective then brings us more flexibility and choice over how we respond *(i.e. we are more able to manage the complexity).* In summary, vertical development helps us build our capacity to see and manage complexity.

Laura vividly remembers a moment early in her career that was characteristic of vertical development. A few years after joining a prestigious management consultancy as a junior consultant, she was promoted to project manager. Alongside many congratulatory emails, she received a handwritten note on thick, old-fashioned headed paper from a mentor, a seasoned director called Paul. After the celebratory opening sentence, Paul devoted the rest of the note to encouraging Laura to make sure that the promotion was really what *she* wanted. He urged her to use this moment as an opportunity to shape her career, and her life, rather than keep putting one foot in front of the other on the consulting career path set out in front of her. Laura remembers thinking 'Paul, what do you mean? Of course getting promoted is what I want. It is a recognition of my hard work. I was lucky to join this sought-after company, and now I am rising through its ranks. Why would I want something different? Why are you pushing me to question myself when it's a time to celebrate?'

Not knowing what to make of Paul's note, Laura pinned it to her noticeboard and went on her winter holidays with friends. Two weeks later, their car crashed at high speed into a mountain rock face, flipped and skidded, and came to a standstill on the edge of a steep ravine. Everyone escaped with relatively minor injuries, but that near-death experience was the first big wake-up call of Laura's life. It opened a small chink in her inner operating system, to think more about what she truly wanted from her life, and question whether the career path ahead of her was *the* map to follow.

When she went back to work after her recovery, it was on subtly different terms: she saw more clearly the benefits and disadvantages of the choices she was making, and indeed that she owned those choices. She reread the note from Paul and was struck by how differently she made sense of it. Only a few weeks previously, she had felt perplexed and slightly resentful when reading it; now she realized the gift he had tried to give her, by encouraging her to ask herself important questions that would help her shape a meaningful life.

We share this story to illustrate what Laura remembers (albeit with 20 years of hindsight) as a moment of significant change in her inner operating system. It was as though she lifted her perspective so that she could see more of herself (especially her inner operating system) and her life. She saw how she had felt driven to pursue a career path that brought much recognition from others. She saw the constraints of this way of thinking, and the impact on other parts of her life. She realized she had more choice, and more freedom to make those choices for herself.

This was a small but characteristic step along the path of vertical development that many adults follow, and you may recognize something similar for yourself or others around you. Round-the-world pilot Gaby Kennard also described to us how, around the age of 30, she realized she was deferring to others for big choices: 'I didn't have the strength or the belief in myself to do what it was I wanted to do. I realized maybe I should take responsibility for the rest of my life and work out what it is I want to do. And that's what led me to make my solo flight around the world.' Like Laura, Gaby saw her inner operating system in sharp relief: how she was holding herself back and what could unfold if she believed more in herself.

Both Laura and Gaby saw their relationships with others at home and at work with more perspective and became more independent thinkers. They realized there was no 'right way' they had to follow, but rather they could define what the 'right way' was for them. They were starting to rely more on themselves and less on external sources (e.g. other people) for their career and life choices. They were more able to create new choices, and to take them.

The parallels in Laura and Gaby's stories are so strong because vertical development follows a predictable path in most adults, although it unfolds over our lifetimes and at different paces. From the starting point described in Laura and Gaby's stories, it might take us years or even decades to fully build independent thinking into the deep wiring of mindsets in our inner operating system, and we might never fully arrive there. But, if we do, the path of vertical development can continue. With more perspective on our inner operating system and the world around us, we might notice the limitations of our independent thinking. With that awareness, we might gain additional flexibility and choice, allowing us to manage even greater complexity.

Vertical development can seem academic, and is much less well known than neuroscience, but it is at least as important for truly understanding how we and others tick, how to get the best out of people and how to navigate difficult situations. It is the core of what our coachees and participants on leadership development programmes tell us makes the most difference to their lives. Versions of it are built into most branches of psychotherapy. It is also central to how busy single dad Nick (described in the Introduction and Chapter 1) took greater charge of his choices and became more effective at work. In the next section we look at why it is so powerful for individuals and for organizations.

Why does vertical development matter?

First, vertical development helps us be more effective. It helps us see more of situations, including different viewpoints, and how the different elements in the situation are related. We can also see more of our inner operating systems and how they are helping and hindering us, which paves the way for us to manage ourselves better. We can also better support others through change and challenges, because we can see their viewpoints and the wider situation more clearly, and channel our own emotions and empathy more effectively. We also have a greater sense of choice when deciding what we do and how to do it, which means we can create more and better options, and feel more able to take them. Nick's greater understanding of his inner operating system allowed him to make better choices about how he used his time at work, and to be more effective in meetings.

Second, vertical development can help our well-being. Nick's greater insight and sense of choice allowed him to better manage his busy life as a single dad, which improved his well-being and that of his family. But it goes further than that: with vertical development we are more able to manage our brain to be at its best, including protect and explore modes. We can see our hidden drivers and hidden driver mindsets more clearly, and simply having this perspective loosens their grip over us. We can also use the greater flexibility of our inner operating system to adapt our hidden driver mindsets, so we channel our hidden drivers more constructively and spend more time in explore mode. We saw the benefits of this to Nick, and the beginnings of benefit to Rachel, in the previous chapters. Spending more time in explore mode will, in turn, benefit our effectiveness: the virtuous cycle of the performance curve.

Third, vertical development makes it easier to develop ourselves so we stay on the performance curve. As we have greater insight into, and flexibility of, our inner operating system, it is easier for us to develop it. Development will feel more fluid and faster: it will be easier for us to catch our inner operating system when it is sending us off track, and redirect it so we bounce back.

There is a positive correlation between the level of vertical development and leadership effectiveness, particularly at more senior levels in organizations[2,3,4]. This is not surprising, given that leaders are often coping with complex environments, which are full of change, uncertainty and competing interests. To be effective, they need to look ahead to the years (or even decades) to come, deep into the workings of their people and their organization, and widely into the landscape around them. As they develop vertically, they will be more able to challenge assumptions and preconceptions, hold and bring together multiple points of view, and look past constraints to find bigger, longer-term solutions. They will also be more able to manage themselves so they can support others and set the tone, even when under immense pressure. Vertical development helps them see and manage the complexity they face.

If vertical development is so valuable for our effectiveness and well-being, what drives it? The ups and downs on the roller coaster of life are often triggers for vertical development, whether it be a first job, moving countries, a car crash, an illness, losing a parent, becoming a parent or separation from a spouse. At these times, it can seem that everything we take for granted (for example, how the world works, what other people mean to us, or our personal power) is thrown into the air. We might have had certain expectations about how life would play out, the results we would get, or what other people would do. Now we must learn to survive and thrive in a new reality. But why wait for a car crash to make it happen?

We can also turn the smaller challenges of daily life into drivers of our vertical development: set-backs, confrontations, uncertainties, or indeed any times we feel outside our comfort zone. The rest of this chapter helps you do just that: i.e. to prompt vertical development proactively. We first cover the typical path of vertical development that adults follow. We then suggest things that you can do yourself (without needing major life events, coaching or therapy), to nudge along your vertical development and help you be on the performance curve.

The path of vertical development

Our early lives are characterized by plenty of development, vertical and otherwise. If you have spent time around young children, you will have observed with delight, and even awe, how fast they learn. They are learning facts and know-how: the lump of metal with wheels outside the house is a car and can take us to grandma's house; strawberries are edible but the spoon is not. They are developing skills: holding a pen to paper to make a mark; balancing bricks to build a tower. And they are also developing their inner operating system, i.e. the deep wiring in their brains that guides how they make sense of situations, prioritize what matters, react emotionally and take action.

Developmental psychologists have long tried to map the development of the inner operating system in children. A century ago, Swiss psychologist Jean Piaget started laying out his theory of developmental stages in children, to show how they build up a more sophisticated understanding of the world and think in more complex ways. There has also been a lot of interest in how children move through developmental steps to build a 'theory of mind': the ability to understand and empathize with others' points of view.

In the last half a century in particular, researchers have extended this mapping of inner operating system development into adults[5]. They have observed that adults follow a predictable path, which we can imagine is like a walk up a mountain with slopes and plateaus. We each walk at different paces, so some of us might spend quite some time on a plateau, or even stay on it indefinitely. Others might continue the climb, though usually in fits and starts rather than at a steady pace. On each plateau, we have a new vantage point, which incorporates the perspectives of earlier plateaus.

Harvard professor Robert Kegan has laid out three main plateaus on the path of adult vertical development, called Stage 3 (socialized mind), Stage 4 (self-authoring mind) and Stage 5 (self-transforming mind). Stage 1 (impulsive mind) is relevant to young children. Stage 2 (imperial mind) is relevant to older children including teenagers, and most people move through it before adulthood[6,7].

Table 4.1 shows the distribution of the adult population across these different stages, based on data from earlier studies of Robert Kegan and his colleagues. These (and similar studies) suggest that most adults are operating at or between stages 3 and 4 (about 80 per cent of people), with a few at earlier stages, and a few after[3,4].

Table 4.1 Distribution of adult population at the different stages of vertical development

Stage	2	2–3	3	3–4	4	4–5	5
Percentage of adults	5	8	14	32	34	6	<1

Notes: Stage 2 = imperial; Stage 3 = socialized; Stage 4 = self-authoring; Stage 5 = self-transforming. 2–3, 3–4 and 4–5 are transitional stages, in which features of two stages are present.

There is strong research to back up this general path of development but, like most models, it is just a guidepost, something to hold lightly and not see the stages as too definitive. We observe people who appear to straddle stages: for example they seem to operate differently at work and at home; or when solving complex problems versus relating to others. This makes sense if you think of moving between stages as the realigning of all the little mindset 'cogs' in our inner operating system: while some cogs might have already realigned to a later stage, it might take decades for the remaining ones to do so. While it will get easier to realign cogs as more of them are already realigned and our inner operating system is more practised at it, some cogs might stubbornly persist in their old positions. The good news is that, while the stages look definitive, a small move can make a big difference to how we operate (as we saw with earlier stories).

Vertical development stages

Children typically move from being impulse-driven toddlers (Stage 1) to the 'imperial' mind (Stage 2) around the time of starting school. They gain a sense of their place in the world, their personal power, and having wishes and needs. They are more self-contained, but still liable to focus on what they want, to think short term, and to see things in binary ways. Under conflict, a child or adult operating out of Stage 2 would likely react in a binary way (seeing things as good or bad, for or against them).

While Stage 2 is the dominant stage of few adults, its characteristic ways of operating can also come out in all of us, whatever our dominant stage of development. This might be when we feel under pressure and in protect mode (and our brain's executive function is not at its best). Stage 2 ways of operating can also be stoked culturally and politically, for example by the discourse surrounding populist movements or conflicts.

Let's now look in more detail at the typical characteristics of the inner operating system at each of the main stages of adult development: stages 3–5. A summary is shown in Table 4.2. We find it helpful to bring alive each stage with stories, but please bear in mind that each story simply illustrates, in our view, characteristics of that stage at that moment in time, or a trend in movement between stages. It does not mean the person is or was dominantly at a stage of development. There are many internal and external factors that influence what we think, feel and do in a particular situation, as well as our vertical development. We also cannot accurately infer someone's stage from isolated examples, given that different mindset cogs in their inner operating system may be pointing at different stages.

Stage 3: the socialized mind

This is the stage of development with which most of us enter adulthood. Around one in seven of all adults will be fully operating at this stage and another third on the slopes beyond it (so largely operating out of this stage, but with some perspectives from the next stage).

As we grow into the socialized mind, we come to see that we can survive and thrive best if we co-operate with others. To make that happen, we defer to those around us, or to 'how things are done around here', to be included and taken care of as one of the group. For this reason, it can also be thought of as the *dependent mind*.

When making sense of situations from a socialized mind, we draw on mindsets that come from outside of ourselves and which we have internalized into our inner operating system (largely unknowingly). We look to these guide rails (such as societal principles or others' views) to get interpretations of situations and find direction. We will likely not seek or even imagine there could be another way of seeing or doing things; rather, what we see is 'just the way things are'. Some of these mindsets might come from those who raised us: such as 'success means joining a prestigious company and rising through its ranks' (as Laura absorbed early in her career), or 'perseverance pays' (which Rachel took on from her father, as described in Chapter 3). Our mindsets might also be influenced by other groups, such as religious orders, celebrities, peers, teachers, experts or bosses.

From a socialized mind, we tend to see our own thoughts and emotions as happening to us, rather than being shaped by us. They just 'are'. We might think or say: 'Being busy at work makes me feel stressed.' The language of 'You made me feel...' is indicative of this way of making sense.

There appears to be strong elements of the socialized mind in how Laura, Gaby and Nick were operating in the situations we described earlier. They were making choices based on rules and expectations they had internalized from others. They were looking outside of themselves (to others at home or at work) for how to interpret what mattered and to set direction. Laura's early career choice to join a sought-after company seemed to be influenced by her socialized mind. Nick's likeability and responsiveness were underpinned by his attentiveness to being liked by others. This helped drive his early career success, but was no longer sustainable in his increasingly complex work and family situation. Gaby describes traits of a socialized mind when talking about her early married life: 'I always deferred a little. I was too influenced.' But over time she came to realize that, to feel truly fulfilled and happy, she was ready to find out and pursue what *she* wanted from her life.

The favouring of collective ways of thinking has been an essential glue in human society for thousands of years. It can help us to get aligned, work to common principles and collectively benefit from each other's accumulated experience and understanding. It has an important place in organizations: Nick and Laura's companies benefited from them fitting in and getting things done. It helps individuals fit in, and can hold families and communities together. However, a tendency to defer to the operating systems of others does have its drawbacks, especially as the world is increasingly complex and uncertain, and we are each needing to find our own path through it. Nick, Laura and Gaby were feeling the constraints of their inner operating systems. What might come next on the path of vertical development?

Stage 4: the self-authoring mind

This is the stage of vertical development that most of us are moving towards, or located in, during our adulthood. Around a third of adults are fully operating out of this stage. Around a further third of people are on the incline between this and the previous stage, and a handful of people are on the incline beyond it.

If we are operating with a self-authoring mind, we are just that: the authors of our selves. We believe our viewpoints and feelings are our choice, and we have taken charge of them (often with gusto). We tend to bring our own view of what matters and how to interpret situations, and to draw on our own internal compass or rulebook when deciding what to do. It can also be called the *independent mind*.

We see that we can each have choice in how we make meaning of situations. We are pickier about taking on others' views than previously. For example, we might come to realize that 'success means joining a prestigious company and rising through its ranks' is just one person's view of the world, and instead we shape our own definition, e.g. 'success is seeking to move forwards every day, whatever the challenges'. And, when we settle on a viewpoint about a topic, we might be quite attached to it, believing it to be the 'right' way to see things, certainly for ourselves and quite possibly for others too. This clarity helps us to cut through uncertainty, be convincing and get things done.

We also tend to look more inside ourselves to manage our emotions. We see more clearly that we have a choice over what we think and feel, and therefore how we react to situations. We might say: 'I let myself get stressed when I have a lot to do at work.' This is subtly different from the example we gave for the socialized mind ('Being busy at work makes me feel stressed'), which lacks a sense of personal control over how we feel. With this awareness comes a greater willingness and ability to change 'inside' to get change 'outside'. We learn to rethink situations, i.e. see them from different or broader viewpoints to create a more helpful overall perspective and balanced emotional response. For example, we might say: 'What really fuels my stress is worrying about letting my colleagues down but, in the end, they are struggling to meet deadlines just as much as I am. Maybe if we all talked more about the priorities, it would help us all feel more in control and less stressed.' This is reappraisal, which we first mentioned in Chapter 2, and it helps settle us down emotionally as well as giving us greater control over ourselves.

Both Gaby and Nick appear to have taken on more elements of the self-authoring mind over time, which helped them be effective and thrive. They started to question what was right, make their own choices about priorities and success, and take charge of how they wanted to live. While a full transition from one plateau to another might take years (and not even happen in a lifetime), Nick seemed to take a couple of steps along the incline in six months. This helped him thrive more at work and as a busy parent. Likewise, Gaby, over a few years, found much greater fulfilment with a solo flight around the world and then her degree. And, using her wings (quite literally) seemed to consolidate her self-authoring mind: 'I realized it was important to work things out for myself, not to believe others. That I must do what I want to do. And, in the process of flying around the world, I realized that I made really good choices and good decisions.'

While the self-authoring mind helps us take charge of ourselves and our choices, this 'taking charge' can also get in our way. Rachel, who was leading her family's business in a difficult market, had many characteristics of the self-authoring mind. She had strong views and used them to be directive, and this worked well in a stable environment when she was on form. However, when the world became more complex, Rachel was unable to draw in the perspectives of her colleagues and be flexible in her thinking. On top of this, she was increasingly in protect mode, which meant that her brain was not bringing its best thinking (her us-or-them mentality about the 'enemy' had echoes of Stage 2 thinking).

Like Rachel, many of us face challenging and uncertain environments at work or home. How could the next stage of development help us have more perspective and flexibility, to help us perform?

Stage 5: the self-transforming mind

This stage of development is relatively rare. It is thought that around 6 per cent of adults are on the journey between the self-authoring mind and the self-transforming mind, and fewer than 1 per cent have a fully developed self-transforming mind.

On our journey towards the self-transforming mind, we become more aware that there are many ways of seeing things. We recognize that our own viewpoints are shaped by our own experiences and therefore narrow, so the idea of being 'right' is limiting. Instead, we have a desire to be able to see or embrace multiple points of view and find ways of shaping reality that bring these together. We tend to look beyond constraints, to seek possibility even when seemingly stuck, and to find the light among the shadows. We can be empathetic in a qualitatively different way from the earlier stages, because we are adept at inhabiting the experience of others and navigating rocky emotional terrain. The self-transforming mind can also be called the *interdependent mind*.

The self-transforming mind can bring different ways of making sense and finding direction. For example, a self-authoring mind might have a single definition of success. A self-transforming mind might be more focused on understanding different viewpoints about success, or the process for getting to them ('I'm so curious about how different people come to their definitions of success, and how that influences them and those around them'). Or a self-transforming mind might reframe the question entirely ('What's behind why we are focused on success as a society? What does it get for us and what does it inhibit? Where else might we place our attention and what might that yield?'). Questions such as these may help us, and others, to see the system around us, and our hidden drivers, with more distance. This perspective can then give us a greater sense of choice.

If we are operating from a self-transforming mind, we have the adeptness of thinking that the self-authoring mind has developed, but are also able to challenge the limits of that thinking. For example, rather than changing how we feel about not meeting deadlines for our colleagues (the self-authoring example on p.77), we might ask, 'How can this period of peak intensity be one of renewal for us?' We might expand our horizons: 'Why are we busy? How could we change the ways our business works to remove this bottleneck for now, and for the future?' This can challenge both us and others to be more creative, to look longer term, to find the simpler way, or to think bigger when setting goals and finding solutions.

Likewise, rather than seeking to control our thoughts and emotions to best serve us in that moment, we might be more tempted to embrace those thoughts and emotions in all their fullness. We might let go of whether they are painful or delightful, and instead simply see them as parts of human experience, each with their own virtues and shadows.

A move towards the self-transforming mind brings us a wider-angled lens. It is as though the few more steps up the mountain path away from the self-authoring plateau suddenly unlock the view of a whole mountain range, with many peaks, and we realize that there is no single route, and that our viewpoint is just one limited perspective. This is akin to cellist Yo-Yo Ma's comments that there are 'many frames for looking at things' or 'many ways to Rome'.

Yo-Yo seems to be illustrating elements of the self-transforming ways of thinking when he talks about the interdependence of self and others in a performance. 'When you are performing, the aim is to make the audience the most important person, not you. You have to know the minutiae of what it takes to get people to pay attention to something – timing, cliff-hanging moments – but, once you have that ability, then it's how you use it and what for. You cannot say, "I am nothing": you need a strong ego to get people to pay attention. And then you are free to give it away.'

In complex situations, self-transforming ways of operating can help get better answers and align people. Wendy Kopp, co-founder of Teach For America and now CEO of Teach For All, told us she used to push to get to a consensus view of the right answer. She tries to lead differently now: 'I try to create the space to surface diverse perspectives. Our energy is then spent trying to integrate all of that. We look for a way through that acknowledges all the perspectives and gets to a higher state. But we stay open to the idea that we may not get consensus ... in which case, whoever is closest to that issue is going to need to make a call, which we will embrace.' This approach has some self-transforming characteristics to it, such as the emphasis on holding the space, surfacing the divergent perspectives and seeking to create something even better from integrating them. And it gets better results than the 'push' approach of driving consensus, in three ways. First, it creates the possibility of a better answer and, perhaps, a simpler one. Second, knowing that someone will make the call, if needed, makes things faster and more efficient than pushing for consensus, which risks stagnation. Third, it can create much stronger alignment because people truly feel heard, rather than shepherded.

But it is not to say that bringing these qualities of a self-transforming mind is always necessary or better. It might open up more questions, more nuances, or a desire to bring in and make sense of more perspectives than is needed or even helpful. Being able to knuckle down and follow others' guidance or absorb others' expertise (socialized mind), or assert a point of view and go for it (self-authoring mind), has merits in many circumstances. This is likely to be true in an emergency, or when we know very little about something and need to get on with it, or when there is little added value in questioning how we do something.

Paying attention to vertical development is not about hierarchy or judgement; it is more about matching the complexity of a problem with the complexity of the inner operating system that tackles it, for the benefit of the problem and the operating system. Another inner operating system might well find a way through, but it might take longer and come at a greater cost or trade-off (leading to the boom-and-bust cycle). The self-transforming mind will have more capacity to stretch up and address more complex challenges, and may find solutions that bring simplicity.

Table 4.2 summarizes what we have described for each of the three main adult stages.

Table 4.2 Typical characteristics by stage of vertical development

	Stage 3	Stage 4	Stage 5
Stage name	Socialized mind	Self-authoring mind	Self-transforming mind
How I see my own mind	There are set ways to see things, and it is best if I follow them	My viewpoints are my choice, and I can therefore choose the right ones	There are many ways of seeing things, there is no one 'right' answer
How I feel about myself and my capacity to grow and change	My thoughts and feelings just 'are'. Trying to change them would go against the grain of how I operate, and might be difficult and even threatening. However, I can learn new skills	It's not always easy, but I can try to manage my thoughts, feelings and actions in line with what I think is right. Learning helps me be more personally powerful	Growing and changing is a part of everything I do, usually with a curiosity about the experience and what it might uncover. It is a group adventure and a life-long process
Where I get my source of understanding and direction about what to do and how	From the interpretations and expectations of people around me, or other trusted authorities (such as experts or cultural rules)	From my own view of how things work and what is important. Or from authorities to whom I choose to defer	Through questioning and integrating different ways of seeing things and operating
How I might relate to others under pressure or in conflict	Look for rules and expectations for the appropriate way to behave	Decide what I think is right (for me and/or for others), then try to guide or direct others towards it	Listen and seek out diverse points of view. Encourage a view of the bigger picture. Support others to move towards a resolution

	Stage 3	Stage 4	Stage 5
How I might deal with a difficult problem	Take the question at face value. Follow the usual problem-solving route. Look for how we or others have tackled similar issues in the past, or how things are normally done	Clarify the question. Come up with a way of solving the problem. Seek to optimize. Challenge pre-conceptions about how things should be done	Reframe the problem into a bigger question. Challenge assumptions. Embrace uncertainty and disorder through the problem-solving process

How developing vertically helps us get in the driving seat of our brains

As we develop vertically, we gain more perspective on, and flexibility in shaping, our mindsets. This is especially useful for shifting our hidden driver mindsets to change our relationship to our hidden drivers. And it works the other way around: if we keep the path of vertical development in mind when we are working with our mindsets and hidden drivers, our inner operating system gets the benefit of a double work-out. Let's see how Rachel and Nick's evolving mindsets illustrate vertical development.

Rachel appeared to operate largely out of the self-authoring stage during the challenges she faced. Her main hidden driver is strength, and you could see this in the hidden driver mindsets that she identified as holding her back during the crisis, such as *strong leaders don't ask for help* and *I can only get into the heart of issues by going into the detail.*

Using the technique in Chapter 3 to channel her hidden drivers more constructively, she pivoted these mindsets to be *strong leaders pick when to ask for help* and *we can get into the heart of issues faster if we look at both the big picture and the detail* respectively. In each mindset, you can still see her hidden driver, but the mindset around it is less black and white; it accommodates more complexity. She is opening how she sees the world and herself, and creating more flexibility and choice to do what is right in that situation. The second one, in particular, hints at integrating two different viewpoints; integration of perspectives would become more prevalent in her ways of thinking as she takes on more characteristics of the self-transforming mind. It is a small first step towards her vertical development, to better manage herself out of protect mode when under pressure, and to getting back on the performance curve.

Nick also brought characteristics of being in transition between the socialized mind and self-authoring mind. His main hidden driver is closeness: it is important to him to feel connected to his colleagues, and for them to like him. You could see this in his hidden driver mindset of *people will resent and dislike me if I try to influence how these meetings are run.*

As he worked on his iceberg (in Chapter 2), it is no surprise that the 'to' mindsets he felt most drawn to were also pivots of his hidden drivers, since they kept meeting the needs of his hidden driver. He came up with *when I try to contribute to how we work together, people will like me because I show that I care* and *we'll feel better together if we are more productive (even if someone resents me for trying).* The first of these mindsets felt very comfortable to him, likely because it is not really stretching his vertical development: it is placing a high premium on other people liking him (a hallmark of how a socialized mind would experience his hidden driver). However, he found the second mindset interestingly stretching, probably because it puts aside 'being liked' and takes a more independent view of the closeness hidden driver, i.e. *we'll feel better together.* If Nick can integrate that mindset into his inner operating system, it will be one cog orienting towards the self-authoring mind and give him more control over succumbing to protect mode.

How can we deliberately go vertical?

So now the million-dollar question is: if it is helpful to operate out of later stages of development, how do we grow the capacity to do that?

If you challenge your inner operating system to manage more complexity, you will likely be giving it a workout that supports your vertical development. There is no single recipe or quick fix, but any exercises that help you see more of any situation (including more of your inner operating system), and give you more flexibility and choice, will be contributing to your vertical development. Most of the exercises in this book have the potential to do that, because they invite you to take fresh perspectives on your inner operating systems and think bigger.

However, we offer some targeted exercises here for a vertical development workout, grouped into three angles: 1) action, 2) reflection and 3) scaffolding. We recommend you pick exercises from each grouping to support your vertical development from different angles.

As you read through these exercises and pick what might be valuable for you to try, bear the following in mind. First, find personal arenas for your development that you care about (such as resolving a conflict with someone close to you, being a parent, or making progress on an issue you feel passionate about). Second, put enough heat or discomfort on yourself that you feel stretched, but not so much that you descend into overwhelm and protect mode. And third, always stay confident that it is possible for you to develop your inner operating system over time (a growth mindset).

Action

Action is about growing by putting ourselves in challenging situations that we cannot navigate without confronting and changing our inner operating system. These situations are designed to trigger our vertical development, without having to wait for life events to do so. It is important to both take the action *and* give the time and attention to integrate what you learn into your inner operating system. Notice what you learn about how you see yourself, others and the world around you. Here are some 'action' exercises:

1) Identify people you profoundly disagree with on high-stakes issues. Walk towards them: spend time with them and understand things from their angle. Explore whether and how this changes how you see things, or create new views that bring your ideas together;

2) Write three speeches about what you believe is important in life. Make them quite different – in topic, angle, tone or intended audience. Try them out, including on people with whom you might not normally share such things. Pay attention to how others react, and how their reaction impacts you;

3) Do something that tests one or more of your hidden driver mindsets (safely and appropriately). For example, if it is very important to you to feel strong and in control, let yourself be vulnerable or dependent when that feels unnatural. What light does it shed on your hidden driver mindset(s)?

4) Put yourself in a new, unfamiliar and uncomfortable situation. How do you feel? Why is it uncomfortable? How does this shed light on, or change, how you see yourself, others or how the world works?

Reflection

We can also support our vertical development by reflecting in a structured way about how we make sense of the world, others and ourselves. We can try to uncover our existing mindsets, and challenge them to get to new ones that better suit our situation. The new mindsets will usually be more nuanced, so we are practising and reinforcing bringing more of the complexity of situations into our thinking. Here are some example reflection exercises. The first three are to do as a one-off or ad hoc, the last is something you might do regularly (daily or weekly):

1) Follow a structured exercise that lays out your behaviours and mindsets, including your hidden drivers. This could be the iceberg exercise in Chapter 2, or an Immunity to Change Map[9]. Anything that gets you to lay out, acknowledge, and experiment with or dislodge the deeper mindsets in your inner operating system;

2) Take a survey that helps you gain insight into your hidden drivers or how fully you are living the different developmental levels (see Notes)[10]. Debrief it with someone experienced, to make sure you get the support you need to digest it and make the most of it for your vertical development;

3) Think through a time (or times) in your life when you went through a major developmental growth spurt. What was the trigger for this development? What helped you develop? What changed about how you saw the world, other people and yourself? How has this impacted how you operate today?

4) Pay attention regularly (e.g. daily) to when you fall into protect and explore mode. What triggered you into protect or explore mode? Was one of your hidden drivers at play? If so, what hidden driver mindsets were contributing to how you reacted? How do those mindsets help and hinder you? (See Chapter 3.)

Scaffolding

Scaffolding allows house builders to elevate themselves to a new level, from which they can build up permanent structures, which then render the scaffolding obsolete. We can also scaffold our inner operating system development with techniques that help us elevate our inner operating system in some way, so we get the immediate benefit and the practice helps build up our inner operating system for the future. Scaffolding is particularly useful for supporting vertical development, for example:

1) Ask yourself questions that encourage thinking out of a particular stage:

   a. To encourage more self-authored thinking, you could ask, 'What would you do if it didn't matter at all to you what anyone else thought?' or 'What do you personally believe is the right/true/ best thing to do? How is that different from what others think? Why?'

   b. To encourage more self-transforming thinking, you could ask 'What are the bigger picture factors at play here?' or 'What are all the different ways to see this? How might we bring all these realities together?'

2) Draw from the heads of complex thinkers or the hearts of emotional masters. Who are the brilliant heads and hearts you know? Try to join a project team, or participate in some of their meetings, or buy them lunch and talk through their challenges or yours;

3) Alternatively, think about someone you know (or even someone you admire from afar) who brings thinking qualities you value. Ask yourself how they would make sense of your situation and get their sense of direction;

4) Pick a hidden driver from Table 3.1 that does not resonate strongly for you, but which you would be curious to cultivate. Have it 'follow you around' for a while, i.e. seek opportunities to meet that need. Pay attention to how it feels and what you get from it.

Up, up and away

Investing in vertical development helps us increase our capacity, so that we can boost both our effectiveness and our well-being, especially in the face of complexity. Like protect and explore modes, it is a useful guide rail to help all of us grow, regardless of our starting point, to maximize our potential and strengthen our well-being.

In the last chapter of the wisdom catalyst, we lay out one more avenue for developing our inner operating system, that of particular mindsets we can cultivate to help us be on the performance curve.

CHAPTER FIVE

Mastering the three performance curve mindsets

Over the past few chapters, we have focused on the wisdom catalyst of the performance curve: developing our ability to see and adapt different aspects of our inner operating system. We have looked at how being in protect or explore mode affects the brain's functioning and learned about the drivers that often send us into these modes. And we have seen that the adult brain can develop vertically, so we are more effective at seeing and managing complexity.

At the very start of the wisdom catalyst section, we introduced mindsets, emotions and habits as building blocks of our inner operating system. We illustrated techniques for recognizing and adapting our mindsets and emotions. In this last chapter on the wisdom catalyst, we are going to zoom in on three mindsets that we have found to be associated with being on the performance curve. Cultivating these mindsets is another way in which we can adapt our inner operating systems to maximize our effectiveness and our potential, as well as our sense of well-being

The three *performance curve mindsets* are:

1) *The accountable mindset* – From this mindset, we see ourselves as being able to influence situations. We understand that what we think, say and do affects the outcomes we experience. We feel personal responsibility for things that have gone wrong and for fixing them. We also recognize that we can shape what we think and feel;

2) *The growth mindset* – From this mindset, we believe that we can grow and develop. We see challenges and setbacks as opportunities to learn and grow. We focus on possibilities and potential – how things can develop in the future – not only on the past and the present;

3) *The big picture mindset* – In this mindset, we believe it is important to optimize for the whole. We pay attention to interests beyond our own, often looking across organizational boundaries. We consider the longer-term impact of our decisions.

Why have we chosen these three mindsets? Actually, we did not choose them! In our 20-plus years of working with hundreds of teams and organizations and thousands of individuals, in dozens of countries around the world, these three mindsets keep coming up. They are the mindsets that leaders most often ask us to cultivate in their teams or organizations and which most often unlock individual and collective performance. When we asked leaders which mindsets have made the most difference to their performance, these mindsets came out top[1].

People tell us that these mindsets help them to be more personally powerful, see more options and possibilities, and be more adaptable. They feel more in control, settled and fulfilled. All this helps them to make sense of, and work through, more challenging, complex and uncertain situations. Shifting to any of these three mindsets is a powerful form of reappraisal, which will settle protect mode in our brains and encourage explore mode[2].

In a moment, we will look at each of these mindsets in turn. We cover what each mindset is and how it helps you to be on the performance curve. We help you recognize when you or others are bringing that mindset (or not) and how to cultivate it. We also look at the nemesis of each mindset, so that you are better able to catch yourself or others and course correct. Our aim is to help you draw more on each performance curve mindset, whatever your starting point.

Deliberately cultivating these mindsets is also a type of scaffolding for vertical development. When we take a balcony view of our thinking, and deliberately choose our way of thinking, we are practising self-awareness, perspective taking and versatility of thinking. Furthermore, we observe that people who show more characteristics of later stages of vertical development can live these mindsets more fully and expansively than people who show more characteristics of earlier stages of development. By practising these mindsets, we will be training new neural pathways that are consistent with later stages of vertical development.

Let's first get a flavour of these mindsets in action, starting with the house of Krug Champagne.

The three performance curve mindsets in action

Maggie Henriquez is a force of nature. Venezuelan by birth and a systems engineer by training, she has built a reputation for leading and transforming businesses in turbulent times. In the 1990s, she turned around Nabisco's loss-making biscuit business in Mexico, sparking a quality revolution in the industry. She then spent eight years at Moët Hennessy in Argentina, carefully developing their wine portfolio during the country's economic crisis. In 2009, with a 30-year track record, she took over as president and CEO of Krug Champagne, owned by the LVMH group. The champagne house was in need of a boost, and it was the midst of the 2008/9 financial crisis.

With Maggie's experience in quickly turning around businesses and her nose for wine, as well as delectable champagnes on hand to win over any sceptics, she seemed well set up. She dived into her new role with gusto and pace, drawing on her previous experiences. After a year, though, it was clear her approach was not working. She recounts: 'I got a D. I failed very badly for the first time in my life. It felt terrible.'

Maggie was invited to an LVMH group training programme and was honest with her fellow participants about how 'devastated and lost' she felt. By luck, she met a fellow participant who had made a similar move from mass-market to luxury goods. He helped Maggie see that *she* was part of the problem. Maggie's mindsets about turnarounds came from working with mass-market brands. The other participant helped Maggie see that the world of luxury required different ways of thinking.

Thankfully, Maggie is a voracious learner and she set to learning about luxury brand management. Her first realization was the importance of the founder for a luxury brand. 'There is no luxury without a brand, and a brand is someone. Founders Coco Chanel, Christian Dior and Louis Vuitton are still alive today through their organizations. How can you set a vision for a company if you don't know its *raison d'être* and values? To know that, you have to know the founder.'

So she and her team set about researching the 170-year history of Krug. They unearthed the original dark cherry leather notebook of founder Joseph Krug from the 1840s, which had survived through bombardments in World War I.

Joseph Krug described in the notebook why he founded Krug. He had been frustrated by how the growing conditions of the year affected the quality of the wines he could produce for clients that year. His vision was to offer the very best champagne each year, and this was realised by blending wines from many separate plots, drawn from current and previous years, to create a unique edition each year. This is known today as Krug Grande Cuvée, and each edition is made from blending over 120 wines from more than 10 different years into the 'most generous expression of champagne'[3]. Maggie shared how putting the dreams of their founder at the heart of everything they do, and how they communicate, has been transformational. It inspires the team to work towards, and push the boundaries of, this vision.

Let's look at some of the innovations that came out of Krug's renewed connection with the founder's original vision. Each Krug Grande Cuvée bottle now shows the edition number on its front label, to emphasize it is a unique expression. Furthermore, a Krug ID sits on every bottle and can be used to connect to a website and also a smartphone app with information about the story of the creation of the champagnes[4]. Krug has also enlisted musicians to taste their champagnes and then choose or create a piece of music to accompany each one, partly for the sensory experience, but also as a metaphor of 'fullness' for their Krug Grande Cuvée as an orchestral composition. The team are also tracking and tightening up the production conditions at every step of their wine-making process, including helping their growers migrate to organic and sustainable methods (no doubt aided by having a systems engineer at the helm!). This will gradually feed through into the wines over the coming decades. As Maggie says with conviction, 'Everything is in place to continue to improve. The best is yet to come!'

This vineyard vignette illustrates that the revitalization of Krug has come through looking backwards in its history, looking forwards to the Krug of future generations, and making links that turn this historic brand into a modern, multi-faceted experience. It also illustrates the cocktail of the accountable mindset, growth mindset and big picture mindset. Let's look at each cocktail ingredient in turn.

The accountable mindset

What is an accountable mindset?

With the accountable mindset, we recognize that what we think, say and do affects the outcomes we experience, and that we can shape what we think and feel. We feel personal responsibility for things that have gone wrong and for fixing them. At the heart of the accountable mindset is a belief that we can influence situations. Psychologists call this having an *internal locus of control* (believing that we control outcomes in our lives, rather than external forces being in control)[5]. We channel any disappointment or anger into redressing the situation and learning from it.

Maggie Henriquez took an accountable mindset when she acknowledged that her approach was getting in the way of progress at Krug. This then led her to remedy the issues by immersing herself in the luxury brands world and the Krug legacy. As Maggie put it: 'We have to take responsibility, to see we are part of the problem. Then we can be part of the solution.'

Interestingly, it does not really matter whether Maggie's action (or inaction) was the primary cause of the issue. Maggie joined Krug at the time of the financial crisis and inherited some challenges. The question is: where did she place her attention? Did she look backwards and outwards to apportion blame, and thereby stay stuck? Or did she look inwards at what she could have done differently and what she could do to move things forwards?

Holding an accountable mindset is not about dismissing what has happened to us, or implying that we are at fault when we are not. Many of us will have experienced being wronged in heart-breaking ways or finding ourselves in sad or difficult circumstances that are not of our own choosing, such as illnesses and losses. We are not advocating for diminishing our emotions, or putting on an artificial 'positive mental attitude'. It is about placing our attention on what we can control and how to move forwards. While not always easy, extraordinary power can come from owning our thoughts and feelings. Nelson Mandela illustrated this when he was released after 27 years of imprisonment and he reportedly said, 'As I walked out the door toward the gate that would lead to my freedom, I knew if I didn't leave my bitterness and hatred behind, I'd still be in prison.'

It is important not to see taking accountability as being heroic or solving things alone. We have seen many examples of how enrolling others in feeling accountable for solving the problem leads to powerful results. Maggie has solved problems by surrounding herself with skilful experts – production managers, financial controllers, wine-makers – and she emphasizes how these relationships bring creativity and motivation. International development leader Lorina McAdam, who realized she needed to change her leadership approach during a strike in her aid organization in the Democratic Republic of Congo, told us how she created a cabinet of people who brought different perspectives. This reduced the risk of a biased response and they were able to solve the problem as a collective.

Finally, we should also be mindful to distinguish between taking accountability and blaming ourselves. As cellist Yo-Yo Ma says: 'Two of the most important words to say in life are "Oh well". Don't fret. Don't stew. Don't punish yourself when things go wrong and you think it's your fault.' Blaming yourself is a form of victimization – making yourself feel smaller and more backed into a corner, whereas taking accountability is about standing taller and stepping forwards.

The nemesis of an accountable mindset: the victim mindset

The opposite of an accountable mindset is often called a 'victim mindset'. 'Victim' is a strong word, and this is not about being a victim of a crime. A victim mindset is where we believe that we have little or no influence over situations. Things are done to us, there is little or nothing we can do to prevent or change them. We feel powerless, that things are happening to us and there is nothing we can do about it.

Most of us will succumb to the victim mindset sometimes. Maggie has a mantra 'leaders aren't victims', yet she felt stuck in her first year at Krug before she realized that she needed to change her own approach. In fact, victim mindset is all around us: in the grumbling at the water cooler, the daily news cycle, and social media. It is a common trap, even for people who are responsible and proactive. Why might that be?

A victim mindset can feel better in the short term than taking accountability. It gets us sympathy and we avoid looking at our own mistakes and shortcomings. Blaming others might also protect us from triggering our hidden drivers. For example, if we admit we contributed to a project going badly, we might have to face up to not being as knowledgeable or valuable as we would like.

It is also possible that victim behaviours are well wired into our brains. In stressful situations, it appears our brains actually default to acting passively but in a heightened protect mode until they detect how to influence the situation (this is freeze, rather than fight or flight)[6]. This response may avoid expending unnecessary energy while keeping us on red alert to figure out what we should do next. However, if we overuse this response, it will keep us stuck.

We observe people with characteristics of later stages of development living an accountable mindset more fully and expansively. They seem to access more perspective and versatility with their mindsets and emotions, and so are more able to spot and shift their victim mindsets and unhelpful emotions. We described in the previous chapter how, as she seemed to develop vertically, round-the-world pilot Gaby Kennard shifted away from a victim mindset and took accountability for her feelings, mindsets and what she did with her life. Working on taking accountability and also on your general vertical development can therefore be complementary avenues for development.

If you are interested in reading more about the accountable and victim mindsets, see Notes[7,8].

Why does the accountable mindset help us be on the performance curve?

We have seen the accountable mindset make a tremendous difference to hundreds of organizations and teams and thousands of leaders. It helps people develop their inner operating systems in a way that unblocks situations, improves working relationships, and transform results. And this is backed up by the psychological research: having an internal locus of control (the psychological term for an accountable mindset) is associated with higher levels of job satisfaction and performance, and lower levels of stress[5,9]. Why?

First, it leads to deliberate, persistent action. Focusing on how we have, and can, contribute to a situation helps us pinpoint what we can do to move forwards. And, assuming we care enough to want to move things forwards, we are more likely to persist. When we mix this mindset in with a strong, clear sense of purpose (see Chapter 8), it is especially potent.

Second, cultivating an accountable mindset in your team or organization leads to more people who are confident to step up and make decisions.

Wendy Kopp, CEO of Teach For All, told us how, when its global organization is supporting social entrepreneurs to create their organizations, it would be easy to offer cookie-cutter templates based on experiences from other countries in the network. However, Teach For All resists doing so, as they are aware that network partners need to think through what will work in their local context and culture. In doing so, they build their own sense of accountability, as well as local capacity. She says it was 'amazingly clear' how important this mindset and capability was during the early days of the pandemic, when each partner was equipped to evolve and adjust, making the best decisions for their local context.

Third, role modelling an accountable mindset acts as a pressure valve to diffuse tension and sets an example. It stops everyone worrying about protecting themselves (and their hidden needs and fears), so it gets everyone's brains towards explore mode, where they can bring their best thinking to solve the issues together. Think about the times when you or others have acknowledged a mistake and the impact this had. Compare it with the times someone did not step up to acknowledge accountability: what effect did that have on you? We usually find that acknowledging our part in an issue can feel uncomfortable at first, but that it is a powerful ingredient for starting any difficult conversation to unblock an issue (more on that in Chapter 11).

In fact, scientific evidence supports the notion that our brains will fare better with an accountable mindset. People who believe they have some control of situations tend to have lower levels of the hormone cortisol in stressful situations[10]. High cortisol levels over time weaken the functioning and structure of our brains, particularly in areas that are important for memory, emotional regulation, and self-control[11]. And the fear that is associated with feeling we are not in control is likely to activate our brain's protect mode, negatively impacting the quality of our executive functioning and creating a vicious cycle as we are less able to problem-solve the way forward.

In summary, taking an accountable mindset faster, more fully and more often, helps us move on the performance curve. From the accountable mindset, everything is possible. But what is needed to help make that possibility into a reality? Let's add our second ingredient, growth mindset, into the cocktail.

The growth mindset

What is a growth mindset?

The growth mindset is rooted in a belief that we can grow and develop, and it profoundly influences how we interpret situations and make choices. It helps us see challenges and setbacks as opportunities to learn and grow. We can imagine possibilities and potential, for ourselves, others, and our projects. It encourages curiosity, a hunger to develop, and a confidence to enlist others to help us do so.

Juan Jose Gonzalez, CEO of innovative medical devices company Ambu, describes the growth mindset when he says, 'You are not a fixed entity, you can evolve. Depending on the circumstance, different skills are required and you have to change…What can the *unrestricted you* achieve?' He learned to bring a growth mindset from early on. His childhood karate career started at four years old with losing all his matches for a decade, but bringing a growth mindset helped him bounce back and persist, and he eventually competed at the national level. Later he beat the odds as a middle-class Peruvian during a period of extreme hyperinflation, political instability and terrorism to get a university scholarship in America, and then summoned up the courage to apply for his first job in a global company despite feeling his English was poor.

Of course there may be limits to what is really possible for any individual. But the growth mindset focuses on the potential for improvement, not on constraints. Pramath Sinha, who has founded two universities and multiple education ventures in India, explains it like this: 'I believe anyone can do anything. I know that sounds bombastic, but I genuinely believe it. You could challenge me by saying that you or I could not become a Formula One driver. Obviously, you cannot do everything. But, in the broad realm of what we are capable of, our potential is way beyond what we can imagine.'

The growth mindset has been much researched and written about by Carol Dweck and colleagues, particularly in the context of education[12]. Here, we want to emphasize two aspects of the growth mindset for being on the performance curve.

The first is to have a *growth mindset about growing our inner operating system*. Learning knowledge (such as the economics of luxury goods) or new skills (such as how to make champagne) may well be just what is needed in a particular situation. But, to be on the performance curve, we need to believe we can develop our inner operating system. We should watch out for distracting ourselves by working on skills ('I just need to get better at writing impactful presentations') instead of confronting our mindsets ('If I can crack the mindsets that lead me to feel threatened when speaking to large audiences, I will connect better with people'). As Yo-Yo Ma says about learning: 'It is about sense-making, about trying to integrate different things.'

The second is to have a *hunger for growth* and to enjoy the growth process. Once Maggie realized she needed to learn a new way of thinking about luxury brand building, she quickly sought out ideas and enlisted her team to help her. In fact, Maggie's openness to growth has helped her throughout her career. She recently completed a PhD in business administration with a thesis in Luxury and Wines, which has challenged her to appreciate the world of luxury, push her thinking and contribute to the field. Maggie is illustrating growth not only as a means to an end, but also as a motivator for its own sake. There is a unique joy and fulfilment that comes from spreading our wings, which further contributes to our effectiveness and well-being.

The nemesis of a growth mindset: the fixed mindset

With a fixed mindset, we believe that we have a fixed set of qualities and abilities that cannot be changed. We therefore see challenging situations as moments to prove our strengths or expose our deficiencies, and likely feel threatened or uncomfortable.

While our inherent talents and previous experiences will affect our capabilities today, our fixed mindset will be a barrier to getting better. As Henry Ford purportedly put it: 'Whether you think you can, or you think you can't, you're right.' From his own struggles, Juan Jose is acutely aware of the trap of the fixed mindset and often tells junior colleagues, 'the biggest limiting factor in terms of how far you will go is how far you *think* you can go. It is important to challenge whatever you are telling yourself is possible.'

Whether we hold a growth mindset or a fixed mindset is not a binary thing: there will be seeds of the fixed mindset in all of us. Perhaps you felt blocked at a particular subject at school or are 'terrible at languages'. Maybe you 'can't sing' or are 'too unco-ordinated to play tennis'.

Like the victim mindset, the fixed mindset is quite prevalent in many societies. Each time a newspaper labels someone stupid, or brilliant, or a genius, it is a blanket statement about that person's ability, rather than a criticism or recognition of something specific that person has done. Through the work of Carol Dweck and others, most teachers and many parents better understand that saying 'good girl' or 'naughty boy' is signalling a fixed mindset to an impressionable young child[12]. Educators are shifting to emphasize effort and progress over judging outcomes.

The fact that we have to be deliberate to signal a growth mindset shows us what a strong tendency the fixed mindset is. The creator of the IQ test, Alfred Binet, was actually not attempting to create a single linear measure of intelligence. He did not believe such a thing existed, and simply wanted to identify children who were struggling, to give them support. Yet we still use it today to assess someone's capacity.

We face possible triggers for a fixed mindset every day. We might see other people performing well, without seeing the effort they put in to prepare. Or we might face a challenge for which we feel ill-prepared. If we worry whether we are up to a task, our hidden drivers could lock us further into a fixed mindset. For example, we might be unknowingly saying to ourselves, 'It's safer not to do this challenging new task, in case I feel out of control.'

Given all this, it is not surprising that we slip into a fixed mindset. Let's look at why it is worthwhile to redirect ourselves (and others) towards a growth mindset.

Why does the growth mindset help us be on the performance curve?

The growth mindset is transformational, for individuals, teams and organizations. It helps them relish and rise to challenges, and improve alone and with the help of others. It helps them persist, overcome barriers, and adapt until they get to their destination. How?

First, people with a growth mindset are more likely to enjoy stretching themselves with challenging goals. Studies by Carol Dweck and others show that a growth mindset really comes into its own when we are faced with a challenge. They have found that, in low-challenge situations, people with fixed mindsets or growth mindsets do not perform very differently. But, once you inject a bit of challenge into the situation, the performance of people with a growth mindset improves, whereas the performance of people with a fixed mindset declines. In a growth mindset, our brain tends to relish a challenge and brings out its best[13]. By contrast, a fixed mindset is likely to trigger protect mode, affecting our brain's ability to bring its best and to grow (a downward spiral).

Second, a growth mindset helps us face results and feedback constructively. We are more likely to pay attention to the progress we have made and look for clues and opportunities to help us improve further. By contrast, with a fixed mindset, we will be alert to what results or feedback might be indicating about our capability (or lack thereof)[14]. Scanning and electrical activity studies of the brain during learning tasks that involve getting feedback seem to show that a growth mindset helps our brains pay attention to and learn from mistakes, pick up reward signals, recognize improvement, and ultimately perform better[15,16].

Studies have also shown that, with a growth mindset, negative feedback tends to lead to better performance next time[13,17]. With a fixed mindset, negative feedback can lead to a decline in performance. If you are not yet convinced about the importance of the growth mindset, read that sentence again. That feedback you give to people in the hope they will improve ... if they bring a fixed mindset, they might get *worse*.

Third, a growth mindset helps us persist and overcome obstacles by being creative and agile. This quality is much like the notion of 'Grit' popularized by Angela Duckworth and it was common in our interviewees[18]. Juan Jose says, 'If you fail, you ask, "What did you learn and what are you going to change?" You should never surrender the ultimate goal but you should evaluate whether there is a need to modify the approach.' The key here is the combination of persistence and adaptability.

A growth mindset can drive performance for organizations, as well as for individuals. Juan Jose needs his people to bring a growth mindset about themselves in order for Ambu to succeed: the company is heavily decentralised and individuals are expected to take fast decisions with calculated risk, to innovate and take on the 'Goliath' incumbents. A fixed mindset acts as a brake, particularly in such an environment. He also nurtures a growth mindset about the business: 'As a leader, it's my role to set ambitions for what the company can become, not based on any limitations in its past, but rather on the possibilities of the future'. Nurturing growth mindsets about ourselves and our businesses is powerful: they can complement each other and fuel us to go far collectively as well as individually.

We have now looked at two mindsets: the accountability mindset and the growth mindset. Together they help us have the self-confidence that we can make a difference and can grow, and the humility to open ourselves up to learn and change. Let's look now at how the third of our mindsets, the big picture mindset, can add some zing to our performance curve mindset cocktail.

The big picture mindset

What is the big picture mindset?

The big picture mindset is founded on a belief that it is important to optimize for the whole, rather than just for us or our part in something. It encourages us to take a more expansive view of what matters. We might put more emphasis on broader performance rather than on our individual results, or recognize the interdependence of other interests and our own needs. We might focus more on longer-term impact rather than immediate results. We will likely feel open, thoughtful, and inclusive.

It is important not to confuse the big picture mindset with a notion of altruism. It is not a requirement for big picture thinking that we are prioritizing others over ourselves, or doing things purely for the common good. Instead, we are taking a very broad (and long view) of performance. We see how, if we can improve the ecosystem and help others do the same, it will benefit us. For example, we might choose not to ask for more budget for our department next year, because we see that another department's results are more critical for the growth of the business, and our department's performance depends on that growth.

Maggie's example illustrates the big picture mindset in several ways. First, she takes the long view. This involves looking backwards: drawing inspiration from, and deferring to, Krug's history. It also involves looking decades ahead: building the legacy with investments in production conditions and the transparency created with the Krug ID. Second, she and her colleagues have sought to enrich the customer experience (e.g. with the smartphone app and the musical collaborations), based on a bigger picture view of the experience their customers are seeking.

Taking the big picture perspective requires skill as well as mindset. Oxford professor Eric Beinhocker described this in how he seeks to bring (and communicate) fresh economic thinking: 'I try to have a holistic view. I am always looking for the bigger picture, putting together ideas. This is both a mindset and a skill gained from experience. The idea is to lift up different strands of thinking into a story. Clear narratives are a powerful leadership tool; they help sense check your strategy and help others buy into it. It's about taking a confusing mess and creating a bigger picture to make sense of it.' (Chapter 9 offers skills to support big picture thinking, to complement the mindset described here.)

As well as the more cognitive aspects of the big picture mindset, there is an equally important social aspect: thinking about 'we' rather than 'me'. If we hold the central belief of the big picture mindset – that it is important to optimize for the whole – then we will focus on what matters to everyone (not just what matters to us individually). We will engage with others: to listen and explore so we understand what they need. We will also be more likely to problem solve together and generate solutions. On page 81 we described how Wendy Kopp has sought to build such a culture at Teach For All, the global network of education organizations she co-founded. They have tried to build a model where they surface divergent perspectives. But they are not always trying to forge a consensus, and they know that ultimately whoever is closest to the issue is going to have to take a call. As she says, 'We try to integrate a way through that actually acknowledges all perspectives'.

The nemesis of the big picture mindset: the silo mindset

With a silo mindset, we narrow our focus to our own interests, including protecting ourselves from our hidden fears. We likely think quite short term: what is the best outcome for me right here, right now? We focus on doing the best for our part, rather than optimizing for the whole. We tend to pay attention to and prioritize those close to us, rather than extending a hand to bridge organizational or societal boundaries. We may well lose sight of what matters to our stakeholders, be they customers, employees, partners or shareholders. We may feel closed or defensive.

The silo mindset is common. When we start coaching a team, the team leader will usually say: 'I want my team to think about the big picture when they take decisions. I want them to work more as a team, not in silos' and 'I wish they would resolve issues together, instead of escalating them to me'. We see this pattern at all levels of organizations. Even if it is hidden most of the year, the silo mindset usually pops up at budget planning season or in bonus/promotion reviews (when each team member is seeking to elevate their budget or their people).

Why is the silo mindset so widespread? First, the big picture mindset is harder cognitive work for our brains. Our brains need to hold more factors in mind – the needs of different stakeholders, etc. Our brain's working memory capacity is limited and it takes extra effort to group things so we can remember more of them and to switch between different factors[19]. It is also extra work for our brains to envisage the potential benefit of our actions to someone who is not close to us (such as a customer we will never meet). While taking different perspectives helps settle our brains in quite positive ways, this is yet more demand on our brains' scarce executive resources. It is far simpler just to zoom in on the most obvious elements to us.

Second, organizational life is both an individualistic and collective endeavour. We need the organization to stay in business to give us a job, and we need to demonstrate our individual value to keep our job. Even if we know we can add most value by making the collective work well, it can be frustrating to face competitive peers or a painfully slow processes to reach consensus. Combined with worries about putting food on the table and the hidden drivers that we are trying to protect, it is no wonder that so many of us spend time in silo mode.

Third, our brains tend to favour what is directly in front of us and certain. We are born very short-termist: young children tend to take one marshmallow now instead of waiting for two marshmallows a few minutes later, as shown by Walter Mischel and colleagues[20]. Most adult brains have more capacity for self-control but they still have to work to envisage future rewards, calibrate their likelihood and value, compare them to what is in front of our noses and then inhibit us from reaching for the reward in front of us[21]. Think about that delicious-smelling cake in front of your nose, compared to fitting into your favourite jeans in three months' time. It is far easier to just eat the cake now. Similarly, as Nobel-prize winner Daniel Kahneman and his colleagues have shown, our brains are averse to losses[22]. Taking the big picture can seem riskier, especially if the payback is uncertain.

In summary, in the silo mindset, we avoid having to make the more effortful, less certain, and often riskier choices. And, if we feel in protect mode as a result of interpersonal or organizational dynamics, the executive functions we need for the big picture mindset may well not be firing on all cylinders, making it even harder. But it is worth cultivating a big picture mindset; let's look at why.

Why does the big picture mindset help us be on the performance curve?

The big picture mindset helps us be more creative, insightful and relevant. It helps us think bigger, draw together pieces of the larger puzzle, and look for knock-on and longer-term consequences. And this way of operating can quickly become a competitive advantage. Eric Beinhocker's skills at bringing together different ideas and collaborators have helped create an international coalition of thinkers and policymakers around a new approach to economics. Pramath Sinha has a reputation as an 'institution builder' in India, having founded two universities in the country, and he attributes this to taking a long-term view.

The big picture mindset also helps people to perform better collectively. It creates more capacity for problem solving and idea generation, because more people bring more perspectives and different ideas, which can then be integrated to get better solutions. Focusing people on what matters overall builds alignment, and involving them early helps them feel a sense of ownership. Many of our other interviewees mentioned this. We described how Wendy Kopp seeks better answers this way. Tom Rippin, CEO of On Purpose, talked about how valuable it is when 'people argue from the organization's or even from the wider system's perspective, not from their personal point of view'.

We are not advocating for painfully slow consensus decision-making. We are simply saying that a big picture mindset boosts the quality of discussion and how aligned people will be afterwards, even if one person ends up taking the decision.

In summary, the three mindsets together help us understand our part in situations so we can take effective action, learn and work with others to improve, and look ahead and around us to get a broad perspective when making choices. We can move forwards faster, collaborate better and find more holistic solutions. Not to say that the nemesis mindsets are never useful. Being able to discern the most helpful mindset in a situation is what helps us be effective and reach our potential, and feel more fulfilled and settled. But these three mindsets are usually not the easy path, at least in the short term. It requires work to strengthen them as defaults in our inner operating system, and they may feel uncomfortable at times. Let's now look at how to do that.

How to nurture the three mindsets in ourselves and others

We can strengthen the neural pathways of these three mindsets so they are more likely to be our default ways of making sense of a situation. We can also get better at course correcting when we are bringing a nemesis mindset. We will now outline three techniques to do this. These techniques can be used with others, as well as ourselves, but with care: we do not know what is going on in other people's heads and we cannot force them to shift their mindsets. Chapters 10 and 11 on the connection catalyst help build the relationship quality required to enter this territory.

1. Experiencing the power of shifting mindsets

In Chapter 2 you learned how different mindsets affect how you experience and approach a situation. This first exercise focuses on how the accountable, growth and big picture mindsets change your experience compared to the victim, fixed and silo mindsets. Since the exercise involves shifting from a nemesis to a performance curve mindset, you will already be strengthening neural muscles to support those shifts in the future.

One of us (Laura) learned an exercise whilst working in California that is almost a magic potion[23]. We and others have used adaptations of this exercise in dozens of organizations all over the world and it can address organizational boundary issues, get post-merger integrations on track, and revitalize broken cultures. It works like this …

Participants work in pairs. They each tell their partner a story of a time when they felt wronged or mistreated. They then each retell the same story, but this time illustrating to their partner how they were accountable for what happened (i.e. everything they did or didn't do that contributed to the situation). After each story has been told, the facilitator asks partners to vote on how convinced they were by what they have heard. As you can imagine, the first round elicits energetic, emotional and compelling stories about being wronged or mistreated. Most people report feeling in protect mode as they relive their story from this victim mindset. Partners listen with empathy and shared indignation, and are usually totally convinced about how wronged or mistreated their partner was. The atmosphere in the second round is very different: calmer, more reflective and even curious. And almost everyone tells an equally convincing story about how they were accountable. Their protect mode seems much dampened down, which is not surprising given that this activity is a form of reappraisal, which settles down our brains.

This exercise highlights how much our mindsets shape how we see things and what we do. The situation is identical in both versions of the story. No doubt there are things that were 'done to' the storytellers. However, when their focus is on taking accountability, it might feel uncomfortable initially, but very quickly they start to feel empowered and see options opening up. Even if it is too late to change the situation in their story, they often start applying this mindset to other current problems and get insights.

Table 5.1 gives instructions for running a simple version of this exercise for each of the three performance curve mindsets. Try it, ideally with a partner. Take turns to tell the first story version, then do the same with the second story version, then discuss the reflection questions. If you do it alone, write down each story version as though you were trying to convince yourself or a friend, and reread each story version after you write it. Either way, spend just a few minutes on each step.

If this exercise doesn't work well for you, you might like to try it with a different story. Overall, it should illustrate to you how much these mindsets affect how you make sense of situations and the actions you

Table 5.1 The power of shifting mindsets

	Accountable mindset	Growth mindset	Big picture mindset
Preparation	Think of a situation in which you felt wronged or mistreated	Think of something you are terrible at, and cannot imagine improving, which has negatively affected you. Any kind of skill or way of doing things, at work or home (e.g. cooking, public speaking...)	Think of something you really hope will work out, for yourself, or those close to you (for example, getting a promotion, or securing a pay rise for someone, or your child getting into university)
Step 1: nemesis mindset story	Tell the story of what happened, illustrating convincingly how completely wronged or mistreated you were	Convincingly describe how totally terrible you are at this thing, and how you know there is no way you can improve	Convincingly describe why it is so important for that thing to work out

	Accountable mindset	Growth mindset	Big picture mindset
Step 2: performance curve mindset story	Imagine you were fully accountable for this same situation. Tell the same story, illustrating convincingly how what you did (or didn't do) drove what happened	Imagine you are capable of improving and feel confident about involving others to help you. List everything you could do to improve. Describe convincingly how much you would improve as a result	List everything else that matters in this situation (alongside or instead of the outcome you want). Consider things that matter for yourself, for others and for the wider world
Step 3: reflection questions	How did it feel to tell each story? What would operating out of the mindset in Step 2 (the performance curve mindset) lead you to do differently?		

take. Let's look now at how you can encourage a mindset shift when you (or others) are drawing on the nemesis mindsets.

2. Course correcting nemesis mindsets

If you spot an unhelpful mindset in yourself or someone else, how can you open up thinking and encourage the performance curve mindsets?

First, we know that the nemesis mindsets are often accompanied by protect mode, and that our ability to get perspective on, and shift, our thinking is likely to be compromised. So, before you even start, you might want to try to reset your brain (and others' brains) from protect mode towards explore mode (Chapter 7 will give you some techniques).

Next, the best technique we have found is to use questions to open up thinking without increasing protect mode. Table 5.2 shows questions you could ask yourself or others to encourage a mindset shift

Table 5.2 Questions to encourage performance curve mindsets

To encourage accountable mindset	To encourage growth mindset
• What might you have done or not done that contributed? • What could you do differently? • How can you move things forwards now? • If you weren't constrained, what might you do? • How could you unblock the barriers?	• What could you learn from this situation? • How could you use it as an opportunity to grow? • What will get you on a steep learning curve now? • If you got out of your own way, what would you do? • Who could help you grow and how could you enlist their help?
To encourage big picture mindset	**To identify mindsets generally**
• What really matters here? • What are other people's priorities and concerns? • What is best for the customer and the business as a whole? • How could you get to some shared goals with others, or help each other? • What will be the longer-term consequences of your actions?	• How are you feeling/thinking? • What are you assuming about yourself, others, or the world? • Which of those mindsets are helping or hindering you? • What might you be most trying to protect? • How could you think differently about this?

away from the nemesis mindsets and towards the performance curve mindsets. The bottom right box includes some general questions that would help raise awareness of what mindsets are at play.

3. Pausing to prepare our performance curve mindsets, especially in challenging situations

You can use the iceberg exercise introduced in Chapter 2 to prepare yourself or someone else to bring the performance curve mindsets, especially if you are facing a challenging situation. Look at Table 2.1 in Chapter 2 for the structure to follow:

- Complete your 'from' iceberg for the behaviours, emotions and mindsets you are already bringing, or are likely to bring, in the challenging situation. What results will you get? Keep hunting until you get to mindsets that relate to your hidden drivers. Notice any hints of victim, fixed or silo mindsets. Circle the mindsets that are most likely to get in your way.
- Draw your 'to' iceberg, noting down what behaviours, emotions and mindsets you would like to bring. Three tips for shifting your mindsets:
  1) If you spotted any victim, fixed or silo mindsets in your 'from' iceberg, introduce accountable, growth or big picture mindsets instead. For example, if your challenging situation were a client meeting about a new topic, you might have a mindset such as 'Clients won't take me seriously because I lack experience on this topic' in your 'from' iceberg (a fixed mindset). You might write in your 'to' iceberg 'Preparing with a colleague can help me plug the gaps in my knowledge and show up well' (growth mindset);
  2) Focus on identifying new mindsets that will help but are realistic. Notice that, in the above example, we did not simply write 'Clients will take me seriously' – we acknowledged the original worry in the new mindset;
  3) Use the mindset pivot technique to embed your hidden drivers in productive mindsets. For example, imagine you had a 'from' mindset of 'If I can't answer some of their questions, clients will think I lack knowledge and am not on top of the brief'. The 'to' mindset could be 'What matters to clients is my ability to understand their issue, and then harness all of our collective knowledge to address it' (hidden driver: being capable/knowledgeable).

Most participants on our leadership programmes benefit from working through the iceberg methodically for a few situations. They then become adept at anticipating, recognizing and reshaping their mindsets on the go and no longer need the iceberg structure.

You may come up with other ways to quickly prompt the mindsets you want. Research by Carol Dweck and others has shown that even quite simple interventions (such as reading an article about how our brains can grow and change) can have profound impact on students' growth mindsets and their results[24]. Little reminders can be enough to prompt your mindsets; our participants often put them on the home screen of their smartphone or on a sticky note by their desk.

In summary, these three techniques will help you cultivate the three performance curve mindsets for yourself and others. Of course, one of the most powerful ways to help others shape their mindsets is to be a powerful role model. Not just in our behaviour, but also in giving others a peek into the mindsets that drive our behaviour, especially in tough situations. So, keep working on how you bring (and talk about) these mindsets, to help others as well as yourself. If you feel that you already bring them some of the time, try to be more consistent. Or, if you feel you already operate from these mindsets most of the time, see if you can expand them. For example, you might think about how you can encourage accountability in others. Or you might expand the reach of your growth mindsets to take on more challenging change for yourself, such as reducing the grip of your hidden drivers. You could make the bigger picture even larger by thinking further ahead or more broadly about an issue. Whatever your starting point, if you keep increasing and expanding your use of these mindsets, you will develop your inner operating system, and hopefully inspire those around you to do the same.

You have now finished this part on the first catalyst of *The Performance Curve*, in which we have looked at different ways we can see and adapt our inner operating systems. We will now turn to the second part of the book, in which we will look at how you can integrate purpose and practices into your daily life to sustainably work on your inner operating system. This will give you the fuel to keep moving along the performance curve.

PART TWO

The Fuel Catalyst

How to Keep Moving on the Performance Curve

CHAPTER SIX

Sustaining the continuous development of your operating system

This chapter introduces the second catalyst for being on the performance curve, the fuel catalyst, and gives an overview of what to expect in this second part of this book. We also lay the groundwork for working with the third building block of our inner operating system: habits.

Being on the performance curve requires fuel, given it is not a leisurely rowing outing on a sunny day. So let's start by imagining you are an Olympic rower. It is the morning after your final race at the Olympics. As you wake up, you feel proud looking at the silver medal hanging on your chair, but also some disappointment; you and your crew were aspiring for gold. In that moment, despite all the pain and sacrifice, you decide to go for gold again in four years' time. And to do whatever it takes, starting now.

So, you wonder, what will it take to win gold? You already gave everything you had this time (and more). Of course, you will keep honing your technique. But new technical ideas will only give you the potential to win. What will fuel you to go all the way and make gold a reality?

One source of fuel will come from *why* you want to put yourself through this again. Is it a quest to set new standards, or reach your potential? Or perhaps to be a role model to others: to show that it is possible to persist until you get what you want? Whatever it is, you will need a strong and renewed sense of purpose – something that makes the long and tortuous path ahead of you worthwhile.

But clarity of purpose alone is not enough: you will need to adjust your day-to-day training habits. Over the last four years, your mind has been a powerful source of momentum – and drag. There were bumps along the road, which often left you feeling frustrated and stuck. You want to do more to train your mind, to be at your best more consistently, and make the most of every day. You start to see a path to success, and it fuels you to jump out of bed. You want to get your crew on board so that, in four years' time, a gold medal is hanging on your chair.

Come back to your own life now. Did you indulge in some sporty daydreaming, or did it seem too removed from your armchair or daily commute? Either way, take a moment to think of times when you were on a journey to achieve high performance. Your challenge might have been academic (such as a degree or other qualification), sporting (such as a race or trek), at work (such as building a new business offering or seeking a new role) or personal (such as improving your health or fitness or becoming a parent). What gave you energy and momentum to stay the course and reach your goal?

Your journey towards high performance will have required fuel, to get you started and keep propelling you forwards in the right direction, especially when the path ahead was foggy or bumpy. You probably needed fuel which endured and yet also injected immediate energy when you needed to rise to challenges and overcome setbacks. Our rower's fuel included a dream of winning and a sense of why that mattered, along with habits for training body and mind. Much like the rower's technique, the wisdom catalyst is the 'technique' of moving on the performance curve. The fuel catalyst complements it, to sustain us on the performance curve over the long haul. Working on the fuel catalyst helps us on the long-term journey of maximizing our potential and our well-being.

The fuel catalyst of the performance curve

Being on the performance curve is more self-sustaining than being on the boom-and-bust curve. It takes less of a toll on our brains and bodies, and we get reward and energy from the boosts to our effectiveness and well-being. However, moving along the performance curve requires fuel too. We need courage and commitment to step into new territories and face our mindset or emotional gremlins. It takes our brains' effort to deviate from established pathways and pursue new ways of interpreting and navigating the world. And, when we challenge the mindsets related to our hidden drivers, it can trigger a protect response because they are linked to our sense of identity and survival circuits. We therefore need good reasons to work on our inner operating systems, and to do so over the long haul.

A crisis can provide fuel to evolve our inner operating system, if it shifts the equation in favour of change. We have witnessed this during the Covid-19 pandemic, when many people made huge personal or organizational changes, which normally would have taken years, in a matter of weeks. However, to be on the performance curve, we want to develop our inner operating system regularly and proactively, whether there is a crisis or not.

The fuel catalyst of the performance curve is the ability to sustain the continuous development of our inner operating system day-to-day and over the long haul. It has two main aspects:

1) *Having a sense of purpose*, so we can focus on where we are going and how to get there, and to give us a reason to inject energy into developing our inner operating system;
2) *Putting in place habits* to maximize traction and minimize friction, especially when the road is bumpy.

Having a sense of purpose brings us clarity of direction and focus. It gives us a reason to face challenges, and is a source of energy when needed.

Almost all our interviewees talked about the underlying purpose of their endeavours. Luke Bradley-Jones, who now runs Disney+ across Europe, loves working on innovative, disruptive projects that improve customers' lives. He has moved roles so he can maintain this sense of purpose. Wendy Kopp, CEO of Teach For All, seeks to bring equality and empowerment through education, and has set up two organizations to make that happen.

Putting in place habits makes it easy for our brains to repeat behaviours that help us move on the performance curve. Habits do not depend on our brain's more constrained executive processing power and are less sensitive to stress[1]. If we build habits to automate bringing our best and growing over time, they will maintain our fuel and safeguard us against slipping into boom-and-bust dynamics when under pressure. One of Luke's habits is to start his day with the hardest item on his to-do list: 'This way I feel like I'm on the front foot. Even if the day is the same, my energy is different.' One of Wendy's habits is a breathing practice to help her centre herself when in protect mode.

From our interviewees, we see that the secret is to combine both of these aspects of fuel, so they are aligned and reinforce each other. Luke takes an annual retreat each year to reflect on his purpose and yearly goals, then translates those into quarterly, weekly and daily goals. Wendy has a similar process and, as she says, 'It's so basic, but it helps me channel my energy.' Luke refers back to his purpose when he feels off track to help him anchor back to what really matters. Wendy knows at what times of day she is least likely to be triggered into protect mode and tries to deal with her most important and most difficult topics then. None of this is rocket science, and both Luke and Wendy were keen to highlight to us that they do fall off track. However, behind this simplicity, we see the power that comes from building and blending purpose and habits.

The challenge is that these two aspects of the fuel catalyst require quite different capabilities. Purpose comes through stepping back from reality and envisioning a better future, whereas the work of building habits is more systematic, analytical and detailed. This might be why some of us struggle to follow through on our dreams, and others of us get lost in the detail of getting things done without a sense of where we are going. It is easy to get stuck with all aspiration and no actuality, or all drudge and no dream.

The aim of this second part of the book is to help you get stronger at whichever aspects of the fuel catalyst would most benefit you, to sustain your journey on the performance curve. It will help you clarify what you find fulfilling and to go wholeheartedly after it. It will also show you how to build habits that support you to go further because you use your energy efficiently, think bigger and grow faster. As a result, it will help you have the energy to maximize your potential and live a life well lived.

What to find in the chapters of Part 2: fuel catalyst

In the rest of this chapter, we cover how to programme our brains to stick to *habits* that help us do what we want to do, efficiently and sustainably. This is useful for implementing all the ideas in this book because it helps us make sure that our daily habits support us to move along the performance curve. But it is particularly relevant for the fuel catalyst, because fuel is about energy and momentum. Building the right habits helps us conserve (and even generate) energy and reduce energy-sapping friction. Habits also help us turn a sense of purpose into more sustained fuel, and not just rely on sparks of motivation.

Chapter 7 then helps you put in place a repertoire of '*performance curve habits*' to support your self-awareness and self-management. This will help you bring your best, especially under pressure. It will also reduce the executive processing power that is needed for growth, thereby increasing the developmental work you can do and making it more sustainable.

In Chapter 8, we focus on *purpose*, a powerful and essential source of fuel. Moving along the performance curve is challenging, and purpose supports us to go through the effort of upgrading our inner operating system. But this does not need to be a grand 'save the world' purpose: just being deliberate or intentional about what we want to create, contribute or experience day-to-day boosts our effectiveness and well-being. This chapter guides you to reflect on what matters to you and why, and to align your efforts with this purpose.

Chapter 9 offers you a technique called *paradoxical thinking*, which boosts our quality of thought, so we improve the quality of the options we generate and the choices we make. Practising paradoxical thinking helps us be more effective, dissolve the trade-off between effectiveness and well-being, and develop our inner operating system. This means it fuels us to perform, and to move on the performance curve. We explain what paradoxical thinking is, why it can be valuable to you and your organization, and how to systematically cultivate it.

Let's now turn to the importance of habits, the science behind them, and how to build them.

How habits drive us and can help on the performance curve

Think about a resolution you have set, at New Year or at another time. Perhaps to lose weight, go to the gym, eat more healthily, spend less or get a better work-life balance. How well did you stick to your resolution? Are you still fully living it now, or did you fall off track?

If you have fallen off track, you are in good company. Studies have long shown that only 10–20 per cent of our New Year's resolutions stick[2]. Fitness application Strava is reported to have recently analysed the data of millions of their users, leading them to nickname a date in mid-January as 'Quitters Day'[3]. These are shockingly bad data points at first sight. But they are also motivating, because they illustrate how much our habits and mindsets are driving us. If we can shift them, we can *harness* their sticky power to be on the performance curve. We have already looked at how to shift mindsets. The rest of this chapter will help you shift habits, using simple methodologies that, when followed, yield a 90 per cent success rate in New Year's resolutions after three months[4].

To successfully change our habits, we need to start by understanding how they exert so much power in our brains and our lives. One of us authors, Laura, knows this only too well. Her PhD research involved studying mindsets and habits in patients with different kinds of brain conditions, but that did not make her immune to her own unhelpful habits: 'When I was studying for my PhD, I regularly drove to my parents' home in London to stay overnight while doing research with patients in nearby hospitals. Midway through my studies, my parents moved house, so the last 20 minutes of the route were different. One night, about nine months after they moved house, I drove home. It was late and I was worrying about writing my PhD thesis. I parked my car, took out my bags and walked up to their front door, only to realize I was at their old home. Almost a year after they had moved!'

Why did Laura's habit of driving to her parents' old house dominate that night? It comes down to how our brain drives action, which is in two main ways:

1) Deliberately, consciously deciding what do and how to do it;
2) Automatically reacting in a certain way (a habit).

Deliberately, consciously deciding what to do draws on our brain's executive functions. We may need to do some self-reflection, analysis or planning. We may even need to stop ourselves from doing what we would usually do. All this draws primarily on the resources of the prefrontal cortex[5]. However, the processing power in our prefrontal cortex has limits[1,6]. When we are in protect mode, our executive centre functions less well and that negatively affects our decision-making[7]. Our executive centre is also not good at doing more than one thing at a time[8]. In the example just described, Laura's brain was strained and distracted, and the deeply ingrained habit of going to the old house won over.

The good news is that the capacity of our brains to guide automatic actions is much larger. We have talked about how mindsets are based on well-worn neural pathways; habits are the same. However, while mindsets are formed from stronger neural pathways in brain areas such as the prefrontal cortex, amygdala and hippocampus, habits are largely formed in the basal ganglia[1]. Because habits do not require our executive functions, we can combine habits (e.g. walking and eating a sandwich), or combine a habit with actions requiring deliberate thought (e.g. walking and having a phone conversation to prepare a meeting). While we might have moments of conscious thought intertwined with our habit (such as whether to do another lap around the block while we finish talking on the phone), our brain largely gets on with our habit without needing deliberate attention. By cultivating habits, we can make use of this larger, automatic brain capacity.

Putting in place habits can help us to be on the performance curve in three main ways. First, when we are feeling under pressure and this is affecting our executive functioning, the right habits will help us to stay effective. Second, since habits do not draw on executive processing power, we can repurpose that power to tackle our most important challenges and do developmental work on our inner operating system. Third, the process of building habits can be a form of scaffolding. When we pay close attention to how we are getting in our own way and experiment with new habits, we develop our perspective taking and our mental flexibility, which helps with vertical development.

Now we have looked at how our habits can automatically drive us (to the right location, and to the wrong one), let's look at how to build habits to make behaviour changes that stick.

How to build sticky habits

As you read the following five steps of building sticky habits, work through an example of your own. You will get a practical and immediate benefit, and your brain will remember the techniques better if it has practised applying them.

Step 1: clarify your desired habit

The first step in building a habit is to be clear what you want to change. You should lay out exactly what you are committing to doing differently, how much and how often. Make sure your habit is something that is in your control (i.e. not about changes other people need to make), feels like a realistic stretch, and will make a big difference to you. Examples of desired habits might be:

- before saying 'yes' to any new projects, I check how I will fit them into my calendar;
- do 10 minutes' journaling every day;
- spend 30 minutes prioritizing and delegating at the start of every day.

If you have in mind a way you want life to be different, such as 'have a better work–life balance' or 'lose weight' or 'get promoted', pick one thing you will do to move towards this outcome. This might be 'stop work at 6 p.m. every day to make dinner with the family' or 'eat modest portion sizes' or 'build two blocks of two hours into my week for strategic thinking'. If you have several things you would like to do differently, pick one: it is better to spend your mental resources on landing one thing at a time and come back to other changes later.

You might wonder how detailed to get at this stage. For example, a habit of 'spending 30 minutes prioritizing and delegating at the start of every day' could be broken down into a sequence of smaller habits, which we call '*micro-habits*'. Your sequence of micro-habits might be:

get a coffee, put my phone on silent mode, make a to-do list in my notebook, rank order the priorities, then finally call or email a couple of team members to delegate tasks. Later on, we will look at your precise sequence of micro-habits, i.e. *how* you make your habit happen. At this stage, stick with answering the more general question of *what* it is you want to commit to doing.

We illustrate the next steps with one of our own personal well-being habits – Laura's goal to swim twice a week – because we have seen that over 95 per cent of our New Year programme participants choose to work on personal well-being topics such as exercise, diet, sleep and mindfulness. But this methodology can equally be applied to almost any change you want to make to what you routinely do at work or at home. For example, you can use it to help you respond better in difficult situations, use your time well, or be more present with your family.

Step 2: hunt down the sources of friction

The next step is to hunt down sources of friction, i.e. *all the things that get in the way of us sticking to our desired habit*. As you read this story about Laura's swimming habit, try to spot sources of friction.

'One recent January, I got back from holiday full of energy and made a commitment to swim a mile twice a week. For the first couple of weeks, I dragged myself away from work and raced to the pool. It was always crowded. "It's just the New Year crowd", the lifeguard told me. "They will be gone in three weeks." Pathetic, I thought, no willpower.

'But then, one day, I was tired and busy. My brain was full after a long day, and I was worried about one of my projects. My last meeting overran and I wasted 10 minutes finding all my swimming kit. Time was tight to make my swim and be home before my nanny needed to leave. I hesitated. Skipping one day wouldn't matter. Swimming is boring. So I turned back to my laptop and forgot the swim. Then the same happened later that week. And before I knew it, I had given up altogether.'

What were Laura's sources of friction? Here are some of them: worrying about her project; her late meeting; struggling to find all her swimming kit; and finding swimming boring. Some friction came from an external source (e.g. the late meeting), some friction was practical (e.g. struggling to find her swimming kit), and some friction was more internal (e.g. finding swimming boring).

Each source of friction was small but, together, they made Laura's desired habit seem further away and harder to get to. The result was a barrier she struggled to overcome that week, especially under pressure. At the start of the year, even though some of these sources of friction were already present, Laura would have drawn on the executive capacity of her prefrontal cortex to control her behaviour and keep her on track. But, when she was worried and in protect mode about the project, her prefrontal cortex did not deliberately control her behaviour, and she defaulted to an old habit of turning back to her laptop.

The key to successful, sustained behaviour change is to *build habits that eliminate or beat friction, so they are sticky enough to keep us on track even when we are under pressure*. When starting our habit building, instead of using our initial motivation to guide our prefrontal cortex to override any sources of friction (which is what Laura initially did), we should use this motivation to deliberately build sticky habits. Not only will it help us stay on track when our prefrontal cortices are not at their best, but it will also free up our prefrontal cortices to channel their executive capacity elsewhere[9].

Hunt down all the sources of friction that will, or might, get in the way of you sticking to your desired habit. You can draw on what has got in the way for you in the past, or imagine what might get in the way. Be quite specific and detailed. Nothing is too small to mention. If it gets in the way, write it down. Consider external sources of friction (i.e. how other people or your environment might affect your plans), practical sources of friction (i.e. equipment and logistics), and internal sources of friction (i.e. your thoughts and feelings).

Step 3: create a sequence of micro-habits that build traction

Once you have identified your sources of friction, the next step is to deconstruct your habit into a sequence of micro-habits (the little steps within your habit) that turn friction into *traction*. *Traction is anything that helps us bust past friction to stick to our desired habit.* At a minimum, traction helps us neutralize friction. At its best, traction turns a source of friction into positive momentum (the habit equivalent of the mindset pivot in Chapter 2). Success comes when you have a bulletproof sequence of micro-habits that you automatically follow, even when potential friction or pressure is high.

To get to this sequence, start by identifying micro-habits that will create traction. Let's look at Laura's second (successful) attempt at

Table 6.1 Friction and traction for Laura's swimming example

Source of friction	Micro-habits that create traction
Struggling to find my swimming kit	Pack full swimming bag as soon as kit is dry after last swim. Keep it in the same place. (The bag is transparent so I can quickly check everything is there)
Over-running meeting	The Friday before, block out a 30-minute buffer to close the day before every upcoming swimming session
Worrying about work issues	Use travel time to the pool to think through an issue or to call a colleague to discuss it
Finding swimming boring	Use waterproof MP3 player (birthday present) to listen to my favourite motivational tunes. (Game-changer, this neutralizes friction *and* creates momentum)

her swimming resolution, when she did just this. Table 6.1 shows the micro-habits she used to create traction.

There are different ways to address sources of friction and we need to judge what will help us most. Laura could have chosen to deal with the late-running meetings by improving meeting planning or setting expectations that she would need to finish the meeting on time (and there might have been other benefits to her and others from that). However, she chose to create a buffer time in her diary, as that was most easily in her control.

Once you have set out the micro-habits that will help you build traction, you will likely see a sequence emerging. There may be some micro-habits that you follow at particular times (e.g. the Friday before, block out 30 minutes in agenda before each swimming session). Other micro-habits will be your default response when faced with a particular circumstance (e.g. if a colleague calls about a work issue at the end of the day, call them back whilst en route to the pool). You may need some micro-habits to take place quite far ahead of the actual event (e.g. packing swimming bag, blocking out buffer time). Without this 'upstream' work, completing your habit in the moment might require Herculean effort (and executive control), which is not sustainable.

The environment around us plays a big part in how we build and change habits[10]. We see this in rehabilitation for addiction: changing the environment of an addict helps them rehabilitate, because the cues for their habits are removed[9]. We can change tangible things in our environment to reduce friction and boost traction, such as throwing out all the chocolate in the house (this sounds awful to us but might be quite effective if your goal is to stop eating sweet treats). We can also make more subtle changes to the environment we are in (such as Laura changing the last 30 minutes of her work day to desk work, rather than a meeting).

Other people are an important part of our environment and can be sources of friction and traction. You might need to ask them to do things differently ('Please try to call me before 5 p.m. on my swimming days if you need something before the end of the day' or 'Please only call me if it is really urgent'). Or you might need new micro-habits of responding to neutralize the friction ('Can this wait until tomorrow? or 'I will call you back from the car in five minutes.'). Spending time with people who have the habits you desire might help you learn their micro-habits and take advantage of the routines and environment they have already created. You may also benefit from the human tendency to take on the norms of people we identify with. Other people can also help your micro-habits feel more rewarding.

You might need some trial and error to create traction but, once you get there, everything will feel smoother, and possibly lighter and more fun. Your desired habit will feel more attainable. And, when the distance to our goals feels more attainable, this encourages us to be in explore mode, so we feel better and are more able to bring our best[11]. Let's turn to how we can use reward to make our habits even more sticky.

Step 4: reward yourself, but in the right way

A cocktail of neurochemicals in our brain accompanies the feeling of reward. The neurochemical dopamine is released primarily in the basal ganglia and is particularly potent; our brains will work quite hard to get it released[12]. That makes our basal ganglia adept at a) learning which actions tend to lead to a feeling of reward, and b) repeating those actions to get more reward. This means that, if you can make doing your micro-habits feel rewarding, your brain will cement them more quickly and more deeply. However, reward is a subtle art which can be counter-productive. Let's look at four ways to ensure rewards are powerful, by making them: immediate, intrinsic, large and surprising.

1. *Immediate* – Our brains are more sensitive to immediate rewards than to delayed ones. In Chapter 5 we talked about how young

children find it hard to resist eating one marshmallow now to get two marshmallows later (so called 'delayed gratification')[13]. While we adults have better developed prefrontal cortices to do the mental work required for delayed gratification, experiments tend to find we also do its opposite, i.e. choose near-term rewards over larger, later rewards[14]. This preference for near-term rewards holds true regardless of timeframe, i.e. whether we are choosing between a reward now vs. in 15 seconds time, or a reward in one month vs. in six months.

We can even see this in the brain's release of dopamine. Our brains release dopamine when they anticipate a reward, which is a way of training us to keep doing things that have historically been rewarding (a bit like Pavlov's dogs). But our brains will be releasing exponentially less anticipatory dopamine if they expect a reward to be delayed: they discount the value of a future reward[15]. Ever succumbed to another box set episode at night, instead of going to bed and feeling fresh the next day? You can thank your anticipatory dopamine for that.

On the upside, we can take advantage of this by making *doing* our habits rewarding, so there is no discounting in our anticipatory dopamine. Best of all is to make the heart of your habit feel enjoyable (such as having your favourite cappuccino while you prioritize at the start of your day, or paying attention to the enjoyable aspects of what you are doing, such as how alive your body feels while swimming). The next best option is to insert a rewarding micro-habit into your sequence (such as ticking a box on a scorecard when you complete a difficult bit of your habit, or giving yourself some extra time in the hot shower after swimming in the cold pool). That will boost your motivation for doing the whole sequence.

2. *Intrinsic* – Intrinsic reward is the internal benefit, such as satisfaction or enjoyment, we get from doing something. Extrinsic reward is given to us, such as praise, recognition, gifts, or money. Intrinsic reward is likely to be a more sustainable motivation for your habits, because it is in your control, and because your brain may

lose interest in predictable external rewards[16,17]. Making your habits feel more rewarding (as described previously) will help generate intrinsic reward. As does putting the emphasis on a different mindset (for example: 'The repetitive nature of swimming balances out the stimulation my brain gets during the rest of my day.').

That said, external rewards might help you get your habits started until they become more intrinsically rewarding. For example, receiving praise from a friend might help you get through the painful phase of starting running again, until you feel stronger and it is more intrinsically enjoyable. Praise or recognition may also help you feel more capable, which could lead to a higher intrinsic reward. The key is not to have your extrinsic reward supplant your intrinsic reward, so we recommend you only use it to cultivate, not replace, intrinsic reward.

3. *Large* – Larger-seeming rewards will generate more dopamine and anticipatory dopamine and so are a greater impetus[18]. You could make the rewards you give yourself during or after your habits bigger: more chocolate sprinkles on your cappuccino, or more time under the hot shower after swimming. However, you can also make your rewards *seem* larger by paying more attention to them, i.e. giving yourself a bigger (maybe even loud, fist-pumping) 'yippee' when you complete a task, or mentally running through why completing your habit is so satisfying.

4. *Surprising* – Surprise is surprisingly motivating[19]. On the one hand, predictability is helpful: our brains know when to put the effort in. But this is where it gets counter-intuitive. As well as firing an anticipatory dopamine signal when we expect a reward, our brains fire a second dopamine signal when the reward comes. (This closes the feedback loop: the size of the second signal helps our brain learn whether it anticipated the reward correctly.) If the reward is surprising in some way (unusual, or surprisingly big), that second hit of dopamine will be bigger. The motivation of surprise draws us into unpredictable activities, such as social media, video games and watching sports matches. By contrast,

predictability reduces the size of the second dopamine signal and predictable rewards can feel less rewarding over time.

Be creative to build surprise into your habits. For example, whilst our colleague Talia was building a habit of keeping up to date daily on current affairs, her partner started conversations with her about random news topics at random times. She experienced her daily reading of the news sites as more rewarding, because she anticipated (and got) surprising opportunities to talk about what she was learning.

These four ways to make your habits rewarding should point you in the right direction. However, reward is a subtle and evolving art, so keep paying attention to how rewarding your habits feel and adjust the rewards if needed. Once you have a plan for reward, you are ready to build a watertight sequence of micro-habits.

Step 5: make your sequence watertight

If you have built micro-habits that draw from the ideas in steps 1–4, you should be well on your way to making your overall change stick. However, even with the best-laid plans, life – and our well-worn old habits – can easily get in the way. To make your sequence watertight, here are some additional ideas and tips.

1. *Substitution* – Do you have a persistent habit you would really like to stop? Instead of eliminating it, replace it. Diverting your energy this way might need some deliberate effort initially, but it is likely to be less demanding for your brain than continually resisting doing something it is used to doing. For example, if you have a habit of reaching for the chocolate (we don't know anyone with that habit, honest), then you could have a bowl of your favourite fruit nearby. Or divert from reading emails on your smartphone when you wake up, to reading a couple of pages of an e-book.

2. *Hooks* – If you are struggling to get your habit started at a regular time, try to hook it to an existing habit. Over time, your brain will

see the existing habit as a cue to automatically do the new habit. For example, if you want to meditate for 10 minutes per day, you could slot it into a specific part of your morning routine, e.g. after getting dressed. Or, if you want to better prioritize your day, organize your to-do list when you first sit down at your desk, before you switch on your computer.

3. *Combining* – If you are struggling to fit your habit in, ask yourself how you could combine it with another activity that would make it, and the other activity, more sustainable and potentially more fulfilling. If you want to walk 10,000 steps per day, could you designate one meeting per day as a walking meeting? Or, if you want to do weekly journaling, could you do it with a close colleague before a lunch or a meeting? You would accomplish two aims in one go, and hopefully both would be enriched by the other.

4. *Upstream intervention* – If you find executing your sequence of micro-habits feels messy, what could you do 'upstream' to make it all run smoother? Think about the difference between packing the night before an early trip vs. scrambling at the last minute to find your passport and phone charger. When we achieve military smoothness in executing a sequence, it feels a lot more reliable and is surprisingly satisfying. Try organizing your running gear the night before to avoid hunting in the dark for your earphones and running socks. Or if you are finding it hard to stick to a diet when eating out with friends, let them know beforehand that you will skip dessert, or plan how you will handle it (e.g. ordering a coffee or fruit plate instead).

5. *Contingency micro-habits* – Things won't always go as planned. You may have unexpected derailers, such as emergencies at work or home, or you might derail yourself. Contingency micro-habits are safety nets to get you back on track. There are two types: 1) rescue habits (to get you back on track in the moment); and 2) recovery habits (to get you back on track after falling off the wagon). In the swimming example, Laura's biggest derailer was getting stuck on a work topic right before

she was supposed to go swimming. She put in place two rescue habits: 1) asking herself or others, 'Can this wait until tomorrow?' (usually yes); and 2) dealing with any outstanding issues while travelling to the swimming pool. She also put in place a recovery habit: 'If I don't go swimming, then I immediately look for a new swimming slot in my calendar. If that's not possible, I plan a run instead.'

6. *Feedback loops* – Once you start building your habit, stay open to learning what works and adjusting as needed. The more frequent your feedback loop, the faster you are going to learn. We call this 'rapid cycle learning' because the daily benefits compound (like interest in a savings account). These questions help you learn fast:

a) How often did I stick to my desired habit, relative to what I wanted to do? (If you make a score sheet with boxes to check each time you complete your goal, this should give you a little hit of dopamine as part of your sequence, making it feel rewarding as well as informative.)

b) What helped and hindered me (including how did I get in my own way)?

c) What am I going to do differently tomorrow/next week to help me stay on track?

7. *Buddies* – Involving someone else in your habit-building process has multiple benefits. You will be more likely to achieve your habit if you commit to it out loud to someone else and, especially, if they hold you accountable. A buddy creates a natural prompt for you to do a feedback loop and evolve your habit to work even better. You might also pick up tips from them or, if you form the right developmental relationship with your buddy, it could lead to rich discussions that support you both to develop. Finally, hopefully it is more fun with a buddy, so you are more likely to enjoy being in the business of building habits. Participants on our leadership programmes get these benefits from peers, but many also find it helpful to have a buddy at home,

such as their partner. Buddies can also come from unusual sources: one of us, Vanessa, joined a Silent Zoom Writing Group while writing this book. Each daily session starts with goal setting and finishes with everyone sharing what they have achieved. As well as being held accountable for her commitments, being able to look at strangers studiously typing away was surprisingly effective for staying on task and not making a gazillion cups of tea. Vanessa got some great writing tips and encouragement, while having company made it more fun!

If you have in mind a habit you want to strengthen, take a moment to consolidate your ideas, to get ready to put them into practice and automate your habit. Alternatively, having now learned about automating habits, make a note of which habits in your life you could apply this to. As Aristotle said, we are what we repeatedly do. Deliberately investing in what you repeatedly do, even under pressure, helps you be who you want to be.

In the next chapter, we will focus on habits that are worthy of your investment, because they are particularly powerful for moving on the performance curve.

CHAPTER SEVEN

Performance curve habits: small things, big difference

Given the extraordinary power of habits to help us take action without requiring precious executive processing power, it makes sense to benefit from them as much as possible for fuelling us on the performance curve. Indeed, in our work and research with high performers from around the world, we have found that each has a set of regular practices or tools to help them build their effectiveness and well-being. They invest to build these into habits over the long haul, so they can easily draw on them when they are under pressure. Let's look at a couple of examples.

Janet Dekker is a veteran Dutch Human Resources executive of large global organizations, including Air France-KLM and the award-winning beauty retailer, Sephora (where she spent several years stewarding its fast growth). Janet's habits for helping her bring her best include yoga, mindset-shifting practices and opera singing. She calls them, 'vitamins for the mind and body which help me find options I might otherwise not have'.

As CEO of innovative medical device company Ambu, Juan Jose Gonzalez seeks to be driven and decisive, but to balance that out with open-mindedness and connection to others. To get this balance, he practises regular mindfulness and karate, which helps him embody qualities he learned in his early karate career. Encouraging emerging leaders is also a practice that helps him keep his own aspirational mindset, especially when he is knocked off-centre: 'In a crisis, rather than cancelling, I'll book in more mentoring meetings. And, if the company were about to go down, I'd book a global meeting with all the top talents. You cannot but feel inspired after trying to motivate the next generation of leaders, and then you can use that inspiration to look at the challenges from a position of strength'.

Habits such as Janet's and Juan Jose's strengthen two foundational capabilities for fuelling us on the performance curve: 1) self-awareness (noticing what we are thinking, feeling and doing in a given moment), and 2) self-management (using that awareness to deliberately make choices that help our effectiveness and well-being). Whatever the ways in which we seek to develop our inner operating system (for example, by shifting mindsets, or cultivating explore mode as our default), we need these two foundational capabilities.

In this chapter, we help you to improve your repertoire of *performance curve habits* to automate how you bring, and strengthen, your self-awareness and self-management. Regularly using tools that build these foundational capabilities a) gives you a strong effectiveness and well-being baseline, and b) codes into your operating system to more automatically draw on them when needed, such as when under pressure. It also increases the developmental work your inner operating system can do, because you will need less executive processing power to follow these practices if you have turned them into habits, thereby making your development more sustainable. This is especially important given that our greatest opportunities for deeper growth are likely to be when our weaknesses are exposed. In those situations, it is quite likely that we will be in protect mode and our executive functioning will be compromised. When that is the case, we don't want to be scrambling for ways to reset. We therefore need habits ready at our fingertips that provide fuel to fall back on, so we can adapt our inner operating system while dealing with the matter at hand.

However, the challenge does not lie in understanding the importance and benefits of these habits. The challenge is in the doing: knowing what habits to practise and making the time for them.

Many of us have a starting point for performance curve habits: the tools or practices we use to feel good and get back on track, such as doing sport, listening to music, or writing in a journal. Lots of people have tried out mindfulness over the past few years. But we authors have experienced that most people reach for the same one or two tools, occasionally trying a new idea from a friend, training course, book or article. It is not easy to get full visibility of the range of tools we might use for different needs. We offer you here a more systematic approach to picking tools and building habits to ensure you practise them. The aim is that you can pick the right tools for you individually, and also to use them with others to build collective effectiveness and well-being.

To help you choose the right tools, we introduce five channels for accessing our inner operating system: head, heart, hand, body and breath. We have identified these channels through exploring different disciplines, trawling the scientific literature, interviewing high performers in a range of arenas, and working with leaders to help them grow and perform. For each channel, we present a selection of tools that strengthen self-awareness and self-management. We then cover how to turn these tools into habits that stick: when done repeatedly, they become second nature and can fuel the development of our inner operating system. We finish this chapter with tips for how you can help others build performance curve habits.

The five channels for performance curve habits

In this section, we offer you a few tools from each of the five channels (an overview of the list of tools is shown in Table 7.1 on p.151). We focus on tools that do not take much time and, once you are familiar with them, many can even be done 'on the go'. As you read through, pay attention to whether you already have practices in the different channels, and how well they support your self-awareness and self-management. Note any tools that could benefit you, or others around you. Don't be constrained by this list: use it to spark other ideas for what would work for you. We do not give very detailed instructions for tools, since there are plenty of examples and instructions on the Internet.

Head – understanding and shifting our thoughts and focus

In the wisdom catalyst, we explored how much of our mental processing is driven by deeply wired neural pathways, formed through past experiences to help us react quickly and efficiently. If we want to do things differently, it is important to train our minds to uncover and re-shape these deeper levels of thinking; and the tools in the head channel target our thinking directly. The wisdom catalyst chapters gave you a number of tools that fit in the head channel, such as the iceberg and hidden drivers.

We can also draw on tools from therapy for our head channel, given that identifying (and shifting) our mindsets is at the core of many forms of psychotherapy, such as cognitive-behavioural therapy (CBT). CBT activates parts of the brain's prefrontal cortex associated with cognitive control and reduces activation in the limbic system (particularly the amygdala), i.e. it seems to help us regulate our emotions before we are too far down the track of a fight-flight-freeze response[1]. A common tool used within CBT is reappraisal, in which we widen our focus to pay attention to potentially rewarding aspects of the situation, and then use those to take a more rounded, constructive view. It sounds simple, but there is a lot of evidence this is a very powerful tool for regulating our emotions before we slip too far into protect mode[2]. Therapy that includes reappraisal can have positive effects on people's mental well-being even when measured a year afterwards[3].

We can use reappraisal at any time to take a more rounded, constructive view of difficult situations, for example by considering what we might learn from a challenging situation, or how it could help us focus on what really matters. As we described in Chapter 3, cellist Yo-Yo Ma illustrated reappraisal to keep him in explore mode for his Proms performance, by bringing his attention to how perfect the venue and audience were for the long, uninterrupted performance of Bach's cello suites. Speeches or readings can also prompt us to reappraise. Laura's partner, French senior executive Olivier Brousse, keeps a stock of thought-provoking quotes that help him set his mindsets: from literary figures (such as Albert Camus), historical biographies, and even movies (such as the critic Anton Ego's discourse at the end of Pixar's *Ratatouille*). Olivier comes back to these quotes when preparing for big leadership moments, to help him get in the right frame of mind. Juan Jose's methods (such as mentoring) that bring him back to an aspirational mindset are also versions of reappraisal.

Another tool to target our mindsets and thinking patterns is *visualization*. Brain scanning studies show that we activate largely the same brain areas when we are visualizing something happening as when we are actually doing or experiencing that thing[4]. This means we can use visualization to set up helpful thought patterns for future events, or we can redirect our brains towards explore mode by visualizing previous rewarding experiences. Visualization is a well-known tool for athletes, but studies have demonstrated a wide range of other performance improvements, e.g. in memory tests and reducing performance anxiety in musicians[5]. Yo-Yo described how he uses visualization to prepare for a performance: he lives through imaginary scenarios of what might go wrong (he lists scenarios such as the conductor collapsing, a protest group in the audience, an earthquake, or a tornado), so that he is ready for anything. He says it helps him have 'an emergency button in my head so that I know what to do if something happens, and can be alert but not panicking' – in our language this is to avoid succumbing to protect mode.

Yo-Yo also uses another head tool: *perspective taking*, which is stepping into the shoes of someone else to see things from a different perspective. He talked about taking the audience's perspective to help him prepare for his performances, but he has found it to be equally important during rehearsals with orchestras and conductors, when time is scarce and tensions can run high. It allows him, for example, to make a choice about when to raise technical details and when to relax and bring the group together with a joke or gesture. Research shows that taking the perspective of others helps us regain higher order capacities, such as empathy, when under stress. That means we can better understand issues and find ways forward with other people[6].

We also include in the 'head' channel *mindfulness practices* that help us build control over where we place our *attention*. They train our minds to be more focused, neutral observers by directly paying attention to one aspect of our experience (e.g. an object, sounds, physical sensations, or thoughts) and bringing the mind back whenever it wanders, without interpretation or judgement. Regular mindfulness practice is shown to improve memory, thinking, mood and well-being[7].

There are clear changes in the brain activity of those who practise mindfulness, indicating their brains are more actively controlling attention and regulating emotions[8]. These changes are often visible after a single session of mindfulness, though of course the benefits will be stronger and longer lasting with regular practice[9]. Even more striking is that the parts of regular meditators' brains associated with sensory attention are thicker than in non-meditators[10]. This is thought to be because meditation has increased the connections between nerve cells. In addition, there is some evidence that meditation counteracts age-related decline of the frontal cortex (which includes the prefrontal cortex). This shows the potential value of regular mindfulness for optimizing your brain performance over the long haul.

Heart – noticing our emotions and eliciting emotions that may serve us better

In Chapters 2 and 3 we talked about how emotions animate our mindsets into behaviours; they prompt action and provide the energy for it through their effects on our brain and our physiology. We also explored how emotions are an important clue as to the hidden drivers and mindsets that are in charge of our 'steering wheel', and can guide us in working with our inner operating system. We all know how powerful emotions can be: in the intensity of an emotional reaction, we may do something that we later regret. We might also have an emotional centre of gravity: certain emotions we spend more time feeling than others or favour as an initial reaction, which we can think of as a 'habit of emotion'. Heart tools help us notice our emotions and elicit ones that may serve us better.

Researchers, such as UCLA's Matthew Lieberman, have shown how simply naming the emotions we are feeling (*'emotional labelling'*) is valuable. It can reduce the brain's reactivity and allows us better access to the brain's executive functioning so we can make more deliberate (and hopefully wiser) choices[11]. When we combine emotional labelling with fine-tuning our ability to name the precise emotions we are feeling, we will also be building our emotional granularity. Emotional granularity has been shown to bring numerous benefits, including healthier stress coping mechanisms and better performance in tests[12]. A helpful starting point for getting from a broad 'bad', to a more specific 'sad', to a precise 'regretful', can be seen in Figure 2.1 (p. 34), which shows four core emotions and a range of 'flavours'.

Of course, recognizing our emotions is also the first bridge to identifying why we are feeling how we are feeling, and what action to take. We also often teach clients to notice and accept how an emotion feels in their body (*'emotion tracking'*). This is done through a series of questions: 'What emotion am I feeling right now?' then 'Where in my body is it strongest?' (taking a few breaths while focusing on that area, simply accepting the physical sensations of the emotion), then again 'What am I feeling now?' and finally 'What can I learn from this emotion?' We can use this short process to be less controlled by intense emotions and to gain more self-awareness and clarity.

Another well-known tool that helps us feel more resourceful and content is thinking of three things we feel grateful for, called 'gratitudes'. We often include this tool in our leadership programmes. One investment professional, Sarah Jones, told us she was recently stuck in traffic, which caused her to miss a flight to an important work event, and she felt very anxious. She used her gratitudes to get perspective and move back to explore mode. She said it was what got her through the whole experience and enabled her to focus on coming up with a good plan B quickly. Indeed, scanning studies show that the gratitudes exercise activates parts of the brain associated with social reward, and might well be training our brain to default to these more constructive ways of thinking rather than becoming stuck in unhelpful thought patterns[13]. We are not suggesting to ignore problems or simply pursue rewards – it is about recognizing where we are on the protect–explore spectrum and having the attentional and emotional control to be able to shift ourselves and be better able to address problems.

Several mindfulness practices also focus on generating specific emotions, such as compassion, joy or tranquillity, to increase our tendency for those emotions and boost well-being. The loving-kindness practice (also called 'metta' meditation) is probably the best known: it starts by practising receiving kindness and warmth ourselves before sending it out to people we like, then people about whom we feel neutral, and finally to those with whom we find it more difficult.

A further important family of tools we put in the heart channel are those related to purpose. These tools help us to identify what matters to us most and to pay attention to that, especially when we are under pressure. We look at purpose in more detail in Chapter 8.

Hand – writing or making something to deepen insight and clarify intentions

Employing our hands, whether through writing or making, can bring perspective, intuition and creativity. We may see things from fresh angles and open up new solutions, or draw on our intuition to get deeper insights or more clarity. 'Hand' tools can also help with emotional regulation by absorbing us (i.e. moving our attention away from unproductive thoughts and emotions), so we step back from our heated emotions and process a situation.

We can use our hands to make things, such as by drawing, painting, modelling clay or crafting. It should benefit us in the same way as art therapy, by focusing our attention on something constructive, strengthening our control functions and bringing reward from having made something. Hopefully its aesthetic appeal will give us a little emotional boost, too[14,15]! There is even research to indicate adult colouring books can reduce anxiety[16].

We also include *writing* here. *'Expressive writing'* is writing down our deepest thoughts and feelings for some time (e.g. 10 minutes). It settles our minds, reduces brain and body stress markers, boosts our immune system and improves academic test results[17,18]. This may be because it helps us label our emotions and process our thoughts (e.g. through reappraisal). Expressive writing even seems to reduce the jumpiness of certain brain signals in anxious people's brains[18]. We authors believe that expressive writing is an underrated gem for improving our well-being and effectiveness, given the wealth of evidence behind it and its broad benefits.

One of our other favourites is a writing exercise we call 'daily review'. We recommend a simple structure to look first at our learnings from yesterday and then set intentions for today. This structure is designed to help a) solidify important memories from yesterday by revisiting them, and b) prime our brains to spot opportunities to make our intentions come alive today[19,20]. This is another example of 'rapid cycle learning' (see also p.137) and participants on our leadership programmes who adopt this one habit daily see their progress skyrocket.

Body – using internal attention or movement to be present, alert and at ease

The brain-body feedback loop works to send signals from our body back into our brains[21]. This means we can use our body to influence how we think and feel, and plenty of research backs this up.

We are using the brain-body loop to help us be on the performance curve when we *take care of ourselves physically*, such as through sleep, food and water, exercise, exposure to nature/green spaces, hot or cold showers or baths, or massage. Let's look at two examples in more detail: exercise and exposure to nature/green spaces.

1. *Regular exercise* – Regular exercise is associated with a thickening in brain areas involved in executive control and memory, likely meaning the neurons are more connected and active[22]. Moderate physical exercise also gives us a boost in both mental and emotional well-being and protects from cognitive decline in ageing.

Many of our high performers have told us that sports involving *rhythmical activity* are particularly beneficial to them. This includes obvious sports such as swimming, running and walking, and also less obvious ones. For example, Juan Jose practises karate and Olivier hits golf balls at the practice range, especially when he is under pressure. Though we have not found direct neuroscientific research on this, we hypothesize these activities bring mindfulness-like focus (i.e. training executive control and reducing activation in the fight-flight-freeze circuitry) and provide rhythmical feedback to the brain (i.e. inducing rhythmical brain activity similar to states of rest and well-being)[23].

2. *Exposure to green spaces* – There are studies showing that exposure to green spaces improves recovery after surgery, psychiatric outcomes and general well-being[24,25]. Why might this be? One theory is that exposure to nature helps the prefrontal cortex regulate unhelpful thinking, by injecting positive stimuli into our environments and drawing our focus away from unhelpful thoughts. Another theory is that being in nature helps our brains to settle into all-important

periods of self-reflection and mind-wandering (what neuroscientists call 'default mode network' activity).

We can also take advantage of the brain–body feedback loop on the go, to get us into a particular mindset or reset ourselves as we transition between different parts of our day. Many people find that a few star jumps, or taking the stairs, can help them. Amy Cuddy's *power pose* has gained a lot of visibility and following, and several studies have found that people say power poses help them feel more powerful and positive[26]. Although there is debate among scientists about the impact of taking a power pose on our body and brain, we say 'if it works for you, go for it'[27].

You can also practise movements that are specific to a habit or mindset you want to shift. Remember the earlier example of how, as a habit, someone's mouth might automatically shut and they may physically sit back during a heated team discussion? Wriggling the jaws or leaning forwards could signal to the brain that the body is not in real danger, shift protect mode and allow more deliberate choice of action.

A less physically active way of using the brain-body feedback loop is *body scanning*. This is a mindfulness-based practice of building a mental map of our bodies that helps us gain attentional control and acuity, and rebalance our brains to centre and calm us[28].

Breath – shifting our mental and emotional state through breathing

Deliberate breathing is a 'remote control' for the brain. This also works via the brain-body feedback loop, because the pattern of our breathing is an important way our body and brain communicate with each other[23]. Our breathing pattern changes depending on where we are on the protect–explore spectrum and what emotions we are feeling. Sighs of relief, angry grunts, sobs of grief, laughter and sharp intakes of breath are just some of the more pronounced ways our breathing changes with our emotions. But, because of the brain-body feedback loop, shifting our breathing patterns helps change how we feel and think. This is especially useful when we are in the grip of intense emotions and our brain's executive functions are compromised.

Breathing practices are central to many ancient wisdom traditions and are often used by elite military units and athletes. Nevertheless, the neuroscientific research into deliberate breathing is in its early stages. Initial studies suggest that deliberate breathing may induce rhythmical brain activity similar to periods of rest or positive well-being[29]. It also helps a number of health conditions, including depression, chronic pain and post-traumatic stress disorder. Slower, deeper breathing helps process stress, reduce cortisol, lower blood pressure and settle our heart rate[30,31].

One of us authors, Vanessa, has used breathing practices extensively with clients suffering from post-traumatic stress, depression or anxiety. She also incorporates shorter breathing practices into her coaching sessions to help clients settle into a clear and grounded learning space or more easily access emotional awareness. An important starting point for any breathing practice is to make sure you use your diaphragm for breathing; the stomach should extend outwards when inhaling and softly draw inwards when exhaling. When reversed, this sends stress signals to the brain and is more likely to send it to protect mode.

Easy-to-pick-up breathing practices involve adapting the *ratio* of inhale to exhale. *Lengthening the outbreath* feels calming[32]. Try inhaling to a count of three and exhaling to a count of six for a few minutes, while lying down, sitting or walking. Both of us authors use this practice to help us fall back asleep in the night. By contrast, *lengthen the inhale* for a more energizing effect, or to reset when feeling more intense emotions. Inhale to a count of six and exhale to a count of three for several minutes. You can also do this sitting or walking.

'Box breathing' is often used by armed forces (such as Navy Seals) to perform well under pressure[33]. This breathing pattern includes pauses after the inhale and exhale, which can be visualized as the four sides of a square (inhale-pause-exhale-pause, hence the name). Take four counts for each side, but you may need to start faster when feeling very intense emotions and your breath is already rapid.

There are also breath-based mindfulness practices, for example *breath counting*. This reduces emotional reactivity, because we build the ability to observe something we are experiencing without interfering, and has a calming and centring effect. Don't alter your breath in any way, just count each breath on the exhale from 1 to 10 and then back down to 1 again. You can do it sitting down, waiting for an appointment or queuing for the bus – but try to complete at least three rounds in one go.

We put *singing* in the 'breath' channel, too. When Janet Dekker is under additional pressure, rather than cancel her singing lessons, she will often book an extra one. The breathing practice that comes with singing helps to settle the mind and get fresh perspectives. Indeed, singing has even been shown to boost mood and immune markers and reduce stress[34].

Table 7.1 Overview of performance curve habits

Channel	Brief description of tool	Purpose of tool
Head Understanding and shifting our thoughts and focus	*Iceberg model and hidden drivers (see Chapters 2 and 3)* Identifying root causes of behaviour	To identify and sustainably shift mindsets and behaviours
	Reappraisal Using questions or speeches/quotes to consider beneficial aspects of a challenging situation	To take a more constructive view of difficult situations and reduce protect mode
	Visualization Picturing ourselves in past, present or future experiences as if we were actually doing or experiencing something	To set up helpful thought patterns, or redirect our brains towards explore mode

Channel	Brief description of tool	Purpose of tool
	Perspective taking Stepping into the shoes of someone else to see things from their perspective	To settle emotional reactivity, better understand current reality and others' perspectives, and generate new ideas
	Attention-based mindfulness practices Practising one-pointed observation (of objects, thought, sensations etc.), without interpretation or judgement	To build control over where we place our attention, strengthen our ability to focus, and improve emotional regulation
Heart Noticing our emotions and eliciting emotions that may serve us better	*Emotional labelling* Naming the emotions we are feeling	To build awareness of emotional states and reduce emotional reactivity
	Emotion tracking Following the sensations of an emotion and identifying its meaning for us	To be less controlled by intense emotions, and to gain more self-awareness and clarity of action
	Gratitudes Listing a few things we are grateful for	To feel more resourceful when tackling challenges
	Loving-kindness meditation (mindfulness practice) Cultivating kindness for oneself and others	To boost well-being and reduce stress, to build more positive social connections
	Purpose (see Chapter 8) Identifying and paying attention to what matters most	To bring direction and momentum, or to reset ourselves when challenged
Hand Writing or making something to deepen insight and clarify intentions	*Draw, paint, model clay or craft* Creating objects or images that express a topic and our feelings about it in non-verbal ways	To bring perspective, intuition and creativity, to step back from intense emotions and process a situation
	Expressive writing Writing our deepest thoughts and feelings for some time, e.g. 10 minutes	To explore deeper thoughts and emotions, reduce stress and boost immunity

Channel	Brief description of tool	Purpose of tool
	Daily review Reviewing learnings from today and setting intentions for tomorrow	To consolidate learnings and prime our brains to spot opportunities that are in line with intentions
Body Using internal attention or movement to be present, alert and at ease	*Physical self-care (e.g. sleep, food and water, exercise, exposure to nature/ green spaces, hot or cold showers or baths, massage)* Taking care of our bodies and supporting brain functioning	To engage our inbuilt mechanisms for recovery and rejuvenation
	Movement boosters (star jumps, taking the stairs, power poses) Actively moving to affect our brains via the brain-body feedback loop	To reset our brains and bodies, release tensions and re-energize
	Body-scanning (mindfulness practice) Building a mental map of our bodies by scanning from head to toe, without judgement or changing anything	To gain attentional control and acuity, to centre and calm us
Breath Shifting our mental and emotional state through deliberate breathing	*Breathing ratios* • *Lengthening the outbreath:* exhaling for twice as long as inhaling (for a few minutes) • *Lengthening the inbreath:* inhaling for twice as long as exhaling (for a few minutes)	• To calm our minds and process stress • To energize, or to reset when feeling more intense emotions
	Box breathing Inhaling-pausing-exhaling-pausing for equal counts of four (over several minutes)	To maintain clarity of thinking when under pressure
	Breath counting Counting each breath on the exhale from 1 to 10	To calm and centre the mind, to reduce emotional reactivity
	Singing Singing a piece of music or chanting	To lower stress, as a natural mood and immunity booster

Now that you have seen all five channels for performance curve habits, you may start to spot some commonalities and links between the channels. For example, writing or 'making' tools from the 'hand' channel can be a physical version of emotional labelling, or indeed the beginnings of reappraisal. Similarly, physical activity will have additional impact through our breathing. Indeed, these five channels are not perfectly distinct. They are a range of different access points for building self-awareness and self-management, and the neuroscientific evidence we have drawn together shows quite strikingly how they have similar effects on our brain.

How to select your repertoire of performance curve habits

Here is our advice for selecting tools that work for you, to complement what you are doing already:

Have regular and ad hoc tools. You will want some tools that you use regularly, ideally daily, for example to set you up for the day or to transition from work to home. Through regular practice of these tools, you will steadily compound the benefits, so your self-awareness and self-management capabilities will build over time. You will also benefit from some tools for ad hoc situations, to help you check in with yourself and bounce back quickly, for example when you are under pressure and not bringing your best. In particularly high-pressure times, you might add in one or two more to help you stay on the performance curve.

Stretch beyond what you know. Avoid assuming that the tools that seem most accessible to you will be the ones to use. There is often great value in pursuing tools that seem less of a fit, because they will complement things you are already strong at. We have an emerging hypothesis that the most effective sets of habits include at least one tool from the two 'B' channels (breath and body), and at least a couple of tools from the three 'H' channels (head/heart/hand). This makes logical sense: it ensures you are using a range of levers to build your self-awareness and self-management, taking advantage of the brain-body loop (through the two 'B's), and targeting your mindsets and emotions more directly (through the three 'H's).

Get the right tools for you. Different things work for different people at different times. Mindfulness practice was not working for one of us, Laura, at a challenging moment when she was returning to work after maternity leave. One strategy would have been to persist with mindfulness, but the expressive writing and breathing she used instead were enjoyable and beneficial to her, so she was more motivated. We lack scientific studies that compare the overall effectiveness of different tools in different circumstances. So, most importantly, you should experiment and pick what works for you. You might like to explore when it is more helpful for you to *zoom out* (i.e. redirect your attention or broaden your focus) or when you want a tool to help you *zoom in* (i.e. identify and work through something):

- Zooming out involves redirecting attention to something more constructive (e.g. through gratitudes), taking a broader view (e.g. reappraisal), or just training a general ability to control our attention (e.g. mindfulness, karate). This stops us being in the grip of unhelpful thoughts and emotions, and helps us access other resources. It might serve you well when you are feeling heavily in protect mode.
- Zooming in helps us constructively engage with something (when we are ready), to eventually get to a different perspective. Example tools would be mindset shifts, emotional labelling, expressive writing and some breathing practices. Over time, this may be more transformational for your inner operating system, rather than zooming out practices which simply help you cope in the moment.

Persist with the tools you have chosen... As you use a tool repeatedly, you should be strengthening neural pathways in your brain and body.

This may take a while to be noticeable to you though, so you will need to persist.

... but change when needed. You can choose and adapt your performance curve habits for your current goals and needs, which is why knowing about this wider repertoire is helpful. Change tools when it feels right for you. Don't chase novelty, but if you are really sure a habit is not giving you enough benefit, try something else.

How to make performance curve habits part of your life

How do you make time for these habits when you are already under pressure and every minute is spoken for? The key lies in not seeing it as an additional task or, worse, a chore. Media executive Luke Bradley-Jones hits the nail on the head: 'All my practices help me be the best version of myself and live with integrity. Living with integrity and staying true to my values is a source of happiness for me...And happiness helps performance.' For many high-performing individuals, strengthening their self-awareness and self-management is a way of life and fundamental enabler of their success.

To make this general advice actionable, below are some tips for building performance curve habits into day-to-day activities (you might also like to review the tips for building habits from Chapter 6).

1. *Small but consistent changes go a long way* – Start with a small investment of time to build performance curve habits into your day, but do it consistently to get the compounding effect. The more you practise, the more benefit you will notice, both at the time of practising and over the course of the day.

2. *Combine your habits with another activity or cue* – Once you are familiar with a specific tool, you can combine it with other activities, e.g. using your habitual commute to work to do your daily review or a body scan. Many tools can be done on the move, while waiting for

the kettle to boil, or even during a conversation (e.g. a long exhale). This means your daily activities can become cues to practise your performance curve habits without needing to make extra time.

3. *Approach these habits with explore mode, rather than putting pressure on yourself* – Be aware and deliberate about how you think and feel about your performance curve habits. If you feel guilty, obligated, frustrated or worried about sticking to your habits (i.e. emotions more characteristic of protect mode), doing them regularly will likely feel like a battle and you might not get the full benefits. Try to approach your performance curve habits with a sense of explore mode, such as with curiosity or hope. Recognize yourself for doing something tremendous for your well-being and effectiveness. Or find ways to make them feel more fun and rewarding, especially if you feel you are investing and not yet getting the benefits.

4. *One new habit at a time* – Don't spread your capacity for embedding new habits too thinly. Pick one tool to do for a little while to become familiar with it and experience its benefits. Then, if needed, onboard another tool or switch back to something else in your repertoire. Over time, your 'muscle' for building and adapting habits will get strengthened, which is a benefit in itself.

Helping others build self-awareness and self-management

If you are in a leadership role, you likely want to bring your best and help others do the same. In today's pressured times, showing up well yourself can already be challenging enough. Our advice is simple: lead by example. Practise your performance curve habits, and tell, or even show, people what you are doing. Make it normal to talk about these performance curve habits, and signal that you believe working on them is a sign of personal strength, not weakness. Explain that building your self-awareness and self-management is an ongoing quest for you, and name and share the tools you use. After doing this for a while, you could help your colleagues create space to practise individually. You could also build time into team meetings to try out practices together, and put them into your training programmes and events.

People have told us that their performance curve habits help them feel more purposeful, clear, in control, content and alive. Sometimes it takes just a little inspiration to get going and reap the ongoing benefits. You could be that inspiration for someone else. It will also be a legacy you pass on to future generations at work and at home, enabling them to start on a stronger footing when it comes to combining effectiveness and well-being into fulfilling lives.

In the next chapter, we focus on how to sustain our journey on the performance curve by strengthening our sense of purpose, and being purposeful. Purpose is an essential source of fuel, because it tells us why maximizing our potential matters and supports us through the heavy lifting of upgrading our inner operating system in numerous ways.

CHAPTER EIGHT

Get purpose-fu(e)l

Wendy Kopp founded Teach For America and Teach For All: organizations that seek to solve educational inequality. When we spoke to Wendy, her face and voice noticeably lit up as she described why she settled on this field. 'In my senior year of college, I felt a huge sense of freedom. I truly felt like I could just do anything I wanted to do. And I realized that the reason I felt this was because of the education I had had.' When she thought about what she wanted to do with her life, she asked herself what matters most that would be worth working incredibly hard for. 'And I just thought: education. That's the thing that makes such a difference. It's why I feel this sense of freedom. And it's just not fair that not everyone feels that. So what can I do?' Wendy is very clear on the purpose behind what she does.

Purpose is a powerful fuel for individuals, teams and organizations. It motivates us to bring our best and aligns people on a common goal. That alone is reason enough for many experts and organizations to focus on purpose[1]. Like Wendy, almost all our interviewees kept referring to the underlying sense of purpose behind their endeavours. This purpose deeply mattered to them and was usually connected to their own life experiences. It was a powerful fuel that sustained and guided them personally, and also helped them ignite others. For the medical device company Ambu, CEO Juan Jose Gonzalez describes having the right vision and aspiration as 'absolutely crucial to deliver superior performance because it not only defines the company, but defines anybody who in one way or another touches the company'.

In the context of the performance curve, we particularly want to help you use purpose as fuel for developing your inner operating system – in other words, to get purpose-fu(e)l! We look at the key features of what makes for a powerful purpose and how to harness it day-to-day. Focusing on a lofty sense of purpose does not eliminate the need for discipline and detail, but it can bring a lightness and clarity to our daily lives to help us stay the course. This chapter also helps you translate your sense of purpose into day-to-day actions and habits.

Why is purpose important for the performance curve?

Purpose is the reason for existing and for doing what we do: the big *why*. It gives us direction, casts the mundane in a light of deeper meaning, and makes facing challenges worthwhile. It evokes potential and possibility for the future. In Wendy's example on the previous page, this potential is the dream of everyone feeling the sense of freedom and possibility that she did as a college senior.

On the performance curve, we deliberately evolve our inner operating system on an ongoing basis, without the additional force of a crisis. That is demanding and, without the external pull or push of a crisis, it requires a compelling internal reason to fuel us. A sense of purpose is that internal reason; it tells us what maximizing our potential is in service of and why it matters.

To get this fuel, we do not need to be able to name a big life or 'save the world' purpose, such as solving educational inequality. Our purpose might anyway evolve at different stages of our lives, or in different settings. To fuel us on the performance curve, it is enough to have (and harness) a deeper reason behind our decisions and actions. For a project, it could simply be 'to get the job done *and* bring warmth and humanity to how we work with our clients'. Or for a pitch meeting, 'to form a connection that will last years, not only sell a piece of work'.

Over time, we might see a common element in these different intentions and be able to name a bigger purpose in the way Wendy does. But that is not essential to be more purpose-fuelled day-to-day. We therefore define purpose quite broadly as *our North Star for doing, or not doing something.* An effective purpose for moving on the performance curve is *one that helps us and others bring and grow our best.*

Purpose can fuel us on the performance curve in three main ways.

First, focusing on purpose can increase motivation and help us be in explore mode, both to bring our best and grow over time. As Tom Rippin, CEO of On Purpose, put it: 'If there is a higher purpose I believe in, I can tolerate some quite mundane and hard work, and very happily go the extra mile. I feel more relaxed and less stressed.' Doing our tax declaration might not feel exhilarating, but knowing we are working towards a bigger purpose can make such tasks seem less painful and perhaps even enjoyable.

The key is that the purpose feels real and achievable. If we envisage something we need or want but have not got, a part of the brain called the anterior insula activates. We feel motivated, and it sends signals to other brain areas to take action towards the goal. And, when we feel motivated, our brain is more in explore mode. How much we feel motivated and in explore mode depends on how achievable the goal feels to us (even if it might take a long time and much effort). By contrast, if our purpose feels unachievable, our motivation will be dampened and we may even undermine ourselves by tipping into protect mode[2].

Second, purpose can make us more focused. The North Star of purpose gives clarity of direction and priorities, which helps our brain be focused and spot opportunities. Wendy mentioned how she is constantly thinking about the tension between current reality and her vision, and how that helps her identify what is needed to make progress, be that how she spends her time personally or the way the organization operates. Purpose acts as a filter for our actions, making sure we move in the desired direction and get the most out of the resources we have. This creates space for us to use our brain's executive capacity well.

Third, purpose provides scaffolding for vertical development. As with the later stages of development, paying attention to what matters encourages us to expand our perspective and include more pieces of the puzzle. It helps us manage complexity by putting front of mind what matters. Deciding what matters also encourages us to feel like we own our own choices: the 'have to' or 'should' is replaced with a 'want to', as with later stages of development.

What makes for a high-fuel purpose?

High-fuel purpose has two common features: 1) a high personal heart factor (i.e. we really care about something and enjoy it), and 2) it serves something greater than ourselves. These two features help us be in explore mode, so we will be more resourceful, more likely to spot opportunities to move towards our purpose, and more able to work through challenges in ways that develop our inner operating system. As a result, we are more likely to forge strengths in, rather than get consumed by, the fires of those challenges. And it is those strengths that lead us to truly unique impact and high performance, as illustrated by any hero's journey.

For example, Pramath Sinha is glad he eventually focused on education: 'I feel a sense of purpose and meaning and fulfilment doing what I do. Education changes people's lives and it has a tremendous knock-on and ripple effect on the country and the society as a whole.' Having this high-fuel purpose has driven Pramath to found two universities and numerous education ventures despite many challenges. Through this, he has developed his strengths as an innovator and institution builder, somewhat to his own surprise. He says 'I was not always like this. I never thought I would be given a tag like "institution builder".'

Let's look at each feature of a high-fuel purpose more closely.

High personal heart factor: fuel from joy

Potent fuel comes from doing something we enjoy. Joy, and different flavours of it, such as love or gratitude, are perhaps the most powerful creative force there is. Joy feels good and boosts our mood and well-being: it helps us to be in explore mode and therefore we are more willing to leave our comfort zone and choose the risks of growth and change. Wendy was full of gratitude for the freedom that education had brought to her own life. By working in education, she is regularly reminded and energized by that gratitude and sense of freedom. And Pramath described how he has become 'enamoured by this idea of creating impact that endures and sustains itself'.

We miss out on this fuel from a high heart factor if we pursue a purpose only because it makes rational sense based on our past, position or skills, or because it seems noble, is trendy or in demand. It is well worth finding out what genuinely resonates with our sense of identity, values and passions. If nature is not your thing and you feel uneasy with too much wilderness around you, then an environmental cause is unlikely to be the right channel to help you access purpose-fuel! A powerful purpose for moving on the performance curve therefore has a *high personal heart factor, i.e. it gives us joy and really matters to us personally.*

Additional fuel comes from also enjoying *how* we serve that purpose. Pramath discovered that he thrives on the diversity and multiplicity of things that he works on concurrently, rather than just burrowing himself deep into one thing. 'I'm doing a variety of things under this broad umbrella of higher education. I am constantly jumping from this to that, picking up dots from here and there and feeding them back. And I do that with people as well, connecting dots between ideas and insights, and between people.'

When we are setting a collective purpose, it is important to make sure there is a high heart factor for everyone. Each individual of a team or organization needs to be able to relate their work not just to any bigger purpose, but one that matters to them personally. As Juan Jose pointed out: 'a vision that is grounded on financials or shareholder return only is not enough to enrol the organization and unlock our full potential. At our core is our desire to have remarkable careers, to do something that has not been done before.' 'Remarkable' will mean different things to different people: for some it might be breaking through frontiers, for others it might be the impact they have on society, the wider planet, or their customers, the company, or their immediate team.

We are likely to be drawn to a purpose that relates to our hidden drivers, because meeting them will feel very important and bring joy to us. This alignment of our hidden drivers and purpose may well fuel us, but there is a risk: we might get attached to realizing the purpose as a means of fulfilling our hidden drivers. That makes us more likely to fall into protect mode when there are challenges. This was the case for US entrepreneur Rachel from Chapter 3: in a stable market, and hence in explore mode, she felt a great sense of fulfilment from her vision for expanding the family business, at least partly because it served her hidden drivers, especially her need to feel strong. But when the business came under fire from a new entrant and sales declined, it meant Rachel therefore felt personally under attack. She made it her purpose to destroy the 'enemy', rather than focus on how she could find new opportunities for the company and, in the process, sabotaged her vision for it.

If we start experiencing high emotions when we are trying to meet a purpose or objective, it is quite possible our hidden drivers are being triggered, which is a chance for us to develop how we relate to them. One of us (Vanessa) experienced this working as a therapist, where helping clients break through their struggles matched her hidden drivers of needing to feel virtuous and closeness. When she had clients who struggled to open up or were not moving forwards, she sometimes felt judgemental, impatient and in protect mode (not exactly helpful for her or the client!). Vanessa learned to use her protect mode as a signal to see how she could better help the client open up or move forwards, for example by asking a question about what was getting in the way. By redirecting her energy, she reduced the grip of the hidden driver and turned it into a gift.

Greater than ourselves: fuel from contributing to the whole

The second feature that makes for a powerful purpose is that it is *greater than ourselves*. Not just greater than us individually, but also greater than our immediate circle of family and friends. Many of our interviewees told us how focusing on contributing to the wider world was important to them. Pramath wants to 'build something that outlasts me, that is not about immediate returns, gains or profits, but meeting a need that goes way beyond'.

Interestingly, focusing on how they can contribute at large is what fuelled most of our interviewees to grow and maximize their potential – even if that wasn't the primary aim. CEO of On Purpose, Tom Rippin, refers to Viktor Frankl, who talks about how, through self-transcendence [i.e. serving a purpose beyond one's self], one may self-actualize [i.e. achieve one's full potential][3]. 'But if one aims for self-actualisation in the first place, it [ironically] won't happen,' said Tom.

Pilot Gaby Kennard echoed that 'purpose has to be bigger than yourself. If I could achieve this round-the-world flight, with no money and no suitable aircraft, this is surely going to be helpful to other people to know that if I could do it, they can do whatever it is that they want to do.' Certainly, Gaby's adventure had a lot of personal meaning to her. She was setting out to prove others wrong who did not believe she had what it takes. Flying also gave her a closeness to her father, who was killed as a pilot in the war and whom she had never met. But seeing how her achievements could help others gave her a different kind of strength to go beyond her limits and persevere through 'a hell of a process'.

It is evolutionarily sensible to contribute to the wider system, because it is good for our individual, as well as collective, survival. Tom Rippin explains this through the analogy of the human body where 'usually cells contribute to the health of the overall body. They don't just maximize their own growth, which can be very unhealthy. Transposing this to individuals and organizations means looking at how we can make the system – be that the economy, be that nature, be that the society – as healthy as possible; as opposed to make where I am as large or profitable as possible.'

This may be why our brains are wired to experience helping others as rewarding in its own right: this 'prosocial' behaviour has an evolutionary advantage of contributing to the well-being of our species, which takes care of us in return, and helps us thrive overall[4]. In some cases, we may even find giving more rewarding than receiving[5]. This additional reward will help us be in explore mode and therefore overcome challenges. The more reward we expect, the more willing we will be to work harder and also more likely to transcend the limits of what we think is possible or we are capable of.

That said, we should be aware of the trap of doing good while denying our own needs and wants in service of others. This might be another example of hidden drivers gripping us and we risk falling into protect mode. When our own needs are not met, this limits what we can give – just as when a cell in the body is not getting the nutrients it needs, it cannot contribute to the health of the whole. We need to be on solid ground to help others: put your own oxygen mask on first before assisting someone else.

Let's next look at how to identify a high-fuel purpose that helps us bring the best of our brains and grow them in the process. If you already have an inkling of such a purpose for yourself, this next section will help you fine-tune or reinforce it.

How to identify a high-fuel purpose

For strong purpose-fuel, we need to find out what has a high personal heart factor and serves others. Joy and a sense of fulfilment fuel us to achieve goals, learn and build strengths more easily. They are also the biggest navigational aid we have for living and working with purpose.

Hang on, you might say, I enjoy playing golf and am pretty good at it, but does that mean I should become a professional golfer? Possibly, but probably not. We suggest you dig into *why* you enjoy golf. What is it that you value about that activity? Is it being out in nature? Or the easeful concentration that golf gets you into? What does that tell you about what matters to you, i.e. what you care about deeply? And how could this benefit others or the wider system?

Often, a high-fuel purpose is linked to our personal life experiences and values, such as Wendy's experience of the freedom she gained through education and seeing it as unfair that not everyone got that. We therefore suggest you start by observing yourself using one or both of the exercises below. Make notes in a journal, or discuss your insights with a friend.

Exercise 1 – Think of a past experience when you felt at your best. A time when you felt alive, joyful, rewarded or fulfilled. Let yourself travel back in time to become the person you were then. Visualize the scene. Where are you? Who are you with? What is happening? Pay attention to the emotions you are feeling, and locate these in your body. Then explore why you might be feeling this way, for example:

- What aspect of the situation inspires or grabs you the most?
- What is the impact on others, or on the wider world?
- What does that tell you about what matters to you? What do you care about that is bigger than yourself?
- What do you dream of?

Exercise 2 – Turn to your current, day-to-day life. Visualize yourself over the course of a normal day or week, doing what you typically do. Pause for any activities that feel particularly joyful or important to you. Once you have finished, take a moment to note:

- Which of the activities bring you joy or satisfaction and make you feel alive while doing them?
- What is the impact of these on others or the wider world?
- What would you like to do more of?
- What does that tell you about what matters to you? What do you care about that is bigger than yourself?
- If helpful, consider what has the opposite effect on you. What really kills your joy? What feels dull or lifeless to you?

For either of these exercises, make sure you dig deeper into *why* you enjoy, or do not enjoy, something, as per the 'I love golf' example. Once you have some ideas, keep these in mind as you go about the next few days, to test and refine them further. Keep note of what naturally lights you up (and what does not).

Nick, our boom-and-bust executive who put his daughter into the gym's childcare so he could do more work instead of exercise, started fine-tuning his purpose compass in this way. It was really challenging at first, because he was used to focusing on getting the tasks at hand done, rather than how he was feeling as he was going about his work. Every day on his commute home, Nick mentally relived his day, to screen for high or low heart moments. That helped him notice them more as they were occurring in real time. Over the course of a few weeks, Nick found and tested the clues he was getting and ended up with a solid insight that, beyond the intellectually stimulating aspects of his work, he really lights up when he can help others bring and experience their best. Nick was surprised what a difference it made to his own motivation and energy at work when he was able to help others shine in some way.

Memories came back to Nick of tutoring younger students at school to augment his pocket money, and how much he had enjoyed that.

The more you pay attention to the physical and emotional signals from your body, the more acute your purpose compass will get. It may take some time until you get a clearer picture, but stick with it! Savour the moments of joy or fulfilment and use them to learn about your values and passions. Dream a little about what having more of these could feel and look like. Who would you be if you spent more of your life in this way? What would it feel like to be that person?

As you identify your joy givers and drainers, do not feel pressure to immediately make changes – big or small. Focus more on observing and learning about yourself, rather than taking action quite yet. Use the gap between where you are now and where you might like to be to get used to the tension between current reality and a future vision. If we want our purpose to help us stay on the performance curve longer term, we need to be able to constructively face this tension.

Translate your purpose into reality

No matter how deeply a purpose might resonate with us emotionally, it has little impact if we do not act in accordance with it and follow through. If purpose is the castle in the clouds, our job is to build the ladder to reach it. In this section, we offer some practical strategies to build that ladder and work with purpose in a way that helps you move on the performance curve. Though these strategies are focused on individual purpose, the same principles can be applied to working with purpose in a team or organization. For both individual and collective purpose, Tom Rippin encouraged us to make sure that the purpose really is the ultimate end, and not fall into the trap of using purpose as a means to other ends, such as financial gains.

Depending on how purpose-fuelled you feel today, you can combine these strategies, or pick what gives you the highest fuel boost for now.

We start by looking at how you can make your actions more purpose-fuelled without having a clear high-fuel purpose, and then see how Nick and others have put their identified purpose into action.

1. *Find purpose anywhere* – Lorina McAdam described how to tap into purpose-fuel when we do not have a clear sense of a deeper purpose. Perhaps unexpectedly for someone working out in the field for international development and humanitarian NGOs, Lorina told us that she is not driven by one specific theme or purpose. 'The more I learn about something, the more curious I am about it. Suddenly everything becomes fascinating, and I can find purpose in it.' If you are feeling quite unmotivated about a task, or lacking clarity about a bigger purpose, how could you become more curious about just that activity – be it a piece of work, walking the dog or doing the dishes? What would shift it from being something you 'should' or 'have to' do, to something that is meaningful to you, something you 'want' to do, and thereby generate more fuel? And if you really cannot muster any curiosity or motivation, then simply give it your all anyway. Do it with complete abandon. Make that activity your purpose, as if it were what mattered most to you in your entire life. You will be surprised at the fuel this can generate.

2. *Set intentions* – Another simple way of being more purpose-fuelled is to set intentions for regular activities. Once you have chosen an intention, you can easily cascade that to behaviours or actions to make it a reality. For example, you can reflect on how you want a meeting to feel and how you will bring those qualities to it, instead of only preparing content for the topics to be discussed at a meeting. You could try out different intentions and see which ones really grab you, as clues towards a bigger purpose.

3. *Start small* – Often, our clients assume that, to harness the power of purpose, we need to have our purpose all figured out and then methodically work out how to get there. However, we do not need to know all that to generate fuel. We are better served to start small and

make our everyday activities more purposeful, aligning them with what matters to us, and drawing satisfaction from our progress[6].

Nick found several small ways he could put into action his identified purpose of helping others bring and experience their best. Before or in meetings, he set an intention for his interactions with his team and other colleagues and how he would follow through on that. He would look out for how he might help someone step up, for example through work assignments. He made a point of acknowledging what someone had done well or improved on, also in the wider company beyond his own team.

Being more purpose-fuelled at work also made Nick reflect on what kind of parent he wanted to be for his daughter, Molly, and changed his interactions with her. By focusing more on how Molly was growing and discovering her own capabilities, the time they spent together felt closer and more fun. Molly was relishing learning new things together with Nick. It also helped transform some key pressure points, such as leaving the house on time in the morning. In the past, Nick would have done a lot himself to get Molly ready because it was faster, even though she was at an age when she could learn to dress herself and brush her teeth. Nick practised those activities with Molly, who was then well set up to do more herself in the morning.

This experience with Molly in turn led Nick to see how at work he had also defaulted to doing more himself, rather than delegating to his team, because it was faster and led to better results in the short term. It took him some additional time in the beginning to ensure his team was set up to succeed on the bigger tasks he decided to delegate, but the investment soon paid off by relieving Nick's workload. And delegating more did not overload his team, because they were being more productive overall as a result of learning more from Nick's experience. They were also feeling more engaged through the additional responsibility they were getting. A win-win on many fronts.

After a few months of making smaller changes to be more purpose-fuelled, Nick started looking at how his purpose connected with his role in the organization. He looked at how much opportunity he had for helping others bring and experience their best, and how much of his week he was spending doing so. It was already a significant amount, but Nick felt ready to do more. When he got an email from HR about coaching training for leaders in the company, he immediately felt drawn to it and signed up. This is not the kind of thing he would have sought out a few months earlier, and it would have been inconceivable for him to take on anything extra. However, because he had built up the capacity in his team to step up, he now had the time and mental bandwidth.

In Nick's case, taking small steps set him up to take a bigger step when the opportunity came. This is common: fuel begets fuel once it is in motion. Gaby Kennard was not struck by a bolt of inspiration that she wanted to fly solo around the world and then methodically set out to do so. 'It was a sort of understanding that slowly evolved. As a kid, I used to look at atlases and imagine that I was going to do some great trick, some great journey, and I did not know how. But then I guess what happened is that I started learning to fly in my thirties. I split up with my first husband and decided to do the things that I really wanted to do. And then I was very passionate about it.'

The important part is to get started. Do not be too linear or determined about identifying a bigger purpose and how to get there. Allow room for discovery, and twists and turns along the way. As Pramath pointed out, 'our potential is way beyond what we can imagine'. Best to hold lightly any specifics of the destination and plans for getting there.

Starting small can also take the shape of mini-demonstrations of what you are discovering through fine-tuning your purpose compass. To continue the golf example: if what you love about golf is being out in nature, you could start by bringing more plants into your workspace, having lunch or 'walking' meetings/calls in a park, or supporting a local wildlife initiative. If you love the easeful concentration golf gets you into, you might like to visualize yourself getting into position on the tee as you get ready for a challenging task or meeting. All this will help fuel you on the performance curve and orient you towards more fuel.

4. *Align 'how' with 'why'* – There is a causal symmetry between 'why' we do something and 'how' we go about it. By causal symmetry, we mean that our success in making a purpose into reality depends on whether we mirror the qualities of the purpose ourselves. For example, in helping others bring and experience their best, Nick was fuelled by his own uncovering of his best. Quite a few of our interviewees with a strong sense of purpose highlighted this symmetry and derived much fuel and sense of direction from it. 'If we are trying to foster the leadership of kids, we need to foster the leadership of their teachers and of the staff members in those network organizations and also of our own staff members. That's the core thing,' said Wendy Kopp. 'Because only adults who feel unleashed are going to truly foster the leadership with their kids. You can't do that if there are any disconnects in the system.'

Yo-Yo Ma was equally resolute about ensuring that how the music is played matches the effect he wants it to have on his audience. So rather than focus on the end goal of the performance and which technical details might contribute to it, he keeps front of mind the relationships and energy among the performers and the audience. 'If that's there, the music will automatically be there,' Yo-Yo explained, and added, 'But that's not something that's taught in schools or professional environments.' While this might be true in many such places, we also frequently encounter individuals and organizations, like Wendy's, who prioritize matching what they want to create externally with how they operate internally. Harappa, one of the education organizations Pramath has co-founded, is another such example. They see it as imperative to be a learning organization themselves and dedicate time and resources to that because that is their core business as a provider of online courses for workplace success. What would it look like for you to mirror your sense of purpose in how you operate day-to-day, including how you interact with others?

Build 'habits of purpose'

Building habits can help you live and harness your purpose day-to-day, especially when under pressure. Habits might sound uninspiring and uncreative. But, crafted in the right way, they can have the opposite effect – to bring lightness to discipline, top up batteries and turbo-charge your purpose-fuel. Habits ensure that we put our time and energy behind the purpose we choose to pursue and do not get distracted or slowed down. This helps us get more out of the time and energy we have.

The key to setting up great habits that maximize your purpose-fuel is that they work for you. The examples below will not work for everyone, so take them as inspiration to help you craft your own (referring back to the section on habits in Chapter 6 if needed).

1. *Build habits for connecting 'why' and 'how'* – Contemplating 'why' we do something is different work for our brain than managing 'how' we do it, and it is effortful for our brains to switch between these two different tasks[7]. Picture yourself deeply absorbed in a piece of work. As you are focusing on the details of the matter at hand, the deeper purpose is probably quite far out of sight. Similarly, a lofty purpose can seem distant from the activities of our hours, days and even weeks. Having a habit that connects 'why' and 'how' helps us with this challenge. Many interviewees described an annual reflection point and regular review cycles as the cornerstone of how they connect 'why' and 'how'. Luke Bradley-Jones has been going on his week-long annual retreats for 15 years. He reflects on his life and his purpose during this time. He also sets annual goals and then uses them to guide his quarterly, weekly and daily goals. 'I share my weekly priorities with my team and then report back every week. I use my weekly priorities to write my daily to-do list.' And when Luke feels off track, he uses his bigger purpose

to reset, often with the help of his wife: 'How important really is this? How important will this be in five years? Will I even remember this in one year?'

There are many other ways to habitually bring 'why' into how you do things daily. When Lorina McAdam gets too absorbed in the administrative minutiae, it is a cue for her to go on a field trip to visit the people she is serving to reconnect with why she is there, 'and suddenly, all the admin is worth it'. Other people find it helpful to have images that remind them of their purpose on their walls or wallets. Building a habit of setting intentions for a meeting, project or day also falls into this category.

2. *Build habits that allow you to do more of what you enjoy* – Pramath, for example, uses what he enjoys doing to shape how he pursues his bigger purpose of changing people's lives in India via building innovative and enduring educational institutions. He has an ecosystem of habits (such as how he builds teams, runs meetings and manages his time). They help him do what he loves to do most (such as connecting the dots and seeing others flourish). In the process, he creates the conditions for others to grow and come up with ideas that he would not have thought of himself.

3. *Build a habit of making your purpose seem more achievable* – The more we *believe* it is possible to achieve a purpose or goal, the more motivational fuel our brains generate[2]. Working on mindsets is one way to increase our belief in the possibility of our dreams becoming reality. Regularly reading or watching stories about people who have persevered with their purpose through trialling times can also strengthen our belief in the achievability of our purpose – if they can, so can we.

4. *Build a habit for 'swallowing the purpose frogs'* – We love the quote attributed to Mark Twain: 'If you know you have to swallow a frog, swallow it first thing in the morning. If there are two frogs, swallow the biggest one first.' Doing the hardest thing on our to-do list helps us feel ahead and start the day with a sense of achievement. In terms of getting purpose-fuelled, ensure that some of your 'frogs' are also important

steps for making progress on your purpose. Often these items have less urgency, because purpose by nature is more timeless. That means they can easily fall victim to the Eisenhower Principle ('What is important is seldom urgent, what is urgent is seldom important')[8].

Tom Rippin described how he used to want to get the small stuff done, to then clear the decks and have a larger amount of time to work on something bigger. 'And then you spend all day clearing the decks and actually haven't got any time left. Or by the time you do, you're actually not very fresh anymore.' Once he identified this example of friction, Tom set in place a number of things that help him make time for 'purpose frogs'. 'I block time in my calendar and I've been working a day a week away from my desk. I spend that day in the institute that I had my sabbatical in, it is a quiet environment that I associate with working in a different way. Even if I do have my e-mails open, I feel less compelled to have to reply to them straight away.'

5. *Build habits that involve others* – How we interact with others can provide both friction and traction to our purpose habits. It can distract us when there are competing objectives at play, and it can boost our purpose-fuel when objectives synchronize or coexist. A shared purpose in a team or organization will generate more fuel through building collective habits that suit their context. For example, most people in Tom's organization, On Purpose, now spend a day a week away from their desk to tackle bigger chunks of work. Juan Jose told us how he has built a habit into his meetings to consider decisions through the lenses of Ambu's three values (results with speed, collaboration and integrity).

We have now covered how to get more purpose-fuelled for moving on the performance curve by fine-tuning your purpose compass and harnessing purpose day-to-day. In the next chapter we look at a final method for fuelling us on the performance curve and maximizing our potential by boosting the quality of options we generate and the choices we make: paradoxical thinking.

CHAPTER NINE

Harnessing the power of paradox

In life and work we often face conflicting demands. Work vs. play. Pace vs. accuracy. Quality vs. cost. Effectiveness vs. well-being (the core theme of this book). When faced with a dilemma between two contradictory ideas, we might first feel stuck in a gridlock: 'Shall I do A or B?' Or we might look for a trade-off by asking, 'How do I divide things up between A and B?' If, however, we can find a way to see past 'A vs. B' and, instead, bring them together so their combined value is greater than the sum of the parts, we can boost our performance.

To illustrate, let's consider who has the power during an orchestral performance. At first, we might say the conductor holds the power, and rightly so: the musicians cannot all decide to play their own interpretation of the music. Therefore, the conductor stands centre stage and keeps the musicians in line with a baton. But what about the musicians? Each is an expert in their own craft and knows how to bring the best of themselves and their instrument to the music. If we gave the musicians the power, the collective force could be much stronger, but we could risk chaos.

Cellist Yo-Yo Ma is acutely conscious of this dilemma: 'The use and distribution of power in a performance situation is very interesting because, if you over-control something, the music dies. Certain people have an inordinate amount of power to say what we are going to do.' (Yo-Yo is likely referring to the conductor, soloist(s), etc.) He goes on to say: 'What you can do is transfer power, i.e. responsibility, to as many people as possible, so that they automatically do what is right for the moment. For that to happen, the individual members of the orchestra have to know what the big picture is – what we are doing, why and for whom – and then to make every moment have purpose and meaning.'

Yo-Yo's approach (of transferring power to many) goes beyond the dilemma of choosing between the opposing ideas of control (and killing the music) vs. autonomy (expressive but potentially chaotic). It also goes beyond settling for a compromise, e.g. controlling some aspects, giving autonomy for other aspects. Yo-Yo is advocating a solution to the dilemma that unlocks the full potential of the individuals and of the collective. In other words, tight control of the shared big picture permits greater autonomy for individuals, which, in the end, leads to everyone controlling the outcome, and greater total control. (As an aside: this also illustrates benefits of the big picture mindset.)

This chapter is about how we can systematically come up with such solutions to the different dilemmas we regularly face. We present a technique – called *paradoxical thinking* – which can be applied to a wide range of dilemmas to help us find better solutions. A paradox is a statement that initially seems self-contradictory and/or contrary to logic, and paradoxical thinking helps us to bring together these seemingly contradictory ideas. It helps us see beyond binary solutions to dilemmas (e.g. power sits either with the conductor or the musicians). It also helps us see beyond trade-offs and compromises (e.g. power is divided between the conductor and the musicians).

With paradoxical thinking, we look at a dilemma both more holistically and more forensically, to unlock it such that the opposing ideas can coexist and reinforce each other. This smarter thinking can help us access greater effectiveness and find ways for our effectiveness and well-being to reinforce each other. Since it can systematically elevate our thinking to help us find our way past barriers and complexity, it is a form of fuel to sustain us on the performance curve.

Paradoxical thinking is found in debates between Greek philosophers, and reportedly helped Einstein and other scientists to develop their theories[1]. It was also rife among the interviewees for this book; each has incorporated their own version of paradoxical thinking into their daily work and sees it as an important part of their effectiveness. You heard another example from Yo-Yo in Chapter 4, where he talked about needing a strong ego in order to be able to give it away. Wendy Kopp described how she was always looking for the 'third way'. For example, she talked extensively about how Teach For All transcends the common dilemma of *local autonomy vs. global consistency* by focusing on strengthening local leadership and creating connections between local organizations, thus building the collective capacity of the network. Lorina McAdam told us stories about helping others to reframe their thinking to reconcile the needs of the local people with the constraints of the humanitarian mission. Pramath Sinha explained how he helps his teams to move beyond constraints: 'I challenge my teams to raise their sights. I try to simplify the world to help improve and enhance their mental models, so they start thinking expansively and differently.'

Defining paradoxical thinking

There are three typical features of paradoxical thinking. The first feature is the *presence of a dilemma or trade-off*. We have mentioned some examples already. Table 9.1 below shows common organizational or industry dilemmas (variations of which also show up in our personal lives).

Table 9.1: Common dilemmas in organizations and industries

- Should we delegate more or control more? (Such as in Yo-Yo's orchestra example.)
- Should we prioritize local autonomy or global consistency?
- Should we raise prices or increase sales volumes?
- Should we reduce the cost of customer service or protect spend per customer?

- Should we prioritize short-term profits or invest in innovation?
- Should we go fast or minimize risk?
- Should we 'do good' (environmental, community, etc.) or meet our targets?
- Should we prioritize short-term performance or longer-term health?

Note: these are written as dilemmas, i.e. either-or questions, to lay out clearly the two contradictory ideas, or poles. However, each could also be written as a trade-off (e.g. to what extent should we reduce customer service levels vs. protect spend per customer?). Occasionally there might be more than two contradictory ideas, in which case the techniques we offer later will work just as well, but we will stick with two ideas in all the illustrating examples in this chapter.

The second feature of paradoxical thinking is *refusing to answer these either-or questions*. We reject settling for unsatisfying choices and compromises, which are ways of merely coping with a dilemma. Instead, we reframe: we shift our mindset from 'this is an unsolvable gridlock' to 'this is a solvable paradox'.

The third feature of paradoxical thinking is that we *look for both-and solutions*. We generate a solution that makes the two seemingly contradictory poles work in harmony, rather than in opposition. We seek to make *both* ideas a reality and unlock further benefits by having them coexist ('both-and'). For example, this book is about working on our inner operating system to unlock the paradox of both effectiveness and well-being, leading to greater overall performance (the 'and'). This is much like the notion of yin and yang, in which two opposing energies mutually reinforce each other, and each contains the seed of the other within it.

This might seem quite theoretical, so rest assured that half the battle of paradoxical thinking is being able to recognize when we are boxed into a dilemma and open our mind to the possibility of both-and solutions. We will give detailed guidance for doing this in the later part of this chapter.

Why does paradoxical thinking provide fuel?

Practising paradoxical thinking sustains us on the performance curve for three main reasons.

First, paradoxical thinking enables us to access higher levels of effectiveness, outsmart the competition, raise standards, and bring our best thinking to some of the toughest issues of our time, such as living sustainably. Individuals who bring paradoxical thinking are more innovative and creative, and there is evidence that leaders who bring paradoxical thinking spur more innovation in their employees[2,3]. Paradoxical thinking helps us get past the dilemmas or trade-offs where we feel gridlocked, so that we (and our team or organization) can perform at our best and maximize our potential. We find new ways through problems that enable us to do more with less. It can bring people together, because it encourages us to stop defending opposing interests and start looking for how to combine interests in a way that creates more overall.

Second, paradoxical thinking fuels us by reframing how we see problems and challenging us to shift our perspectives and mindsets, so it helps us evolve our inner operating system. People operating out of the later stages of development mentioned in Chapter 4 have more versatility of thinking. This naturally leads them to deploy paradoxical thinking without necessarily being aware of it, because they see past initial answers to come up with solutions that better address the complexity of problems. Paradoxical thinking techniques are a form of scaffolding we can use to reliably get the benefits of these more complex ways of thinking to tackle our immediate problems, whatever our stage of development. In addition, the more we practise paradoxical thinking, the better our brains will get at it, and the more likely we will be to make use of it when we are faced with a dilemma.

Third, paradoxical thinking breaks the vicious cycle we see between binary thinking and being in protect mode. If we bring binary thinking to face a dilemma, we are likely to feel stuck, under pressure and in protect mode. In protect mode, our brain's executive functioning will likely be impaired, affecting the complexity of our thinking. And the causality could work the other way: if we are already in protect mode and we come across a dilemma, our brains will be focused on the source of threat and we are unlikely to bring our most complex thinking to the problem. In protect mode, it is either us or the tiger: we are not wired to explore nuanced solutions with a beast who wants to eat us! By contrast, being comfortable with embracing paradoxes and the resulting explore mode has been shown to help people perform and innovate[2,3]. Integrating paradoxical thinking into our inner operating system should therefore encourage explore mode and help us recover from, or avoid, protect mode.

However, paradoxical thinking is not easy. It is hard work. It requires time and deep thinking, but it also requires confronting contradictions, rather than avoiding them. There is some evidence that our brains find contradictions mentally and emotionally unpleasant, and that this dislike drives us to remove those contradictions (the theory of 'cognitive dissonance')[4]. Oxford professor Eric Beinhocker, whose work on big economic challenges is rife with paradoxes, told us, 'I feel uncomfortable and slightly irritated when there is lots of messy stuff and I want to make sense of it. But that discomfort is also a signal of opportunity, a missing piece of the puzzle waiting to be discovered.' So don't be surprised if sitting with your dilemmas feels uncomfortable: scanning studies have seen this in other people's brains, too! Sit with them, because paradoxical thinking depends on a tolerance for uncertainty and confusion, for frustration and craziness, and a hunger for finding solutions that take you on new adventures.

In the rest of this chapter, we will help you train your paradoxical eye and show how to cultivate paradoxical thinking systematically for yourself and your team. We share with you the techniques we and our colleagues have developed and used over the years to help client teams apply paradoxical thinking. Two books by Roger Martin, and Colin Price and Sharon Toye first piqued our interest in paradoxical thinking, in case you wish to explore this field further[5,6].

A beautiful paradox

Let's enter the world of beauty. Sephora, the world's leading prestige beauty retailer, has been conquering the world with its distinctive black-and-white striped stores. It is now present in more than 35 markets across five continents, having doubled its bricks-and-mortar presence to approximately 2,500 stores over the past decade, as well as building a powerful online presence. It has also won plenty of awards, such as global retailer of the year in 2018. Sephora is adept at using paradoxical solutions to grow and perform.

One example is how Sephora unlocks the paradox of *reducing cost of customer service and increasing customer spend,* looking specifically at the cost of customer service at cash desks. The main driver for this cost is the number of cashiers. For any retailer, reducing the number of cashiers risks longer queues and dissatisfied customers, who might be tempted to abandon their purchases or avoid that retailer's stores in the future. By contrast, increasing the number of cashiers should lead to shorter queues. This might entice customers to buy even if they are in a hurry, and encourage them to come back in the future because they can make their purchases quickly. However, having more cashiers costs more and risks lowering productivity.

What helps Sephora unlock this paradox of reducing the cost of customer service and increasing customer spend is the sales racks that line the queuing area. Many retailers have these racks, but we are particularly impressed by Sephora's 'Beauty to Go' ones because they are stacked full of convenient mini-sizes and cutesy lip balms, and shoppers find them irresistible. So much so that we authors feel cheated if there is no queue to give us an excuse to peruse and pop a few small items into our baskets. But this is not at all insignificant: the price tags are mostly not mini-sized and we imagine that popping a few of those items into a basket is going to add 10, 20, 30 or more euros to a customer's bill.

This means Beauty to Go helps reduce the cost of customer service at cash desks in a way that actually increases customer spend and satisfaction. Queuing is less annoying (and mostly quite enjoyable) for customers who are perusing the Beauty to Go racks, so Sephora store managers can worry less about queue sizes (i.e. reduce customer service at tills), and get a revenue uplift at the same time from the sales of Beauty to Go products. And it goes further: Beauty to Go mini-sizes are a great way for customers to try out new products, new brands and even new beauty categories, potentially increasing their future spend. When we see signs of virtuous circles such as this (a 'both-and'), we know a paradox has been unlocked. It is like nuclear fusion: bringing the elements together generates extra energy.

How do paradoxical solutions come about? Often, there is a story of joining the dots. Beauty to Go is a creatively executed version of the checkout confectionary display that supermarkets have had for decades to tempt customers (and their kids). Sephora then blended this idea with the trend for 'mini items' (cute, affordable and irresistible items … think mini ice creams, mini notebooks, Mini cars…).

You will likely also have examples in your own work and personal life where you found paradoxical solutions. Some of these might be even quite simple. For example: it is a rare sunny day in the UK today as we write this. Should we take time off this afternoon to enjoy the sun, or finish this chapter? What if we reframe that as a paradoxical (both-and) question: how could we take some time outside today in a way that would help us finish this chapter? A walking meeting, perhaps, which might help inspire us to crack a couple of tricky points and give us energy to work more effectively on our return. This seems obvious and straightforward, but what can you do in situations where a paradoxical solution is not evident?

We now give you techniques to make paradoxical thinking systematic: to help you and your organization repeatedly generate ideas that unlock dilemmas. Before you move on, take a moment to reflect on how paradoxical thinking might be relevant for you:

- When did you (or those around you) manage to unlock a paradox? What was the key to the unlock? In what way did it generate extra energy?
- What are the common dilemmas you face at work or at home? How do you tend to cope with them?

With some of your common dilemmas in mind, the rest of this chapter will give you a five-step methodology for reframing dilemmas into paradoxes and solving them with both-and solutions. We will help you boost your quality of thought, so you improve the quality of the options you generate and the choices you make. The tools we introduce will also help you be on the performance curve more generally, because they challenge you to look at your thinking and to think in more integrated and expansive ways. You can draw on any one of these tools in isolation, but of course they are most powerful when used together.

Practising paradoxical thinking: five steps

We use five steps to apply paradoxical thinking to solve dilemmas (see Figure 9.1). Since these steps are designed to take you on a quest, the steps spell out *GRAIL* (you might want to add 'holy' to it, once you discover what power paradoxes contain – especially if you are a Monty Python fan). In a moment, we will walk through each step, illustrated with an example. You could pick an example of your own to practise with as you read (or afterwards). Before we dive in, here are three tips.

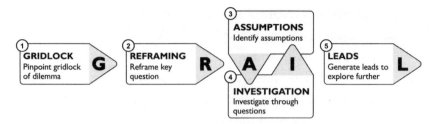

Figure 9.1 Five steps to paradoxical thinking (GRAIL)

First, work loosely from left to right. Begin with *GRIDLOCK* (pinpointing the gridlock at the heart of the dilemma), then move to *REFRAMING* (reframing the key question), then iterate between *ASSUMPTIONS* (identifying assumptions) and *INVESTIGATION* (investigating through questions), and finally let *LEADS* (generating leads to explore further) arise spontaneously as a result of all that. This is not meant to be a rigid linear process; rather, it is a toolkit from which you will likely use the left-hand side tools early in your problem solving, and the right-hand side tools later on. You will almost certainly move back and forth between the steps and might even uncover things later on that cause you to loop back to the first step.

Second, whatever you do, just channel your inner Einstein (sounds attainable, right?) Yes! This quote is popularly attributed to Einstein: 'If I had an hour to solve a problem and my life depended on the solution, I would spend the first 55 minutes determining the proper question to ask, for once I know the proper question, I could solve the problem in less than five minutes.' Whether it came from Einstein or not, we like this quotation a lot, because it reminds us to avoid going straight to Step 5 (LEADS). Not laying the groundwork of earlier steps can constrain the solution with our incoming thinking.

Finally, one way to improve your thinking is to involve others in your GRAIL quest who are not as used to dealing with your problem as you are. Being an expert on a topic can lead to cognitive inflexibility, as we tend to follow the most familiar solution. Research with high-functioning chess players illustrates this[7]. We have seen great value from bringing in people with multiple, more diverse, or distant perspectives to the GRAIL problem-solving process. This could be people who know little or nothing about your topic and are happy to ask you questions (even basic ones), i.e. bring a beginner's mind. Or people who know quite a lot about the issue, but can to see things from other angles. Perhaps they have faced a similar issue before, or have a parallel role in another division, or work on different aspects of the same issue.

We will now walk through each step of GRAIL, using an example to illustrate the process. The example is a business one, but GRAIL also works equally well for paradoxes in our personal lives. Here is the example:

Imagine we are executives in a retail company (since Sephora has just beautifully warmed us up to that sector). We are considering how to open stores in a new country. It is a sizeable, potentially profitable market and some of the team are bullish about our ability to build scale quickly. Others know that the competition is fierce and are bruised from a previously unsuccessful market entry. The more bullish team members think it is better to open several medium-sized stores in different cities, to get some early coverage. The others want to open one large store in the biggest city so we can establish ourselves solidly and learn before expanding. Our starting question could be summarized as: 'Should we start with one large store or several medium-sized stores?'

Step 1 GRIDLOCK: pinpoint the gridlock at the heart of the dilemma

If you want to turn a dilemma into a paradox and unlock it, the first step is to know exactly what the dilemma is. What two things would you really like to have but which seem to be working against each other? What is at the heart of the gridlock, or impasse?

You should find two poles, i.e. underlying qualities you are struggling to reconcile. Academics Jennifer Riel and Roger Martin call these 'Opposable Models' and advocate for laying out the two extreme choices, so that you can really see the dilemma in full technicolour[8]. Table 9.1 on pp.179–80 laid out some example dilemmas. Step 1 is to write down your dilemma as one pole vs. the other (even if this feels more binary than you know to be true). In the Sephora Beauty to Go example, the poles were *reducing cost of customer service vs. increasing customer spend.*

What is the gridlock in our store-opening dilemma, i.e. the poles we are struggling to reconcile? It is not one large store vs. several medium-sized ones. These are two competing solutions, not poles of the underlying gridlock. A little thought might help us see that one pole is minimizing risk, in this case by going slowly and thoroughly. The other pole is fast pace: there is a desire to scale quickly and every day without a store is seen as a day of missed revenue. So the dilemma can be boiled down to the two poles of *low risk vs. fast pace.* Note that these poles could have been different. For example, if our principal concern were how best to get critical mass, the poles could be *focus vs. breadth* (i.e. a large store in one city vs. several medium-sized stores in different cities). The poles could also have been *quality vs. scale* (i.e. devote our efforts to one quality opening vs. divide and conquer to get scale). While the options for each of these sound similar (i.e. one store vs. several), it is the different poles that will lead us to different solutions further down the process, so it is important to make sure we are clear about what really matters.

To check the relevance of the poles we identified, we can go back to the bigger picture, particularly our bigger goals or purpose. If we were Sephora executives, we might look to their desire to surprise and delight customers. This could lead to articulating the dilemma as *surprising and delighting as many new customers as possible at launch time vs. minimizing risk now so we can surprise and delight in this market over the longer term.* When we bring our bigger goals or purpose into the dilemma, it can help us see what is really at stake.

A note: if you are struggling to identify the poles at the heart of your problem, you might want to pause and check it really is a dilemma. Is it actually a gridlock, where two things are working against each other? Or is there really one pole that is far more important than the other? Not every problem is truly a dilemma.

Step 2 REFRAMING: reframe the key question.

Following Einstein's advice, now it is time to look at our original question and reframe it as a paradox that we seek to unlock. We call this new question the *key question*, because it will drive what we eventually solve for and the solution space we consider, as well as helping us to be in explore mode[9]. This means our key question influences the quantity, quality, range and choice of potential solutions we come up with. It is the North Star that guides our quest to paradoxical thinking. How do we reframe our key question to help unlock the paradox?

Figure 9.2 shows a ladder to paradoxical thinking, which is inspired by Colin Price and Sharon Toye's 'levels of thinking' framework. Each rung represents a more expansive mindset about the outcome we expect. That mindset drives the questions we ask and therefore the solutions we get. The top rung encourages paradoxical thinking, but we find it valuable to understand the different rungs that build up to it. Let's look at each rung in turn, starting with the bottom.

1) *Either-or* – On Rung 1, our 'either-or' mindset is based on a belief that we have to choose between one thing or another. We are looking for an 'either-or', or binary, solution;

2) *Trade-off* – On Rung 2, our 'trade-off' mindset is based on a belief that the right solution is to find a compromise or divide things up. We are assuming the answer will be in a range;

3) *Best of each* – On Rung 3, our 'best of each' mindset is based on a belief that the best we can do is optimize, i.e. find some kind of balance between the competing poles. We might pay more attention to optimizing each of the poles, but we still see them as contradictory so we settle for getting the best of each through being savvy or hard working;

4) *Both-and* – On Rung 4, our mindset is 'both-and', i.e. paradoxical thinking. We believe we can find a way to have the two seemingly contradictory poles actually be reinforcing. We believe we can find a solution that gets us 'both-and': both poles, and some extra energy from their fusion.

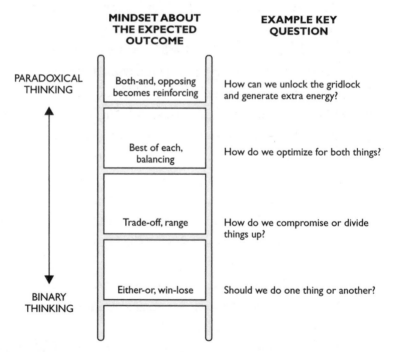

Figure 9.2 Paradoxical thinking ladder
Source: Price and Toye, *Accelerating Performance*. Wiley, 2017

Taking our retail example, below is what the key question might look like at each rung (using the poles we identified earlier of low risk and fast pace).

1) *Either-or* – Our question would be something like, *'Should we go for low risk or fast pace?'* This question will likely open up a discussion about risk and pace, so is already more interesting than the narrow starting question of, *'Should we start with one large store or several medium-sized stores?'* However, it still points to a narrow solution space, because we are confining ourselves to choosing between two competing options;

2) *Trade-off* – On Rung 2, we realize that we do not have to make a binary choice. We might ask, *'To what extent should we go for low risk vs. fast pace?'* Now we are into trade-off territory and you can see this already opens up a range of possibilities compared to Rung 1. For example, we might decide that we could have an acceptable balance between risk and pace by going for one large store and a couple of medium-sized ones;

3) *Best of each* – On Rung 3, we try to get the best of each pole. We might ask, *'How could we optimize for manageable risk and decent pace?'* It is a subtle change from Rung 2, but the question points us away from moving between the two poles and opens up ways we can optimize for both. We might look at sequencing openings, or optimizing the locations or customers we target, or other smart ways to minimize risk and increase pace. For an important but sticky issue, a question of this kind will almost always get to a better answer than the earlier questions. And in many cases, this question might well be enough to get you a great outcome. But what happens if we move up to the top rung?

4) *Both-and* – On Rung 4, we ask a question that turns the gridlock into a paradox to be solved. We are seeking for the two poles to come together and be reinforcing. The key question we might pick is, *'How*

could we enter this new market at pace in a way that reduces risk?'
We also could have had an inverse question, such as, *'How could
we de-risk our market entry in a way that allows us to accelerate our
pace?'*, but this first question seems more positive and encouraging
of explore mode. Whatever we choose (and we could come back to
an alternative key question later if needed), these questions are much
bigger than earlier ones: they bring a spirit of possibility and send us
on a quest for radical ideas.

The questions on Rungs 3 and 4 are both *'How could we...?'* questions,
which makes them much more open than earlier questions. *'How
could we...?'* is a decent template for the first three words of your
key question.

You may notice that Rung 4 is qualitatively different from the
other rungs. On these lower three rungs, we accept that the two poles
or qualities compete and we become progressively more savvy at
arbitrating between them. Our complexity of thinking and the range
and sophistication of our answers increases, but we are still stuck in the
same paradigm. We are coping with the gridlock, rather than breaking
it open and generating extra energy or benefits as a result.

However, on Rung 4, we refuse to accept that the poles work in
opposition, and we look for a solution that breaks open the gridlock. It
is not about looking for a reasonable solution, such as the 'manageable
risk and decent pace' in the Rung 3 question. It is about being
unreasonable. As Juan Jose Gonzalez, CEO of Ambu, told us, 'We set
our own limitations. What boundary we set has significant impact. I
hate the word "reasonable". You have to set goals that reasonable people
would reject. The diagnosis has to be based on facts but the conclusions
are chosen by the team and can be more transformational.'

Asking Rung 3 or 4 questions is a form of scaffolding: it trains our
brain to approach problems with a more complex way of thinking,
as well as helping us solve our immediate problem. For example,

repeatedly generating both-and questions should, over time, train our brain to ask both-and questions instead of either-or questions. If asking both-and questions proves rewarding, these pathways should get even stronger[10].

All that said, don't overthink it. Try to get a question on Rung 3 or 4 and then, if it seems intriguing and you, or others, have energy to explore it, go with it. If you get stuck, check whether you have boxed yourself in with thinking at Rung 1 or 2, or come up with a new question on Rung 3 or 4.

Step 3 ASSUMPTIONS: identify assumptions.

Now that we have a new key question, we might well be ready to jump to answers. But we are still not out of the woods: we risk defaulting to our old thinking patterns and the more limited set of solutions with which we started. To get our thinking out of the metaphorical box (our original solution space), we need to be able to see more clearly the sides of the box we have built up, and find ways to break them down or make the box bigger.

We can do this by naming assumptions, in particular those that lead to constraints. Take a look at everything you have noted down so far, and start spotting assumptions. Pay particular attention to assumptions that might reinforce the dilemma in your mind. Think of assumptions about you, others and the situation more broadly. Do not worry how much these assumptions reflect reality or not (whatever reality is!), nor indeed how strong, common or relevant they are. Just treat this as a brainstorming of assumptions: write each down and move on. Table 9.2 shows a list of questions that will help you to identify assumptions, and sample assumptions from our retail example.

If you dig, you will likely come up with a dozen or more assumptions. This is invaluable, because the assumptions might contain a golden clue on your quest to unlock the paradox. At this step, we often

Table 9.2 Questions to help identify assumptions

Questions that help identify assumptions	Sample assumptions from retail example
• What are we assuming about the *situation*? (e.g. about each pole, what is possible and not possible, how things work around here)	• We have to choose between one larger store or several medium-sized stores • A larger store is lower risk • The number and size of stores is the only way to get pace • If we do not get critical mass early on, we will fail
• What are we assuming about *ourselves*? (e.g. our capabilities, preferences, tendencies, relationships)	• The number and size of stores is our main way to manage risk • If we fail, we will never be able to re-enter
• What are we assuming about *others*? (e.g. customers, colleagues, shareholders, other stakeholders)	• If we fail, we will lose credibility with our shareholders
• What are we assuming about the *wider context*? (e.g. business environment, societal considerations)	• The market is at least as competitive and hence risky as when we failed before

see unlocking start to happen. When we suddenly realize that an assumption is just that – an assumption – a side of the box can fall down and we can suddenly see a possibility emerge. If this happens, explore that possibility further, using the techniques outlined in the next two steps.

Table 9.2 shows a few assumptions from our retail example, but we could have generated many more. Nevertheless, can you see how, even for this brief list which was generated in a couple of minutes, there are clues for new solutions? What if we could find other ways to get pace, or manage risk? Some of those assumptions might well be very true (for example, analysis might show that the market is still very competitive and therefore as risky as before). But this might trigger us to look for products or services for which we have a competitive advantage over the competition. And some assumptions might seem more about us and our worries (risk of a repeat failure, losing credibility), which could unlock some ideas about how we engage our shareholders.

Spelling out assumptions almost naturally opens up a new set of questions that will stimulate new thinking and help us better understand the issue or lead us towards a paradox-solving solution. The next step is to identify and ask such questions.

Step 4 INVESTIGATION: investigate through questions

In Step 4 of GRAIL, we investigate further through questions that help us get depth and impetus for moving forwards. First, we pick the assumptions from Step 3 that feel most important (i.e. they feel like major constraints) or fragile (i.e. we suspect they might not be fully true, however much we are influenced by them). Next, we can create questions that challenge each assumption and stimulate us to think. Some questions will be more about depth: digging for more understanding, to help us unlock our paradox. Some questions will be more about forward momentum, i.e. leading to potential solutions, and will often start with *'How could we...?'* We should aim that all our questions stimulate new thinking, rather than put us back in our box. In our retail example, we might get to questions as shown in Table 9.3.

We can also look back to our North Star (the key question outlined in Step 2) for inspiration. It might help us add useful questions, such as *'How could the ways we might get pace also help us reduce risk?'* or the inverse question *'How could the ways we might de-risk also help us get pace?'* or *'What does pace really mean to us?'*

Table 9.3 Investigative questions for retail example

Assumption	Example question
We have to choose between one large store or several medium-sized stores	What different combinations of store sizes could we use?
A large store is lower risk	What features of a large store make it low risk, and how could we translate those over to medium-sized stores?
The number and size of stores is the only way to get pace	How else could we get pace?
If we do not get critical mass early on, we will fail	How could we reduce our dependency on getting critical mass early on?
The number and size of stores is our main way to manage risk	How else could we manage risk?
If we fail again, we will never be able to re-enter … and we will lose credibility with our shareholders	What really is the risk appetite of our shareholders? How could they help us make this a success?
The market is at least as competitive and hence risky as it was when we failed before	What was it about the market that really drove failure before? How true is that today?

We might also throw in some other generic questions that bring depth or forward momentum, such as:

- What are we not seeing here?
- Who could help us with this?
- Who has cracked this before? What can we learn from them?
- If we could change one thing about the situation, what would it be and what would it get us? How could we change that thing?
- What would customers most value?
- What matters in the bigger picture, or for our purpose? How could we use that to find a way past this gridlock?
- If we saw this as an adventure or a learning opportunity, what would we do?
- What are we most afraid of? If we weren't afraid, how would we unlock this?

You might find it is helpful to list many questions, or you might find that your attention is quickly captured by one assumption and the question(s) that come from it, and you are naturally drawn to generating leads. We now look at that final step.

Step 5 LEADS: generate leads to explore further

In this final step, we identify leads. Leads might be possible solutions, but they could also be avenues for further exploration, which lead to a solution further down the track. They are like the clues a detective would use to guide where to look next.

This step is born out of all the previous work. The biggest mistake is to jump to this too early. It is tempting to take a shortcut, but we really encourage you to hold back and do this only after you have listed at least some assumptions and questions. There is no framework or structure for this step, other than to follow the energy of the questions you have generated and start exploring or answering some of them.

From the rich list of questions we generated for our retail example, several might well unlock the paradox. Let's take a couple: 'How else could we get pace?' and 'How else could we manage risk?' Perhaps our online retail platform could help with these two questions: we could invest to strengthen our online customer base in certain cities or demographics, or plan activities that drive online customers into the stores. Or perhaps pop-up stores offer a low risk, faster alternative. We could also partner with others. What could we do differently with influencers in this market? Or could we opt for a different model: a franchise or joint venture? Or what about partnering up with a department store to open store-in-stores? We could draw on the partner's local knowledge, store traffic, client databases and brand image, and it would be much quicker and cheaper to build store-in-stores than separate shops.

This last idea of store-in-stores might well be one way to resolve our key question, i.e. to enter the market at pace in a way that would reduce risk.

There could be other benefits from a partnership (e.g. lower costs leading to better margins, ability to have presence in smaller towns that might not sustain a standalone store), so it could be a 'both-and' solution. In fact, this last approach has been a cornerstone of Sephora's entry strategy in well-served beauty markets such as Switzerland and Germany. But this is just one example. Franchising helps the world's largest fast-food groups manage pace and risk. The eventual solution might well combine several ideas, some fresh and innovative, and others that we or others have applied elsewhere. Regardless of where you end up, paradoxical thinking opens up the thought process, leading to more and better options.

Here are some more tips for generating leads:

- Treat this as brainstorming. Anything goes, just get ideas surfaced and written down. Be sure to generate a few leads, so that you have multiple avenues for further investigation;
- Watch out for binary or trade-off thinking. If people start saying. *'No that won't work,'* you might ask, *'How could we get past that?'* or *'What would it take to make it work?'* or *'What could we do instead?'* As Pramath Sinha put it: 'Your own comfort zone holds you back. You have to challenge yourself to not settle for something that worked in the past, but rather to bring all of your best fresh thinking.';
- Keep using your original key question as a North Star that guides what you come up with. Likewise, remember the bigger picture, for example customer needs and the overall purpose or vision for the organization or, if it is a personal paradox, your personal purpose and values;
- Embrace simplicity. You might do all this and realize that a simple idea is staring you in the face. You might well already be using that simple idea in other ways. Paradoxical thinking is not about innovative or creative solutions as such; it is about seeing your way past problems. Sometimes that might be by doing something new, but other times it might simply be about getting out of your own way;
- If you are feeling stuck, take a break and do something totally different. Insights seem to come from quite subconscious processes, and brain-

scanning studies suggest they are preceded by a moment of inward attention as our brains are joining the dots[11]. If we give our brains space to do this (rather than deliberately trying to control our thinking with analytical problem solving), we might just find the answers pop up (this is why people say they often get their best insights in the shower or when out for a jog);

- Accept that knotty problems are unlikely to be solved in one go and you might need to revisit the topic, possibly involving others. For example, the questions: *'What was it about the market that really drove failure before? How true is that today?'* might require going back to the team who analysed the market and asking them to dig into this, or even back to the original team who worked on the first attempt;

- Be prepared to start again. You may realize through this process that none of the initial options you considered are viable, or even that you have been working towards the wrong poles. This process is iterative: and your first work-through of the steps might simply lead you to a better key question from which to run the process again.

How will you know if you have found a Rung 4 answer? First, what matters is a good answer, not a Rung 4 answer. But here is how to know the difference between Rungs 3 and 4. Rung 3 can feel like hard work, with lots of juggling and optimizing. Things suddenly feel easier from Rung 4. The unlock brings simplicity and clarity and might not, in retrospect, feel like rocket science. But suddenly everything works together and the feeling of friction or drag goes away. And it often brings people together, because they are no longer defending competing poles. Once you arrive at a Rung 4 unlock, it feels qualitatively different.

In conclusion: go slow to go faster (and further)

You have now seen the (holy) GRAIL of paradoxical thinking, and how we can apply the five steps systematically to get past a dilemma. But these techniques are flexible: they can be used alone or in combination, on small or large, personal or work issues, to help you and others be on the performance curve. For example, simply paying attention to when you or others seem stuck in a forced choice and asking, 'How could you get both those things?' might trigger some Rung 3 or Rung 4 thinking. It will lack the depth of the systematic approach, but our guess is that it will usually provoke interesting new perspectives.

As mentioned at the start of this chapter, using paradoxical thinking in any form should also act as scaffolding for you or others, strengthening neural pathways that support the thinking capacities that are characteristic of later stages of development. We see Rung 1 (either-or) as equivalent to the early stage thinking of a young child, while Rung 2 (trade-off) would help us transition into socialized thinking. Rung 3 (best of each) would help us transition from socialized thinking to self-authoring thinking, and Rung 4 (both-and) would help us transition from self-authoring thinking to self-transforming thinking. Practising paradoxical thinking will help you to develop your thinking capacities, wherever you are in your vertical development journey.

Paradoxical thinking is not always possible, nor indeed desirable. Sometimes, choosing clear priorities and saying 'no' to other possibilities can be incredibly valuable and energize our performance (the paradoxical wisdom of 'less is more'). But, for your biggest work or personal dilemmas, we hope you gain value from the power – and the paradox – of paradoxical thinking: go slow to go faster and, above all, further.

This was the last chapter of the fuel catalyst, and we will now turn our attention to our third and final catalyst, connection, which covers how we can help each other be on the performance curve.

PART THREE

The Connection Catalyst

How to Build Developmental Relationships

CHAPTER TEN

Going far and fast, together

The wisdom and fuel catalysts cover the inner work that supports us to be on the performance curve, and the habits and practices that can fuel that work. The third catalyst – connection – helps us build developmental relationships to do this inner work together. Relationships can be wonderful containers to get us moving on the performance curve. Perhaps you have experienced how working with a good coach or therapist can be life changing. But this catalyst is not about professional support: it is about building everyday relationships that help us and others grow.

Our clients and interviewees tell us countless stories about how others – at home and at work – have helped them get unstuck. This might be close colleagues or family members, or even people they do not know well. Maggie Henriquez got the key to turning around her unsuccessful start at Krug when she was courageous enough to share how 'devastated and lost' she felt at an LVMH training programme. A fellow participant was then able to help her see how she was part of the problem and how to unblock the situation. 'Seeking help is very important,' Maggie told us. 'Sometimes in life you have to accept that you need help and you look for it.'

The problem is this: too few relationships help us grow and be our best. If they did, businesses would not need to spend billions on coaching and 'soft skills' training to address trust and collaboration issues. Nor would the personal development industry have such a market for books, seminars, coaching and therapy to help us improve our relationships.

Sometimes it is helpful for someone more distant from our situation, or with complementary experience, to bring a fresh perspective. In Maggie's story, she learned from someone outside her situation. But Maggie also emphasizes the importance of cultivating developmental relationships in her day-to-day work, to support business success and to help herself and others grow. 'Together we are a source of motivation and creativity for each other. It's about caring and being open. About giving and getting, serving through leadership'.

What if we could get collectively better at building developmental relationships, at work and at home? This would help us and others grow daily, spot and tackle issues sooner, and reduce the need for rescue interventions. The connection catalyst helps us strengthen the relationships in our daily lives so they support us and others to develop more deeply. It also helps us more quickly form developmental relationships with people we know less well.

We authors are acutely aware that the diversity of how our brains have developed as a result of our genetics and experiences will play a role in how easy (and appealing) building developmental relationships is for each of us. We include a wide range of ideas and techniques in the connection catalyst and we hope that this enables you to grow in whatever way makes sense for you and your context. As with everything in *The Performance Curve*, we welcome your feedback and suggestions.

The connection catalyst of the performance curve

Connection can take different forms, and will mean different things to different people. For some people it will mean how close they feel to colleagues, life-long friends, or even the world around them. Cellist Yo-Yo Ma emphasizes the connection he seeks to build with others, and then how he seeks to help them connect the content of his music (or words) to their own lives. We define the connection catalyst of the performance curve as *our ability to form developmental relationships.*

In developmental relationships, we interact in ways that bring out and grow our best, i.e. we develop our inner operating system. This is different from liking, having fun together or understanding each other (though these experiences may well be part of developmental relationships).

There is a proverb that says: 'If you want to go fast, go alone. If you want to go far, go together.' The connection catalyst is about how to do both – go far *and* fast together. Developmental relationships help us go *far* because they grow us in ways we cannot on our own. They encourage us to take responsibility for and shape how we think, feel and act and the results we are getting. They also power us to go further than we can imagine. They help us go *fast* by quickly bringing to the surface the real issues and their causes, so we can get more quickly to solutions.

There are two main aspects to the connection catalyst:

1) *Creating emotional bond*, a heartfelt connection that enables dialogue about our inner operating system;
2) *Providing stretch* that develops each other's inner operating system.

By *emotional bond*, we mean a connection that runs from heart to heart and allows for our deeper development. Emotional bond is beyond simply caring about or supporting the other. With emotional bond, we can rely on each other to be authentic, seen and accepted as we are. We do not need to hide parts of ourselves, because we know our vulnerability is in safe, empathetic hands. This gives us the solidity from which to dive into our inner operating system. We have deliberately chosen the term emotional bond rather than more general terms such as trust or psychological safety, because we are talking specifically about a way of relating that supports highly personal dialogue about mindsets, emotions and behaviours.

Stretch invites us to go below the surface of our iceberg to challenge and develop our inner operating system. Stretch might involve feedback, questions that stimulate deeper reflection, or giving someone a responsibility that requires them to grow.

The analogy of an elastic band connecting two people helps illustrate how emotional bond and stretch complement each other in a developmental relationship. Pulling on the band can lead to the other person stepping away from their current position to a new spot, from which they gain a different perspective on how they are operating. This is akin to stretch. But the elastic band needs to be thick and elastic enough in order not to snap or overextend when stretched. This is akin to emotional bond.

What to find in the chapters of Part 3: connection catalyst

The chapters of Part 3 on the connection catalyst cover different ways of cultivating developmental relationships that support you to reach your potential, individually and collectively. Developmental relationships draw on many aspects of the other performance curve catalysts – wisdom and fuel – and so Part 3 brings together all that we have covered in the book so far.

In the rest of this chapter, we cover the groundwork and science of the first aspect of the connection catalyst: forming emotional bond. We explore how emotional bond helps us increase our effectiveness and well-being, what might get in the way of emotional bond, and how to overcome those barriers and strengthen our capacity to build emotional bond.

Chapter 11 explores the second aspect of the connection catalyst, stretch, and shows what one-to-one developmental relationships look like in action when emotional bond and stretch are combined. As relationships are built on conversations, we will offer you practical ways to make conversations more developmental.

In Chapter 12, we turn to cultures that nurture developmental relationships. We will paint a picture of what these cultures can look like, and offer a range of methods you can apply to your team, group or organization.

Let's now explore emotional bond.

How emotional bond helps us move on the performance curve

Emotional bond helps us move on the performance curve for three reasons.

First, having strong emotional bonds helps us acknowledge our blind spots and grow beyond them. An important starting point for growth is to acknowledge our shortcomings. If we see shortcomings as a dent on our worth as an employee, colleague, boss, friend, parent and so on, we may fear losing something by being open about them (to ourselves or others). Emotional bond gives us the security to be open and in explore mode about areas for growth, including our underlying mindsets, needs and fears. It also helps us take in and make better use of feedback from others.

Second, emotional bond can help us manage our brain's protect and explore modes. If we are in protect mode, emotional bond allows us to express that openly. Labelling our emotions helps us get perspective and settles our protect mode, as well as invites help from others[1]. Furthermore, when we are less afraid to reveal what is below the surface of our iceberg, we are more likely to be in explore mode. More time in explore mode and less time in protect mode means we are able to bring our creativity and problem-solving abilities and will display fewer protective behaviours, such as downplaying problems or assigning blame. Issues will be flagged sooner and resolved more quickly. We will be faster to rally together and adjust course when needed. And there will be less friction and fewer political battles.

Third, emotional bond helps dissolve the paradox of effectiveness vs. well-being, because it boosts them both. When we have this quality of emotional bond, we will pay attention to each other's well-being so everyone will be more likely to bring their best. We will also be more likely to invest time, thought and energy into helping others be effective, and relish the satisfaction of joint success. In challenging times, we will be more likely to stay united rather than fragment to self-protect.

Our interviewees told us how having these kinds of connections – at home or at work – helped them and their teams be their best. For example, Luke Bradley-Jones's success at leading disruptive projects relies heavily on individuals coming together as cohesive teams that help each other push the boundaries. To do this, he says 'In a tightly bonded team, people care about each other and want each other to succeed: they are interested to help others achieve their objectives. They don't feel threatened by each other, and this means they are open-minded to what others say, they listen and seek advice.'

Large-scale studies of psychological safety and trust (which are more general concepts, but share features with emotional bond, such as empathy), also show a link with effectiveness[2]. Research at Google found that a team's culture of psychological safety – a 'shared belief held by members of a team that the team is safe for interpersonal risk-taking' – was the characteristic most associated with team performance[3,4]. Similarly, companies with high trust are better at collaboration, more productive, and have better economic performance[5]. What is amazing is *how much* trust is related to performance. In a survey of 1,095 nationally representative working adults in the US, their self-reported work performance was compared to a calculated level of trust of their organization. Comparing employees in the top and bottom quartiles of companies indicated the following differences: 50 per cent higher productivity, 41 per cent less depersonalization of colleagues, and 41 per cent greater sense of accomplishment[6].

There is also plenty of data to support the idea that trusted relationships are associated with our well-being. Employees in high-trust organizations report 76 per cent higher engagement, suffer less stress, stay longer at the company, and are happier with their lives. Harvard's Study of Adult Development has tracked lifetime emotional and physical well-being for more than 80 years. According to its director, Robert Waldinger, the clearest message of the study is this: 'good relationships keep us happier and healthier. Period.'[7] This phenomenon is not driven by social class, money, IQ or even genes. People with close ties to family, friends and community are happier, physically healthier and live longer than people who are more isolated. 'Loneliness kills,' Waldinger states, 'people who are more isolated than they want to be from others find that they are less happy, their health declines earlier in midlife, their brain functioning declines sooner, and they live shorter lives than people who are not lonely'.

But it is not just any kind of relationship, it is the *quality* of relationship that matters. From her work as a palliative care nurse, author Bronnie Ware advises us to reduce what takes us away from building strong emotional bond (working too much; always looking ahead to the next thing instead of enjoying what we have) and strengthen what builds it (having the courage to express feelings; having the courage to live a life true to ourselves, not the life others expected; staying in touch with friends)[8]. Some problems are just too big to carry around on our own, and helping each other through challenges and partaking in others' happiness are both rewarding for our brains[9,10].

To summarize, it seems that everything is stacked in favour of having strong emotional bonds with each other: there are developmental, performance and well-being benefits. It is therefore not surprising that the human brain has generally evolved to find social connections rewarding, and lack of them painful[11,12]. Indeed, lack of social connection activates similar brain areas as lack of basic needs such as food and water.

Yet there are indicators that, overall, we are not doing too well in forming strong emotional bonds with each other. There is an increase in individuals reporting feeling lonely, and a reduction in the average number of close confidants, which the Harvard Study of Adult

Development describes as essential for living well and healthily[13]. A 2016 global CEO survey reported that 55 per cent of CEOs think that a lack of trust is a threat to their organization's growth[14]. Gallup's global survey puts engagement among employees worldwide at only 22 per cent[15].

So what is driving this gap in emotional bond? And what does it take to strengthen it?

The source of emotional bond: vulnerability and empathy

We have found that the *heartfelt connection of emotional bond results from an interplay of vulnerability and empathy.* Lorina McAdam described how these qualities quickly form emotional bond in the conditions of humanitarian fieldwork. 'You don't have your usual support network there. You don't have people whom you've known for a long time, who know where you're coming from, what you've been through before, what you can deal with, what you can't deal with. So you either open up to them and ask for what you need [vulnerability]. Or, you have to be very attuned to what other people need and try to offer that [empathy]. If you do both, you bond really quickly.'

Vulnerability in a relationship *means exposing something we feel shame about or are worried might expose us to attack, judgement or punishment.* Maggie showed vulnerability in opening up to the training group about how 'devastated and lost' she felt. In fact, Maggie's honesty about her struggles makes her incredibly inspiring and a popular guest speaker at leadership programmes. Her vulnerability allows others to empathize with her, and make achievements like hers more accessible to them. Vulnerability also begets vulnerability, as the other person is more inclined to reciprocate.

Empathy is *experiencing the feelings, thoughts and experience of another as our own.* We pick up cues from the other person's eyes, facial expression, tone of voice, body position and so on, and use these to put ourselves in the other's shoes – mentally and emotionally. It is a higher-order capability, drawing on multiple psychological processes and brain areas[16].

Empathy is also a great prompt for vulnerability. When we feel seen and not alone, we will likely feel more comfortable to share openly. But it works the other way round too: vulnerability is a great prompter for empathy. When we are vulnerable, we are likely to make the other person feel that we trust them. When someone feels we trust them, it tightens their sense of bond to us. We can see this in their brain's production of oxytocin, a neurochemical that is often associated with increased bonding, empathy, trust and generosity[17,18]. Our vulnerability also makes it easier for the other person to empathize with us, because we allow ourselves to be seen as we are and don't put up masks of how we think we should be or want to be seen. The more vulnerable we are, the clearer the cues for the other person to pick up and relate to.

Vulnerability and empathy go hand in hand – they mutually reinforce each other – and make emotional bond grow stronger over time. So what does it take to bring vulnerability and empathy, and what might get in the way?

The basis for vulnerability and empathy: socio-emotional cognition

Empathy and vulnerability depend on what can be called *socio-emotional cognition*[19]. This is our capacity to be aware of the underlying thoughts, beliefs, emotions, intentions of others – even when they are not telling us about them – and co-ordinate those with our own. We have developed a particular network of brain connectivity to support it (which is thought to be altered in people with autistic spectrum characteristics)[20, 21].

Socio-emotional cognition is very different to the cognitive processing we use when we have a non-social task to perform, be it a maths problem, assembly of flat-pack furniture or planning a budget (what we call *task cognition*). And neuroimaging suggests that these two types of cognition draw on quite different brain areas. Task cognition usually draws on the executive function areas associated with planning and problem solving, often grouped together to be called the 'task positive network'[19,22]. Socio-emotional cognition usually draws on a network of brain areas which has been labelled the 'default mode network', because it is activated in brain scanners when we are resting between tasks. (This is presumably because most of us tend to stray into socio-emotional thinking when we are 'off task' and doing nothing in particular, because of the importance of our social world[23].)

Socio-emotional and task cognition can often be brought to bear in the same situation, though they can lead to quite different results. Imagine a friend told you their partner broke up with them. Using your task cognition, you might start problem solving what they should do (let it go, since they never seemed very compatible) or think through what they are looking for in a partner and suggest how to find a better match. Drawing on your socio-emotional cognition would have you listen attentively, give them space and encouragement to share how they are feeling. You would pay careful attention to whether they were ready to talk about dating someone new. Both responses are well intended and valuable – at the right time. Adept switching between the two would be powerful.

But imagine if we systematically approached such situations with just one of these two forms of cognition. It would be akin to stepping on the tennis court with one hand tied behind our back and only allowed to play forehand. We would be able to hit back some balls aimed at our backhand using our forehand, but we would need to do more running and a portion of balls would simply be outside of our reach.

So why might we do that? And, in particular, why might we be contributing to the gap in emotional bond by underusing our socio-emotional cognition?

What might get in the way of socio-emotional cognition?

There can be plenty that gets in the way of us bringing socio-emotional cognition, or at adeptly switching between it and task cognition. This can then compromise our ability to bring vulnerability and empathy. For some people, socio-emotional cognition may simply feel incredibly hard (perhaps like the tennis analogy above), and this may be at least partly due to how our brains have developed. If you feel this way, you may well have already learned approaches to help you navigate socially, and you may find additional ideas to layer on top of these in the next couple of chapters. Other people will simply be underusing their socio-emotional cognition, often without realising it, and this section explains the reasons why this can happen.

First, while the capabilities of socio-emotional and task cognition are complementary, they work like the two sides of an old-fashioned balance[24]. When activity in one goes up, the other goes down, likely because both carry a heavy cognitive load on the brain. This means that, when we are focused on a problem-solving task, our brain's cognitive load is high and we will have less capacity to process our own or others' mental and emotional states. We will be less connected to our own thoughts and emotions, potentially less able to genuinely share what we are thinking and feeling (i.e. be vulnerable), and less empathetic: and all this will affect our emotional bond with others. Cellist Yo-Yo Ma told us that, over the years, as experience helps him worry less about the technical details of the music, he has created mental space to be empathetic: 'Through being relaxed, I can figure out where the tensions are. Is it inside the conductor? Is it inside the musicians? Is it between the conductor and

213

the musicians? Is the conductor having a hard time? Is the orchestra having a hard time?'

Second, when we are focused on task cognition, we may miss the cues that draw us into socio-emotional cognition. Here is an example of when we fell into this trap. We often train our clients on how to have difficult conversations, i.e. how to put emotionally charged issues on the table constructively, work through resistance and find common ground. We had developed a tool that helped clients lay out the issue, why it mattered and what they wanted to talk about as a result. However, when we coached people to prepare for their conversations, we kept finding that there was a powerful piece missing: making oneself vulnerable by taking accountability for having played a part in the situation. We had used task cognition, but missed how role modelling accountability and vulnerability invited the other person to reciprocate it and to be empathetic: i.e. strengthen the emotional bond to set up for a deeper conversation. Once we started focusing on 'How do we create emotional bond to have a productive conversation?' rather than 'How do we lay out what the problem is?' this element became evident and the conversations became more constructive.

What about you? Can you think of times when you brought task cognition when socio-emotional cognition was needed? Perhaps you focused on the 'nuts and bolts' of a project rather than giving space for the individuals involved in it to build working relationships? Or with family and friends, talking a lot about tasks or activities, and not enough about feelings and experiences. How often do you answer the question: 'How was your day?' with a description of *what* you did, rather than *how* you felt and what you learned? Children can be great 'canaries' for missed socio-emotional cognition; their behaviours are less shaped by social etiquette and more honestly reflect how well we are connecting with them.

Third, letting someone else take a peek into parts of ourselves about which we feel protective can seem scary, or outright stupid. As children, we learn how and when to express emotions based on the reactions others have to us doing so. This shapes and develops our default patterns of thinking, feeling and behaving. We learn whether opening up to others via vulnerability and empathy is rewarding or not, or in which circumstances that might be so. We might have learned the hard way that being vulnerable and empathetic does not lead to a stronger emotional bond but in fact exposes us to the opposite – rejection, embarrassment or disappointment.

In some families, we might have been outright taught that showing emotion is weak or awkward, or that certain emotions are not acceptable for gender stereotypes. For example, we might have learned that getting angry makes girls ugly, or crying makes boys weak. Our brains have evolved to avoid these types of social pain with the help of hidden drivers and related mindsets. Designed to protect us from painful experiences, they may also lead us to prioritize task cognition and prevent us from connecting well with ourselves and others (thereby actually causing the very thing they seek to avoid!). Our individual life experiences may therefore lead us to embed mindsets that contribute to a task cognition bias as a form of self-protection.

We might also simply copy the adults around us to get recognition or fit in. If they were not strong in bringing their socio-emotional cognition, we might not have had much chance to develop it ourselves. Or we might have learned (at home or at work) to prioritize task cognition. This training often starts at school with a focus on sitting quietly on a chair, paying attention to a teacher at the front (instead of also one's classmates), absorbing factual knowledge and applying it in logical ways. We then get rewarded via graded tests for individual mastery of that knowledge. Though this is changing, until recently, most school curricula placed little or no emphasis on helping our social thinking systems develop to navigate the web of human interactions.

Finally, if we have tended to develop our task cognition – at school or early in our careers – it is easier for our brain to default to that than to use our relatively weaker socio-emotional cognition. In the tennis analogy, this might well make our already strong forehand truly fantastic and that could have many benefits. But, the more we use only the forehand, the more the muscles needed for a backhand weaken or do not get the chance to strengthen. This reinforces a task cognition bias because our brain is always looking for the path of least resistance, and becomes a vicious cycle.

If the 'soft side' is a backhand we haven't played much, and later in life we want to use it more, this can feel challenging and take time, because our brains need to build new neural pathways. Pilot Gaby Kennard referred to changing childhood patterns of the way she was interacting with close people in her life as 'the hardest thing I've ever done' – harder than flying solo around the world! Programme participants sometimes comment 'how tough the soft side is', once they have embarked on this journey in earnest. The upside of neuroplasticity is that, regardless of our starting point, we can make better use of and upskill our socio-emotional cognition capacity, benefiting all our relationships and, in particular, to cultivate developmental ones. Let's now turn to how.

How to build more emotional bond

When looking to strengthen our socio-emotional cognition and build stronger emotional bond, drawing on our task cognition can be useful and comfortable. For example, we often help participants in our leadership programmes break trust down into different components and analyse their relationships against each of them[25].

However, to truly strengthen our socio-emotional cognition, we should try to move beyond task cognition and give our socio-emotional cognition a workout. Bringing more authentic vulnerability and empathy, connected to what we are feeling inside, is what will best help us strengthen our emotional bonds, whatever our starting point.

As a result, the following exercises are designed to get us up close and personal with the socio-emotional parts of our inner operating system. They can help us remove the barriers that get in the way of our socio-emotional cognition, build emotional awareness in our brains and bodies, and build habits to prime our socio-emotional cognition to engage from the outset.

Whatever you try, remember to pick what feels comfortable for you, but stretching enough to move you forwards. If these exercises bring up painful experiences or feel very difficult, remember that you have a choice about whether or how to pursue them. Additional support (such as a coach or therapist) to work through these topics may also be a life-long investment.

1. Mindset gymnastics: identify and shift mindsets that limit your vulnerability and empathy

The first step is to become aware of, and let go of, the barriers that affect you building emotional bond through vulnerability and empathy. You could do this through *observing yourself,* and/or *journaling.*

Observe yourself in interactions with colleagues, friends or family and pay attention to the thoughts playing out in the back of your mind. When are you focusing more on the task aspects of a situation vs. the social ones? When are you moving towards more empathy or vulnerability and when are you retreating from it? Then journal about what you observe in yourself, such as any patterns.

Alternatively, journal using some of the sentence starters below. For each, keep writing without censoring what comes out of the pen:

- The situations in which I would like to build stronger emotional bond are…
- What is getting in the way is…
- Vulnerability is… If I am vulnerable, I fear that…

- Empathy is… If I really put myself in the other person's shoes, I fear that…
- Emotions are … and that means I'd better…
- I believe relationships are…

After writing for a while, or the next day, review what you have written and spot your mindsets (look for the assumptions and beliefs behind what you have written). Identify any mindsets that seem too rigid or 'black or white' and see if you can come up with a new mindset that would be more helpful to you. For example, 'The closer I get to people, the more I get dragged into their problems', would hinder you from building emotional bond. An alternative mindset, such as 'By leaving people with responsibility for their own problems, I can get close to them without getting dragged into their issues', would allow for greater emotional bond while protecting you from unwanted involvement in their problems.

When we are unsure about where to start in identifying mindsets, the emotions we are feeling in social interactions are great starting points. The more we are aware of our emotions, the easier it is to spot mindsets, so let us move to the emotional side of the coin.

2. Emotional weightlifting: building our emotional awareness in our brains and bodies

Both empathy and vulnerability require emotional awareness. To increase emotional awareness in our brains and bodies, we suggest two exercises: *emotional labelling* and *emotion tracking* (building from what we covered in Chapter 7). We call these exercises *emotional weightlifting*, because they strengthen our emotional muscles.

Emotional labelling (see also p.145) quickly switches on our socio-emotional cognition, so we will be more aware of our and others' emotions. To make this more automatic and be able to distinguish emotions in the moment, try naming your emotions three times a day for two to three weeks. Combine labelling with a more extensive list of emotional flavours than you usually use, and you also get the benefits of building emotional granularity.

When one of us, Vanessa, did this for a couple of weeks with the help of a list of emotions on her fridge, she also noticed how her increased emotional self-awareness helped her be more attuned to what others were feeling, beyond what they were saying. In other words, practising emotional labelling helped boost her empathy, and it was because she was strengthening a capability called *affect matching*. Affect matching is an important component of empathy for most people, in which we generate the emotional experience of another person in our own body[16]. This includes imitating the other person's subtle facial expressions (a consideration for those of us who have wrinkled foreheads and are tempted by Botox!)[26,27]. By replicating their emotion, we are more able to empathize with what they are truly feeling. And, the finer we can distinguish different emotional flavours in ourselves, the more refined and accurate the picture we will have of their feelings.

Emotional labelling can also work well in groups. For example, a client told us about a difficult team meeting to solve a crisis. The discussion was tense and unproductive but, when he expressed his vulnerability by saying how he was feeling about the challenge, the collective mood changed. People felt more in it together and less defensive or threatened. Being more in explore mode and more confident to share uncooked ideas meant they came up with a better solution together.

The second exercise, *emotion tracking*, builds our ability to observe and regulate emotions in the moment. To do emotion tracking, practise feeling and observing the *sensory aspect* of emotions, i.e. the location, nature and intensity of sensations in your body. Do not follow any impulse for action contained in the *interpretive aspect* of the emotion, i.e. the meaning you apply to a sensation, such as whether you like it or not[28]. When feeling a stronger emotion, sit with it. Literally. Sit down and close your eyes. Approach the emotion with curiosity as if you were feeling it for the first time. Notice where you feel it in your body, describe the sensation (hot or cold, sharp or dull, light or intense). Keep watching it, and don't be surprised if it changes into another emotion. If you get distracted or it feels too intense, take a deep, slow breath as if you were breathing into the sensation, giving it more room. Keep watching and feeling until you decide to stop. Do this with emotions you find pleasant and those you find less pleasant.

Why is emotional tracking helpful? We usually experience emotions as a single phenomenon (joy, impatience, etc.). However, our brains are thought to be integrating the sensory aspect of an emotion and the interpretive aspect. This interpretive aspect is underpinned by mindsets, which kick in at lightning speed, often with little awareness on our part. By learning to distinguish between the sensory and the interpretive aspects through regular emotion tracking, we get much more control over our emotions and resultant behaviours. For example, if we are distressed by emotions we associate with vulnerability, such as helplessness, we will likely supress these emotions and struggle to share them or withdraw from others who are experiencing those emotions. However, if we learn to simply observe our experience of helplessness without letting our interpretations drive us to action, we will gain perspective, self-awareness, and emotional regulation. All this will give us more choice to be vulnerable, and more space and capacity for empathy.

You might wonder, why do emotion tracking, rather than work directly with the mindsets that are contributing to our interpretation of the emotion? First, these mindsets kick in so quickly and in combination with our physiology (often protect mode) that it may often be more effective to work directly with our emotions. Second, only focusing on mindsets also risks us moving into task cognition, rather than building our socio-emotional cognition. Finally, feeling emotions from an observer position is very settling for our brains, as it helps us stay in explore mode at times of emotional intensity that might otherwise trigger protect mode. This in turn makes it easier for us to unhook from the emotional grip of mindsets, and work on noticing and shifting them. As a result, mindset gymnastics and emotional weightlifting are beneficial in tandem.

3. Habits to strengthen emotional bond

Habits automate action that would otherwise take deliberate processing power, and we can use them to automate how we draw on socio-emotional cognition. The exercises above build your socio-emotional cognition, but the exercises below train your brain to automatically engage it.

Prime your socio-emotional cognition before situations in which you need it. Identify in which situations or relationships you would like to pay more attention to emotional bond. This might be certain types of work meetings, or before engaging with your family after a day of task cognition at work. To get your socio-emotional cognition ready to focus on emotional bond, you can build a habit that engages it by default. Many of the performance curve habits from Chapter 7 would work here, such as emotional labelling, a quick body scan, or perspective taking about what might be on others' minds. The cue to trigger this habit could be marking particular meetings in a different colour in your calendar, the act of walking to a meeting room, or your commute home (even if it's just down the stairs from your home office to the kitchen). Maybe there are some visual cues you can use, such as a painting on the wall where you can pause for a moment to take in the image and the emotions it evokes in you.

Use rituals to build emotional bond. Embedding unique rituals into relationships at work or at home is a wonderful way of building emotional bond. They allow us to partake in a joint activity and experience it through our own and other people's eyes. Luke Bradley-Jones sends a couple of short appreciation emails at the end of each day and regular handwritten notes. He finds it helps him and others 'correct the genetic imbalance we have to focus on bad stuff, i.e. to focus on the tiger outside the cave rather than the taste of the stew. It takes a lot of work to correct that.' On a lighter note, we authors send each other cute stationery from time to time and have a giggle about indulging in this shared fetish. There is a vulnerability in extending our appreciation (and our foibles) to others, not knowing if they will respond or reciprocate, and this builds emotional bond when it is received with empathy. We may come to count on these rituals as a way of strengthening emotional bond, yet they also include an element of surprise, which keeps it fresh and increases the reward we associate with them.

The deeper these rituals take us below the surface down the iceberg, the more bond can form. Luke ensures quality time with his family by keeping Sundays free, going on a long walk, and talking about what they enjoyed during the week. During the first peak of the Covid-19 pandemic, many of our client teams instituted a daily check-in each morning, principally to connect with each other and reinforce the mindsets they wanted to bring to the day. They commented on how this brought them closer than ever before.

We have now covered the first aspect of the connection catalyst, emotional bond. We looked at its benefits in terms of effectiveness, well-being and development, as well as how to strengthen it. With those foundations in place, the next chapter looks at how emotional bond can be combined with the second aspect of the connection catalyst, stretch, to build developmental relationships.

CHAPTER ELEVEN

Developmental relationships in action

This chapter covers how to build strong developmental relationships with other individuals that support one or both of you to maximize your potential and strengthen your well-being. Let's look at a developmental relationship that helped Nick to get out of the hole he was in at the start of this book.

As Director of Operations and Project Management for new products, Nick interacted with many leaders from across his company. Because he had such a broad overview and was always willing to help, Nick was often sought out by his peers (including, Ali, the new marketing director). Ali had noticed how hard Nick was working and that he seemed to put himself last, so Ali would often treat him to a latte or some sushi.

One afternoon, Nick and Ali were due to meet about marketing plans for a new product launch. Entering Nick's office, Ali noticed Nick's crumpled face and asked, 'Are you OK?' Nick inhaled sharply. 'I'm not,' he replied. Ali saw the pain in Nick's eyes, sat down next to him and said warmly, 'No, you're not.' Feeling Ali's genuine interest and empathy, Nick let out all the accumulated pressure of his work and home life, sharing his fear that he was at breaking point. Ali didn't say much to Nick at first and simply let him unload his exhaustion, frustration and concerns. Eventually Nick took a deep breath and said, 'Well, I'll just soldier on. I have to.'

Since Nick had been so open with him, Ali asked if he could share an observation about Nick's working style. Nick nodded and Ali said, 'I've noticed that many people ask you for help, even when it's not really your job.' Nick frowned a little hearing this, not sure where this was going. Ali noticed his questioning look, took a deep breath and bravely continued by asking Nick how he was prioritizing so many spontaneous requests. 'It all needs to get done,' Nick replied defensively. 'And does it all need to get done by you?,' Ali continued to probe. 'Hmm ...', Nick's face grew more thoughtful.

Ali asked Nick a few more questions and Nick realized that one cause of his busy-ness was people asking him to help with things they could do themselves but found easier to have him do. He liked being asked for help and getting the recognition for it. He had become excellent at moving difficult issues forwards, but it also created an inflow of such requests.

By recognizing how he had contributed to his own overload, Nick realized that he had more power to change it than he had previously thought. And being so overwhelmed helped him realize the price he was paying in exchange for recognition, which in turn made him more open to question his behaviour and look for alternatives. 'Ali, nothing has changed, all the work is still there, but I feel really different about it. I can see a way out. Thank you.' Ali smiled. 'I'm glad I could help you for a change.'

Though Nick realized he needed to get better at saying 'no' to colleagues who had relied on him in the past, he knew it would be uncomfortable and he had some more work to do on this. He asked Ali if they could talk through another time how he could deal with such requests. 'Under one condition,' Ali countered with a grin. 'I am struggling with one of my team. Can I get your help to figure out where I'm stuck when we meet next?'

This conversation with Ali was a real turning point for Nick and kick-started a new phase in his developmental journey of looking at how he was going about things, what was driving him, and finding better alternatives. This not only benefited his own well-being and relationship with his daughter Molly, but also the business. Nick set clearer priorities for himself and his team, what really mattered got more attention, and, after a bit of discomfort, his colleagues got better at handling the issues themselves that Nick had previously taken on. This in turn led to a step up in everyone's effectiveness – a typical example of the multi-dimensional benefits of moving up the performance curve and how one person doing so can have a ripple effect on those around them.

Nick did have a professional coach for some time but, long after the coaching had finished, Nick and Ali kept having conversations like this one. They formed a developmental relationship that became very valuable to both of them for bringing out and developing their best. How did they do that? How do developmental relationships work and how can we build them?

The essence of developmental relationships: emotional bond and stretch

Before that afternoon, Nick and Ali had built the beginnings of an emotional bond: Nick had helped Ali settle into the office and Ali had kept Nick going with lattes and sushi. As a result, Nick felt secure enough to let Ali know how overwhelmed he felt. That brought new levels of vulnerability and empathy which reinforced each other and significantly increased their emotional bond (Figure 11.1). This helped Nick admit to Ali, and perhaps also to himself, all his struggles.

However, building emotional bond and acknowledging there was a problem didn't get Nick to see and deal with the actual cause of the problem: how he was handling requests from colleagues and the deeper mindsets driving his behaviour. Nick was steeling himself to 'soldier on' and continue operating as before. The emotional bond

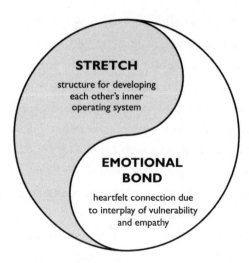

Figure 11.1 Developmental relationships

didn't nudge him out of his comfort zone into a growth zone to learn and do something differently (it was his comfort zone because it was known, familiar territory, not because it was terribly comfortable!).

What Ali did differently at this point in the conversation compared to their prior interactions was to offer Nick some stretch. *Stretch provides structure for developing our inner operating system.* It invites us to go below the surface down the iceberg, for example to challenge mindsets and hidden drivers. Ali stretched the (figurative) elastic of their relationship by sharing his own observations and asking questions about Nick's deeper thought processes. That helped Nick get on the balcony and look at himself and the situation from a different perspective. Nick discovered assumptions he was making about how to act and behave to get recognition. By drawing out Nick's underlying mindsets and challenging them, Ali also supported Nick to take accountability for his contribution to the situation, a necessary condition for being able to do something about it. It was the stretch from Ali that allowed Nick to see that there could be other options for handling the situation that would lead to better outcomes. Stretch ensured that the conversation didn't just temporarily make Nick feel better, but instead it started to help him evolve his inner operating system – to actually *be* better.

For relationships, or conversations, to be developmental and help us go far and fast, they need both emotional bond and stretch, in appropriate amounts. The way emotional bond and stretch come together is more of a dance than a formula or sequence, and empathy helps us discern the right amounts and timing of each. A certain amount of emotional bond is needed to open up about a challenge or problem. We then require stretch to gain a different perspective and expose the deeper causes of the problem that lie within ourselves. But stretch cannot be forced. We cannot make someone else shift perspective or open up about their deeper mindsets, fears and needs. We see stretch as an invitation to be offered – which might be accepted, or not.

Stretch can feel uncomfortable and trigger protect mode, both for the person offering the stretch and the person accepting it. When Ali started sharing his observations about Nick's working style and probed into what Nick was doing and why, we could see Nick close up a little. Ali noticed it, too. Nick had taken a risk in being more vulnerable with Ali and when Ali went beyond his previous empathy into stretch, Nick wasn't sure where Ali was going. Was he going to criticize or judge him? Nick's protect mode could have taken over and prevented him from looking at his part of the problem and hence his way out of it. Ali's continued empathy and the warmth with which he asked Nick those challenging questions stopped Nick from succumbing to protect mode. The comfort of the emotional bond helped both persist through the discomfort of stretch.

We therefore see emotional bond as a prerequisite and enabler of stretch. But stretch also helps build emotional bond through experiencing someone helping us realize and grow our potential. Stretch signals a vulnerability on the part of the person offering it: 'I want the best for you so much that I am willing to pull you out of your comfort zone, at the risk of that triggering resistance towards me, instead of letting you stay where you are right now.'

Ambu CEO Juan Jose Gonzalez emphasized the importance of genuinely putting the other person first: 'Your objective is not for them to stay in the company or deliver a specific financial result; it is for them to become the best executive they can be, whether it is in the company or not. When you do that, some of them will achieve extraordinary things, also for the company'. Stretch shows we believe in someone's greater potential and are willing to climb that mountain with them to help them realize it. And it can have a profound impact on us, too. 'Giving is not just for the one receiving,' Juan Jose pointed out. 'Every time I do it, I am reminding myself that it is applicable to me as well; what would I like to do differently?' That is how emotional bond and stretch reinforce each other in a virtuous circle and build a developmental relationship that helps us bring and grow our best.

Low or high stretch relates to the extent to which we encourage and provide structure for other people to grow in their inner operating system. High stretch is not about throwing people in at the deep end, hoping they will swim, and also does not reflect how challenged someone is feeling. Lorina McAdam described a situation which illustrates this distinction. Having been newly appointed (prematurely, she believes) to her first role as country director of an NGO in the Democratic Republic of Congo, Lorina got a text from her boss while on a break on a Madagascan beach: 'Staff on strike. Security forces involved.'

Rushing back from her holiday, Lorina felt in over her head. She had previously requested help from headquarters that might have mitigated this escalation, but it wasn't forthcoming. Once the crisis erupted, her boss said, 'Everyone is watching you right now to see how you handle this situation. This is your test of leadership.' Understandably, this added to how challenged Lorina was feeling. Not only did she have a crisis on the ground to handle, but her career might also be on the line. This is not what we mean by stretch. High stretch would have been

Lorina's boss asking her questions such as why she thought the staff had gone on strike; how she might have contributed to that; what was the real problem she needed to solve to have impact; how she might have to shift her role in the team to unblock it; and what mindsets might be holding her back from doing that.

Lorina was resourceful enough to put in place a support structure for herself that gave her stretch and emotional bond. She surrounded herself with a small local team whom she trusted and who would balance out her weaknesses and blind spots and give her confidence in the decisions she was making. She resolved the crisis and grew massively from this experience, but her boss missed an opportunity to build a developmental relationship that would have helped Lorina grow through the crisis at hand into her role, rather than add to her stress and risk a protect mode response.

What happens when we lack emotional bond or stretch?

Figure 11.2 illustrates the relationship outcomes for different combinations of emotional bond and stretch. Emotional bond without stretch provides comfort. In the face of a problem, comfort may give us the courage to face it and spark an impulse for change, but might not be enough to see it through. Emotional bond on its own can even become unhelpful when it is keeping us in the habitual 'comfort' zone, not addressing the real issue when there is a problem and letting it fester – like providing pain medication but not setting the broken bone. A relationship based on emotional bond with little or no stretch is neither good nor bad, it depends on the context and what we want from the relationship.

By contrast, stretch alone, even when it is high, is also not sufficient to form a developmental relationship that helps us bring and grow our best. Stretch by itself would feel cold, like an investigation or even a threat, prodding into our inner worlds. Without emotional bond, the

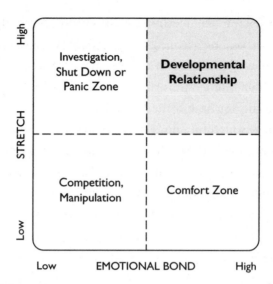

Figure 11.2 Relationship outcomes

elastic band of the relationship isn't thick or elastic enough, and stretch could make it snap: overstretching the individual beyond growth into the panic zone and protect mode, or a shut-down in relating. Stretch without emotional bond can then actually erode performance and bears a considerable, and unnecessary, risk for the individual or an organization.

When there is both low emotional bond and low stretch, then the relationship is likely to be characterized by self-protection, disengagement and competition, seeking to gain advantage over another or even harm them.

If you are familiar with a 2 x 2 matrix of challenge x support, or radical candour (challenge directly x care personally), you will see Figure 11.2 is a similar idea[1]. But we have chosen the terms and definitions of 'emotional bond' and 'stretch' because we are specifically interested in relationships that support inner operating system development. Emotional bond is not about support or care in general: we focus specifically on the connection that comes from the interplay of empathy and vulnerability and creates the conditions for deeper development of our inner operating system. Similarly, stretch is specifically about techniques that go into the territory of inner operating system development. It is not about challenge in general, or about being direct, though those features may often be a part of stretch.

To build developmental relationships, you don't need to be a coach. As part of our work with organizations, colleagues are often paired to give them the opportunity to form developmental relationships, like Nick and Ali, outside of the actual programme. At first, the stretch they offer to each other might not be as slick as that from a seasoned coach. But that does not matter at all. As long as there is positive intent for helping each other grow and they are open about their own icebergs, those two buddies will dig up something useful. Stretch can also come from the person looking at their own situation, for example by saying, 'I am not yet seeing how I'm contributing to this situation.' In fact, it is very important that both parties in a developmental relationship take responsibility for the interchange of emotional bond and stretch and communicate directly if either element is insufficient, so that it can quickly be adjusted.

Let's turn to practical ways to help you bring emotional bond and stretch to conversations and build developmental relationships.

How to build developmental relationships: developmental conversations

Our aim is to help you build, strengthen and use developmental relationships, to help you and others perform and grow. Since relationships are largely formed through conversations (of whatever kind – in-person, virtual, email), our focus is on how you can have conversations that move into developmental territory.

In the rest of this chapter, we offer you several techniques you can weave into one-to-one conversations to help you do this. They are not meant to be formulaic, but rather for you to get insight into how to expand your existing repertoire. Though the focus is developmental conversations, you can also use many of these techniques for constructively discussing challenging topics, regardless of what kind of relationship you would like to build with the other person.

Pause to prepare

Before jumping into action, be clear about your intentions for the conversation beyond simply getting the immediate work done. You will be priming your brain to spot opportunities to live up to these intentions and engage socio-emotional cognition. And true intent helps you be authentic: it is better to have genuine heartfelt intent and to do it clumsily than a slick delivery without genuine emotion behind it. You might ask yourself:

- What does a good outcome look like for our work – in the short term and the longer term? (In terms of results and how it feels to get there?)
- In what ways am I seeking to evolve the relationship I have with this person?
- What might be my opportunities for growth in this discussion? And how might I help the other person grow?
- What mindsets can I bring to the discussion, to set us up for success?

In our leadership programmes, we teach participants to *pause to prepare* conversations, by working through questions such as the above. But, as with much of what we introduce in the book, once they have done this a few times, it becomes a habit: something they just do automatically on the go, at speed and with relatively little executive processing power. That said, for high-stakes conversations, it is often helpful to deliberately slow down and work through questions like these.

Contracting and recontracting

Here we are not talking about legal contracts, but rather about the implicit 'contract' of a relationship, i.e. what it is for, the territory that the relationship covers, and the boundaries of what you do not go into. For most existing relationships, you have a default social contract based on the existing relationship. You might gradually evolve that contract over time, or an emergency might suddenly move it forwards. For example, you might notice that a neighbour is struggling with their relationship with their child, and one day find a way to put that issue on the table sensitively. Recontracting is when you explicitly ask to change that social contract, so it is a technique you can use to transform a relationship into developmental territory.

Ali saw Nick was struggling and wanted to change the way he related to him, to make it a more developmental conversation. He simply asked if he could share an observation about Nick's working style. This is a very light form of recontracting – it signals an intent to enter developmental territory and checks the other person is happy to do that. He could have done it in a more structured and complete way, for example by saying, 'I have noticed you seem really stressed the past few weeks, and I wondered whether you would be open to talking about getting your stress levels down. I worry about the impact on your health and on your team. I've tiptoed around it up to now and probably exacerbated things by asking you to help me out a few times at the last minute. But, rather than talk about the product launch today, would you like to tell me what is driving your stress?' Whether you take a lighter or more structured approach will obviously depend on the situation and existing relationship, but both approaches will change the nature of the conversation.

Many of our clients have told us that they get frustrated with the regular one-to-one meetings they have with colleagues (for example, monthly or weekly meetings between a manager and their direct reports, or between two peers running different divisions). The usual complaint is that the meeting feels like an update: focused on good news stories rather than problem-solving issues; a broad brush tour of everything rather than getting into any depth and substance; or staying purely on the work content and avoiding dealing with relationship issues. If you have any kind of meeting that you would like to shift into more developmental territory to make it more productive and developmental, you could use recontracting to accelerate this change.

Frame the real conversation, constructively

What you do in the first five minutes of a conversation sets the tone. It is easy to fall into two opposing traps. First, being so nice (to avoid triggering protect mode in the other person) that you do not put the real issue on the table. Second, putting the real issue on the table, but triggering protect mode in the other person (and possibly yourself). The art is to get the real issue on the table early and constructively. The structured version of recontracting by Ali two paragraphs earlier is an example of doing this (though we can use framing to set up any conversation constructively, not just recontracting). The framing sequence in Table 11.1 helps do that.

This structure is not meant to be formulaic: you might change the order, or only touch on some steps briefly if they are already well understood between the two of you. However, we usually find the best framing statements cover all these steps, and are also concise (a maximum of a couple of minutes). Once you have made your statement, the opening question signals to the other person that you want to hear from them, and gets them talking so you can understand their perspective. A good opening question also funnels the conversation in a constructive direction (for example, focusing on purpose or reinforcing growth mindset).

It is important to do Step 4, whereby you take accountability for your part in the situation and reveal some vulnerability. It helps

Table 11.1 Framing constructively

Step		Example statements
1	What do you want to talk about?	I wondered whether you would be open to talk about getting your stress levels down today
2	Why do you want to talk about it?	I have noticed you seem really stressed the past few weeks
3	Why does it matter?	I worry about the impact on your health and on your team
4	What is your contribution to the issue?	I've tiptoed around it up to now and probably exacerbated things by asking you to help me out a few times at the last minute
5	Opening question	But, rather than talk about the product launch today, would you like to tell me what is driving your stress?

create the sense of being on the same side of the table, and reduces the likelihood of the other person moving into protect mode. In many of our leadership programmes, two of our coaches will demonstrate this framing sequence live in front of participants on a real topic. It is remarkable how, every single time we do this demonstration, the observers can see how the conversation transforms when the person doing the framing takes accountability. It is as though the blood pressure of the person receiving the framing drops 20 points when they hear their colleague taking accountability, and it sets them up to take accountability for their own contribution.

That said, sometimes when we take accountability, the other person will at first use this as an invitation to avoid their own accountability (consciously or unconsciously). If they respond with a victim mindset, for example by sharing their frustrations about what you or others did, it may feel uncomfortable and that you opened yourself up to be blamed. Our advice is to let them express their experience, while keeping an eye on your brain's protect–explore mode. You will learn about their perspective (that doesn't mean you have to like it or agree with them).

And this process of voicing emotions and being heard should settle down their protect mode, such that they are ready to engage. You can then ask them questions to move things forwards, which brings the accountability firmly back to them. You might need to draw on other techniques we outline in a moment (such as feedback). However, we tend to find that working through this process in the first few minutes of a conversation usually reduces the heat (i.e. protect mode) so dramatically that the rest of the conversation is collaborative and pragmatic.

Lorina McAdam told us that creating an opportunity for others to voice emotions has been an essential leadership technique for her when leading humanitarian missions. 'I deliberately let people vent, to offload. Then, once they get it all out of their system, I ask them questions such as, "What can you do next? What do you need to do that? Is there anything I can do to help you?"' Lorina went on to say, 'One of my colleagues in the Democratic Republic of Congo once said to me, "We don't always agree, but I always leave your office feeling better than when I walked into it." And that was one of the nicest things anyone could say about me as a leader.'

Pay attention

First, pay attention to how others are feeling and acknowledge this. Sometimes simply calling out what you are observing will open a door to a deeper connection and richer conversation, for example, 'You seem really energized today' or 'You look unsure'. Alternatively, you can show empathy without saying a word: Ali signalled to Nick that he had noticed his overwhelm by bringing him latte and sushi. You need to pick what feels right in your culture or relationship.

Second, pay attention to yourself. Where are you on the protect–explore mode spectrum? Are your hidden drivers popping up in your inner chatter? Building up a moment-to-moment awareness of your iceberg will help you see how your iceberg is 'bumping up' against that of the other person, and helping or hindering the discussion. Before conversations that you anticipate will be particularly charged, you might prepare a couple of the tools from Chapter 7 to use in the moment if you need to settle your brain's protect mode. For example, you might take a couple of deep breaths, or remind yourself (and the other person if appropriate) of a couple of gratitudes.

Ask questions

The framing statement we mention above finishes with a question. But our advice is to ask tons of questions. Questions can help you both challenge your inner operating systems and gain insight. They also show the other person that you are interested in their perspective and help them get on the balcony to see their own inner operating system.

Here are some tips for how you might weave questions into developmental conversations.

- *Spot the 'emotional and mindset' doors and walk through them.* In other words, when the other person alludes to their emotions or mindsets, find a way to open the door to talking more about emotions and mindsets. Ali spotted and opened several of Nick's emotional and mindset doors, for example when Nick admitted he was not OK, and when Nick shared his mindset of 'it all needs to get done'. It might seem uncomfortable or confronting to take the conversation into this more personal space, but our experience is that, if people show you those doors, it's usually because they are prepared for you to open them. And if not, they will find a way to keep them shut. Even if they open them a little, it allows you to step into their world and accompany them, making it easier for them to explore their inner operating system. If you hear an emotion popping up, you might ask, 'Could you tell me more?' or 'How do you feel about that?' or 'What leads you to feel that way?' If you hear a mindset popping up, you might ask, 'What are you assuming about the situation?' or 'What leads you to believe that?' or 'How does that assumption help and/or hinder you?'

- *Scaffold the three mindsets: accountability, growth and big picture.* Especially when you spot the nemesis mindsets (victim, fixed and silo), ask questions that send the other person (or yourself, or both of you) into the more constructive mindset. Juan Jose Gonzalez of Ambu expresses and encourages a growth mindset (in himself and others) by asking questions in one-to-ones such as, 'What could the *unrestricted you* achieve?' or 'If fear of failure were absent and you believed you were going to go very far, what would you do with your agenda?'. Refer to the questions in Table 5.2 on page 113 to help you do this;

- *Harness tensions.* Tensions might feel uncomfortable and send us into protect mode. However, similar to heightened emotions, they are also data about what really matters to each of you. Building that understanding and finding ways forward that reconcile both of your needs enables deeper collaboration. Exploring tensions is also a way to find areas for growth in your inner operating systems, paving the way for its development.

First, get some distance from the situation, to settle your own protect mode. Next, try asking questions (of the other person and also sharing your own answers to the same questions), to uncover: the dilemma at the heart of the tension; the assumptions that are driving your behaviour today; and how you might move forwards. For example, you could ask: 'What is it that matters most to each of us? Why?' and 'What are we assuming about the situation today?' and 'How could we find a solution that meets both our needs?' (You might spot that this uses parts of the paradoxical thinking process outlined in Chapter 9.) You might not resolve the tension straight away (especially if you need to build more emotional bond first), but laying out the issues should already feel like progress.

Get feedback flowing

The faster and more frequently our inner operating system gets quality feedback and takes it on board, the better it can develop. To move along the performance curve, ideally we would be getting quality developmental feedback quickly and constantly, and be able to respond to it well (which starts with being in explore mode). Unfortunately, this is far from reality for most of us. In most organizations, feedback flows too little, too late or with too little emotional bond. It is often avoided because it is seen as 'not being nice' or saved for the annual performance review, when it would have been far more beneficial for the person and the work to do it much sooner. Or it is kept very shallow (focused on the work product, staying away from the iceberg). And who doesn't move a little towards protect mode when they hear the dreaded words 'Can I give you some feedback?' Though many organizations have worked hard over the past few years to change their feedback and performance management processes, there is still massive potential in most organizations for feedback to flow more fluidly to help people be on the performance curve. Here are some tips to effectively weave feedback into your one-to-one conversations, to move in that direction:

- *Stop seeing feedback as a separate activity.* Start seeing it as one type of conversational tool. Try to have feedback take place in all your conversations, both ways (i.e. you are giving it, and getting it). For example, you might highlight when someone does something you appreciate. Juan Jose Gonzalez talks about the 'teaching opportunity' of when someone disagrees with him. He pauses, thanks the person, and stresses the importance of disagreement. Or you might ask for feedback that allows you to course correct during a meeting by asking, 'How helpful is this? How could I be more helpful?' Of course there will be times when you need to have a dedicated feedback conversation, but if you get feedback flowing much more often, you might avoid pain later on;

- *Give feedback much more smoothly.* In Chapter 5, we talked about how giving feedback to someone with a fixed mindset can make them perform worse. And, if we go towards protect mode when we hear, 'Can I give you some feedback?', our brain's executive centre will be impeded. So your aim is to maximize growth mindset and minimize protect mode when giving feedback. Many of us will have been taught a classic feedback formula such as 'what I observed … the impact it had on me … what you might do instead/next time…' However, while this structure works brilliantly on a training programme when everyone is primed to be in growth mindset, it is often a red rag to the bull of protect mode when done in the middle of a meeting, or simply not in sync with the flow of the conversation.

  We find a light touch can be far more effective. Here is an example of feedback, following the classic structure: 'Can I give you some feedback, Jack? I experienced you as focusing mostly on presenting the risks. The impact it had on me was to stop taking your argument seriously, because I thought you were biased. Could you share more of the pros as well as the cons?' Here is a lighter-touch alternative: 'Jack, I've noticed you are focusing mostly on presenting the risks. I'm curious about why you are taking that approach … I value hearing both sides of the argument. Would you be open to sharing the upsides too?' Notice that there is no use of the word feedback, even though it is obviously feedback;

- *Blend feedback and questions.* The other problem with the classic feedback structure is how it finishes. Feedback givers are often taught to shut up at that point, and feedback receivers are often taught to 'Say thank you, ask a clarifying question if you want, and don't take it personally.' That's fine as a coping mechanism for not reacting from protect mode and taking some time to reflect on the feedback first, but it is a missed opportunity to get feedback flowing both ways and to deepen insight to support inner operating system development. Questions allow us to take this opportunity. In the Jack example, 'I'm curious about why you are taking that approach' is not technically a question, but it has the intent of a first powerful question to get Jack to start to look at his mindsets. Questions (and responses to them) allow for a dialogue that gets feedback flowing both ways, for example: 'Now I see that you told me about the risks because you thought I knew all about the upsides. What could I have done differently to let you know that I really wanted to hear your view on them too?' Now both your inner operating systems are getting a workout of perspective taking, mindset shifting and taking accountability, as well as helping you work better together next time.

Close well

Whatever the nature of the conversation and where you are with it, be deliberate about how you finish it. A good ending could send you into the rest of your day in explore mode and on the performance curve. A bad ending might trigger protect mode along with some unhelpful mindsets that knock you off the performance curve for the rest of the day ... or beyond. Your empathy will tell you the right way to close, but here are some ideas you might consider for your repertoire.

- Expressing something for which you are grateful, for example acknowledging something about how they handled the conversation. You get the benefit yourself of doing a gratitude practice (as outlined in Chapter 7), and they get reward and reinforcement for something you appreciated;
- Highlight or reinforce what you learned, to help consolidate memories by revisiting them and role model growth mindset. Or ask them what their most important learning is/how they will think differently as a result;
- Role model an accountability mindset. For example, you could acknowledge something you learned during the conversation about your accountability in a situation, without relieving them of their accountability. 'Involving you in this project quite late contributed to this issue, and I'm really sorry about that.';

- Ask questions that send them out of the door in explore mode and with forward movement, for example: 'What should we each do now to get the very best from this situation?' or 'What's the positive step forwards we seek by the next time we talk about this? What's the biggest thing that we can do to get there?'

The techniques in this chapter will help you to have conversations that support development, and strengthen developmental relationships, so you and those around you can be on the performance curve. But you will have even more impact if you are able to get others having these types of conversations routinely with each other, not only with you. That is the focus of the next chapter: building cultures that support developmental relationships. The techniques outlined in this past chapter are a helpful starting point for much of what we propose in the next chapter, so they are designed to be put into practice together.

CHAPTER TWELVE

Building performance curve cultures

Imagine yourself in this scene. It is a Friday in mid-February. You arrive at the office and make a double shot latte to get ready for a big day. This afternoon is your first annual appraisal since joining the company. Your boss, Priya, seems happy with your work: she comments on how to improve your reports but never questions your competence. The feedback you have received via the company's smartphone feedback app is bland ('Helpful analysis, thanks.') or tactical ('More client photos in the slides please!'). Priya told you at mid-year that you were on track and said your next step would be to get exposure to other areas of the business. It should be fine, but you feel a flush of adrenaline. You distract yourself by heading to your desk.

Mid-morning, you attend the monthly meeting for Priya's team. Priya debriefs her recent meeting with the CEO to share the team's strategic plan. The CEO wants the team to be more ambitious, and Priya asks everyone to increase their revenue projections by 10 per cent. Everyone nods, but you guess they are, like you, wondering how on earth they're going to find more revenue. Other departments seem to have cracked this, but not yours. Next, your colleague Leon gives a presentation, which gets the debate going, and he seems pleased with the ideas he received.

After lunch, you attend the kick-off of a new project team. You are excited to finally get exposure to another part of the business. Everyone introduces themselves. Then Carlos, the project leader, shares the project plan. He asks each person what they would feel comfortable taking on, and you volunteer to do some analyses. You feel reassured: it is familiar work, you know you can do a good job on this.

Finally, it is time for your appraisal. As you walk into her office, Priya says, 'Relax! You have done a good job of fitting into the company and this is going to be an easy conversation.' You breathe a sigh of relief. Priya asks you to summarize how you think you are doing and your learning goals for the coming year. She comments that the new project will be a good learning opportunity, now that it is finally off the ground.

You summon your courage to say you would like more ownership of client relationships, knowing that might seem pushy. Priya says, 'Yes, you will need that to get promoted. Let's discuss it at mid-year.' She pauses, then says, 'Actually, first I need you to be more confident in client meetings.' You blush. No one has ever raised that before, but you do feel nervous in client meetings and hesitate to speak up, so it is not surprising she has noticed. Priya says, 'Hey, it's not a big deal. But let's do something about it. I think HR have a presentation skills course that could build your confidence.' You are relieved and write that into the 'training plan' box on the appraisal form. You leave with a spring in your step. A big day, but a good one.

Or was it? You might remember a film called *Sliding Doors* from the late 1990s. It shows how momentary decisions or events can send us on different paths with profound effects. The protagonist (played by Gwyneth Paltrow) plays out two parallel realities. In one reality, she catches the train home to find her boyfriend in bed with another woman. In the second reality, she bumps into someone, misses the train, and misses her boyfriend's mistress. You are now going to channel your inner Gwyneth Paltrow and rerun this scene.

It is that same Friday in mid-February. You make your double latte to set you up for appraisal day. You feel a little apprehensive, but that is nothing new: the past year has felt anything but comfortable! During your job interviews, you learned how, after losing their biggest client a few years ago, the company culture changed enormously. One person described their boss to you as being 'like a personal trainer who smiles but never lets me hide'.

You feel a shot of adrenaline and pause to pay attention to your emotions, following a technique you learned on the personal leadership programme for new joiners. What are you really worried about? You have had almost daily feedback and coaching from your boss, Priya, and everyone you work with, so there will be no nasty surprises in the appraisal. Instead, you realize, you are worried about failing in whatever challenge Priya might spring on you next. You constantly feel at the edge of your capabilities and, though you have always had good support and runway to learn from mistakes, what if you finally let people down and feel incompetent? Maybe something to raise with Priya later.

At the monthly team meeting, it is your turn to bring the opening and closing exercises. You invite each person to set an intention for how they want to contribute in the meeting. Your intention today is to challenge early and concisely. The exercise settles everyone down and brings them together.

The team discusses a recent meeting between the whole team and the CEO, to talk about the team's strategic plan. He had emphasized how important speed was (for customers and for revenue generation), and congratulated the team on halving the time to launch new products by using methods from another department. He asked what it would take to halve the launch time again. The team had challenged him on what this would mean for the company's mindsets about risk and the CEO said the discussion got him thinking. Today, one of your colleagues, Leon, says, 'I wonder if we could find a way whereby halving our launch time actually *reduced* our risk.' People raise their eyebrows initially, but the subsequent discussion leads to some interesting avenues to explore.

At the end, you pair people up for feedback on how they lived their intention during the meeting. Leon had already called you out during the meeting for not raising your concerns early, but you improved later in the meeting. You talk about what it would take for you not to need prompting next time.

Since your mid-year review, you have worked a little with other departments, but you are excited about kicking off a proper cross-department project today. The project leader, Carlos, asks everyone to introduce themselves by sharing their personal development goals. He then shares a draft project plan and asks the team to do a 'pre-mortem' of the project, recounting a couple of times when pre-mortems helped the company avoid major mess-ups. You discuss two questions: 'Imagine in six months we succeeded, what did we do to get there?' and 'Imagine we failed, what did we do or not do?' The team makes a few improvements to the plan and you learn a lot from others' ways of thinking and previous mess-ups.

Everyone is asked to rank how challenged they would feel on each workstream. Carlos proposes pairs for each workstream: someone for whom it is a challenge, and a 'coach' who knows the topic well or has relevant experience. You feel apprehensive about your workstream, but you have seen this past year how fast you can learn, with the right mindsets and support.

As you arrive for your appraisal, Priya spots you are nervous and says, 'Hey. Let's agree how we approach this conversation to get the most out of it and set you up to grow well this year.' She shares her past nervousness about appraisals, and hearing her honesty and vulnerability helps you feel ready to open up.

After looking back over the past year, Priya asks, 'What development do you want from this year?' You mention you want to work towards getting promoted into a client-facing role, although you are nervous about overchallenging yourself and letting people down. She immediately jumps in. 'Hold on. Let's not focus on promotion – that's just a badge. And let's not focus on being overchallenged – that's just going to hold you back. Let's ask, "How can you grow into a client-facing role in a fast but safe way?"' That feels more comfortable but, as soon as Priya talks about sending you to client meetings by yourself, you feel nervous again. 'What's making you nervous?' she asks. You say, 'However much I prepare, I'm anticipating the client will ask me questions I can't answer and I'll seem amateur.'

You have long worried about feeling or being seen as incompetent; you learned at the new joiner training that it is an important hidden driver for you. You realize that the only way to build your confidence (and competence) is to go to a few client meetings alone and get used to handling questions you cannot answer. Priya asks you to write a vision of you in a year, and the mindsets, habits and relationships that will get you there. She suggests you talk it through with someone, and you decide to ask Carlos.

A big day but, in many ways, no bigger than any other. You think back to the perfunctory performance reviews at your last company. This challenging environment is not for everyone, but it is setting you up for life.

Take a moment to reflect on these two scenarios. Each of them consists of real examples from our clients or interviews. We intended the first scenario to be a decent developmental experience, with a well-meaning manager who wants to help her people grow, and training and performance management processes that bring structure to people's development. The second scenario is intended to illustrate a culture that helps its people be on the performance curve. It paints a picture of the experience of being in such a culture: the emotional bond between colleagues; constantly feeling challenged to the edge of your capabilities; and the fact that inner operating systems are never far from people's minds, and often brought into the discussion so people can bring their best to those challenges. It also shows the business benefits that come from this work, such as better teamwork, greater collaboration across departments, more honest conversations (including with the CEO), challenging people to aim higher, and more effective learning from failures.

In a performance curve culture, people's mindsets, habits and interactions encourage each other to be on the performance curve. It is an environment that supports people to: bring their best and grow their potential (wisdom catalyst); strengthen their sense of purpose and the habits that sustain them (fuel catalyst); and form developmental relationships (connection catalyst). A performance curve culture helps boost effectiveness and well-being, individually and collectively, by creating the conditions for people within it to be on the performance curve (see box below).

A performance curve culture helps people to...

- Observe and adjust their mindsets, emotions and behaviours;
- Get out of protect mode and stay in explore mode, even when under pressure;
- Expand their perspectives, choices, and flexibility;
- Bring an accountable mindset, a growth mindset and a big picture mindset;
- Build sticky habits that support their effectiveness and well-being;
- Bring a sense of purpose or intention in everything they do;
- Move from either-or thinking to paradox thinking;
- Build developmental relationships, formed through emotional bond and stretch, to evolve their inner operating systems.

While a true performance curve culture will support people to develop their inner operating systems, it will also be a fertile environment for people to develop in other ways, for example learning technical skills or managerial skills. Since the focus of this book is developing our inner operating systems, the ideas in this chapter will be skewed towards that. But most ideas can easily be adapted to support other kinds of learning, and that may be an accessible way to start as you build up people's comfort with learning together.

This chapter will help you see how you can strengthen cultures to help you and others to be on the performance curve. While we will mostly use workplace examples, contributing to a performance curve culture is something that anyone can do, whatever their role or setting. Each of us has the potential to influence the culture around us, whether that is in our team, organization, family or community. So these ideas are meant to be useful to you, whether you are a team leader, a human resources professional, an educator, in your first job, a senior executive, a stay-at-home parent, a community activist or any number of other roles. Before you read on, we encourage you to reflect on to what extent your current culture supports people to be on the performance curve (see the box on p.248).

The three mindsets of performance curve cultures

Successful performance curve cultures are built on collective mindsets, which then support habits that bring the culture alive. In this section, we lay out the three collective mindsets we have found make the most difference. Helping everyone involved to understand, and embrace, these mindsets is an important step towards building a performance curve culture. The last part of the chapter will then lay out everyday habits that, when combined with these mindsets, support collective development.

Mindset 1: we can prioritize people development in a way that helps us get results faster and better

Most managers we work with believe in the importance of developing their people, but end up prioritizing getting results at the expense of people development. For example, they may avoid staffing someone less experienced on an assignment because it is too risky, or they do not have time to coach them. They are seeing getting results and supporting development as an either-or dilemma, and quite understandably favour getting results.

The first mindset of a performance curve culture rejects that dilemma and looks to unlock the paradox, by finding ways to develop people in a way that gets better, faster results. This mindset then supports people to adopt habits such as you saw in the second scenario, which both build capabilities and deliver business results. People with mismatched skill sets were paired up on workstreams to reduce risk and increase pace of learning. Cross-staffing between departments happened as soon as people were ready, which accelerated learning and collaboration between the departments. Priya encouraged her direct report to go to some easy client meetings by themself, thereby freeing Priya up to focus on other things.

Mindset 2: we all have the potential to improve our inner operating systems, and it is normal and helpful to talk about how we can develop them

While most of us know how much our inner operating systems influence our effectiveness, most on-the-job coaching is about improving technical skills and deliverables. It is often seen as taboo to talk about our mindsets and emotions: a sign of weakness, risky or just not done in the national or company culture. This second mindset tries to unblock that taboo, by helping people see that everyone's inner operating system affects their effectiveness, and we can strengthen it just like we can strengthen technical skills. It also helps people see that, rather than hiding the potential weaknesses in our inner operating system (from ourselves or others), we can learn faster by talking about them. Of course this is a challenge, because it is a vicious cycle: it feels risky to open up if others are not or you fear the consequences. It takes small steps and time to change this mindset, and the habits in the next section are a good place to start.

Once this mindset takes hold, it allows working on our inner operating systems to be a collective and individual daily habit, as you saw in the second scenario. Mindsets were at the heart of a high-stakes strategic discussion with the CEO. No one's mindsets were off the table: it was assumed that everyone's inner operating system was up for development, including the CEO's (importantly). Hidden drivers came up between Priya and her direct report. The protagonist also paid attention to their own mindsets, hidden drivers and emotions (whereas in the first scenario they avoided confronting their worries). They also paid attention to the mindsets of others, for example on the new project team. Rather than being a distraction, discussing mindsets helped the groups be more effective: to aim higher, overcome issues and learn from the past.

Mindset 3: we grow best by working on our development together, as part of our daily work

The most important word in this sentence is 'daily'. If, every day, we develop as part of our normal work, our growth compounds like interest in a bank account (at a far steeper growth trajectory than periodic training courses can lead to). Training and coaching become a complement to and enabler of growing on the job, rather than a replacement for it (for example, by teaching skills that enable us to develop our inner operating systems and help others do the same). This is not a new idea: models like 70:20:10 (the idea that we optimally learn 70 per cent on the job, 20 per cent from others and 10 per cent from training) have been around for a long time. The point is to apply these models to working at the bottom of our icebergs, not simply to technical skills or traditional 'soft skills'. The other important word is 'together', because it emphasizes how much faster we can learn with others, who can help us give our inner operating systems a good workout.

This mindset leads people to build in habits that support development every day. In the first scenario, a training programme on presentation skills was seen as the fix for the person's lack of confidence in meetings, i.e. the solution was outside of the day-to-day work with colleagues. In the second scenario, development solutions were built into daily work, such as the cross-staffing between departments. The flagship new joiner training programme built mindsets and habits that would support people to grow individually and collectively, rather than building pure technical skills. The project team kick-off built the beginnings of empathy and vulnerability (i.e emotional bond) and stretch, to pave the way for developmental relationships.

A change in culture will come best by working on mindsets and habits in tandem. The next section lays out habits that you can build into teams and organizations. Robert Kegan and colleagues' book *An Everyone Culture* contains further valuable examples[1].

Building habits of a performance curve culture

We recommend infusing habits that will support a performance curve culture into three central elements of teamwork, i.e. how you:

1) Build teams and assign work;
2) Hold meetings;
3) Encourage feedback plus coaching.

We will now take each of these elements in turn, sharing example habits you could build into teams' ways of working. This is just a short list and it may spark other ideas for what you could do to strengthen the performance curve culture in your team(s). There is no single recipe for cultivating a performance curve culture: choose what will work for your team(s) or organization. Our own role modelling is also key, so we will look at that at the end, as well as the way we can use an organization's training plan to support a performance curve culture.

1. Building teams and assigning work

The way a team is set up provides the environment for supporting individual and collective development. In a fertile environment, the team feels a strong emotional bond and their thinking is challenged daily. Team members work together to bring their best and develop their inner operating systems. We can create a fertile environment by paying careful attention to who works with whom, how the work is allocated and how teamwork begins and ends. Even if we have a permanent team structure (rather than a project team structure) there is usually plenty we can do. Here are some ideas:

- *Make sure everyone has a challenging assignment.* Give people assignments that force them to see things from fresh angles, build new skills or integrate multiple perspectives. This can be a small reassignment of tasks, such as rotating the responsibility to run the team meeting (or part of it), as in the second scenario. Tom Rippin, CEO of On Purpose, highlighted how important it is to come up with these creative ways of challenging people in smaller organizations like his own, where there are fewer opportunities for doing so by moving them through different roles. Or it can be something larger. For example, Ambu CEO Juan Jose Gonzalez explains how a student presented them with her university thesis on cross-contamination in scopes, and soon after they brought her into their health economics team and published her results. When their competitors queried these findings, Ambu sent the new hire to present her results to them, one of whom had a team of 100 experienced healthcare economists;
- *Support the challenge.* With such a level of challenge needs to come good support for the individual, not just to learn required new skills

but also to ensure their inner operating system sets them up to succeed, especially to avoid succumbing to protect mode. Pairing people, e.g. one more experienced and one less experienced team member, is an age-old technique for transferring skills. However, you can set up pairs to specifically help people do inner operating system work together, for example by observing each other at work, or talking through their challenges and asking each other questions. Lots of our clients have implemented buddy systems across organizational boundaries. It is motivating, builds muscles for forming developmental relationships and accelerates the learning across department lines. Each person will 'lose' a little time on their direct work, but will get that time back in spades through the deep learning and stronger relationships;

- *Launch the team with developmental interactions.* Ideally, this would include some individual sharing and some collective exchange, which builds emotional bond through empathy and vulnerability and provides structured stretch, to accelerate the formation of developmental relationships. You saw individual sharing of development goals in the second scenario at the start of this chapter. A step up would be to invite people to share their hidden drivers and how they show up at work. The collective exchange could be anything that involves practising talking about inner operating systems together, so that people are able to do this later when they are under pressure. The pre-mortem in the second scenario was an example of that. The team imagined themselves in the future and looked back to brainstorm risks and success factors. (This is a type of perceptual positioning, with the benefits we covered in Chapter 7.) You could also run this as a visualization or with a 'hand' exercise, such as drawing. The key is to get to the depth of the inner operating system: how can we think and feel differently to bring our full potential and make this a success (and minimize risk of failure);
- *Ensure your team has regular check-ins and post-mortems that include talking about how the team's inner operating systems are helping and hindering performance.* For example, when identifying lessons learned

and what to do differently, talk about how to adjust mindsets and habits, or how to help each other get back into explore mode when under pressure. After the first few months of the Covid-19 pandemic, one of our clients asked us to run check-ins for their country leadership teams all around the world. Although most teams felt the pandemic brought them closer together, these sessions acted as a pressure valve, made it normal to talk about mindsets and emotions, and set the teams up for the difficult winter ahead. While using a facilitator helps the team have a better session, it doesn't need to be an external coach. You might consider training people from across the organization to run sessions for other teams. We first did this for a manufacturing client who wanted to keep running post-mortem sessions after we stopped working with them. Everyone loved it: the facilitators were proud of their wider contribution and learned a lot, and it was an efficient way to strengthen learning and collaboration between departments.

2. Holding meetings

How much of your working time do you spend in meetings? Participants in our leadership programmes typically say around 80 per cent. That's a lot of time. But we are not focused here on diary management or having efficient meetings. We are focused on what we can do in meetings to help people bring their best and grow their potential over time (i.e. making people more effective individually and collectively, so that all their work, including meetings, is more effective). For example, we might support people to be in explore mode, or to think in more complex ways, such as through paradoxical thinking, perspective taking or paying attention to purpose. Here are some ideas, each of which might take a few minutes to set up but will pay back in development, discussion quality and team cohesion:

- *Send invites and allocate roles with development in mind.* Juan Jose Gonzalez regularly invites leaders to bring their team to meetings with him, rather than come alone (he was the inspiration for the CEO in the second scenario). This allows him to expand people's thinking, reinforce company priorities and values, and encourage productive mindsets. Once at the meeting, you can also allocate roles to support development. Rotating who 'chairs' the team meeting builds facilitation skills in the chair and is a scaffolding opportunity for them, as they have to practise taking different perspectives, integrating opposing ideas, switching between paying attention to the content and the process, and asking questions that unblock issues. It helps build the mindsets and skills that support bigger-picture thinking. You could start this gradually by having a team member lead a part of the meeting, as in the second scenario. Our clients have found this to be very motivating, especially for more junior team members, who put a lot of thought into how to make their slot impactful. An alternative approach is to have team members champion alternative views (e.g. the customer view, contrarian view, optimist view or risk-averse view), to flex their perspective-taking muscles and bring fresh insight;
- *Start the meeting with a shared practice that gets everyone ready to bring their best.* Many of the tools from Chapter 7 could be used here to settle protect mode and encourage explore mode. You could run a short mindfulness practice, simply allow a couple of minutes of quiet, or invite each person to share something they are grateful for. You could also prime people to bring their best, by asking them to set an intention for a quality they will bring to the meeting (e.g. curiosity, persistence) or how they will contribute (e.g. ask questions, be kindly challenging);
- *Infuse a sense of purpose into the meeting.* Bringing purpose into the meeting helps people keep the bigger picture in mind, take the focus off themselves and their needs, and encourage better-quality thinking. This could be as simple as starting a meeting with a recent customer success, or inviting team members to share what is on their customers'

'worry lists'. Juan Jose constantly looks for opportunities to reinforce the company's vision and values. He will use it to learn from the past: 'We lost an opportunity to move towards our vision there...' or to expand thinking: 'How could we get results here with more speed?' (a question based on one of Ambu's three values). Pramath Sinha, the Indian education entrepreneur and institution builder, says, 'I always try to get my teams to go back to the original real problem, then try to solve it. That's the way to bring fresh thinking, and create something enduring';

- *Ask questions that help people get perspective on, and be more versatile with, their thinking.* Both Juan Jose and Pramath use questions in meetings to build thinking capacity and get better answers. What sorts of questions can help accomplish this? We can use questions that reinforce helpful mindsets, such as, 'In what ways might we have contributed more to this situation than we realize?' (accountability mindset) or 'If we consider all the different needs, what might we do?' (big picture mindset). We can also use questions to encourage paradox thinking, such as, 'What is really at the heart of this dilemma?' or 'How might doing X actually get us more of Y?' As well as asking questions ourselves, we can also encourage others to build their capacity for asking questions that open up thinking, which will also be developmental for them as it forces them to take a balcony view, for example on different mindsets around the table.

3. Encourage feedback plus questions

In Chapter 11 we introduced the idea that frequent, informal feedback supports people to be on the performance curve, especially when it is combined with questions that trigger insight into our inner operating systems. Our vision for a performance curve culture is that everyone in the organization is getting quality developmental feedback plus coaching daily, in one-to-one and group settings.

But that feedback is so woven into ways of interacting that people do not see feedback discussions as something separate from doing work and growing on the job. Here are some ideas to move in that direction in teams:

- *Inspire people with a positive vision of the culture you are seeking to create.* Make clear the benefits to them and others. Call your culture something positive, such as a 'performance curve culture' or a 'development culture', rather than a 'feedback culture'. 'Feedback' sends many people into protect mode and, more importantly, it is just a means to an end. If you wanted your family to be fit and strong but you have mixed feelings about abdominal crunches, you would call it a 'be fit culture', not a 'sit-up culture';

- *Make it routine that everyone knows what everyone else is working on.* This helps people help each other, and also encourages a growth mindset, because it shows everyone is a 'work in progress'. You could get everyone to share their development goals quarterly, or at the start of a project, as per the second scenario. Or you could go one step further and put up a poster on which everyone writes their current development goals;

- *Create little moments where feedback flows.* You could hold a feedback discussion in a group, starting with 'How effective was this meeting on a scale of 1–10? If it wasn't a 9 or a 10, what could we do next time that would make the meeting a 9 or a 10?' or 'Share one input from someone else that really helped shift your thinking.' Or you could close a meeting with a quick round of feedback. An efficient and safe way to start is to have pairs give each other feedback, as you saw in the second scenario. Encourage people to not just give feedback on the work product (e.g. 'your analysis was really clear') but also touch on the inner operating system (e.g. 'I noticed you go quiet when X topic came up but I really felt we could have benefitted from your view'). And encourage them to add in coaching questions (e.g. 'Did you notice that? What were you thinking or feeling when you went quiet?'). You can save these feedback exchanges for the end of a meeting, but you could also put them in the middle of a meeting, to accelerate the learning cycle;

- *Create a buddy system.* You could pair people up with other team members, or with people from other departments, or with people of different seniority levels. Buddies can then meet regularly, or you can build in time for buddy exchanges as part of team meetings. They can exchange feedback, or share their daily/weekly review. The key is that the buddies bring empathy and vulnerability, and intertwine feedback and asking questions that encourage their partner to gain insights for their inner operating system. Rotating buddies periodically helps people build developmental relationships with more people. Using trios rather than pairs builds everyone's comfort with giving feedback in front of each other, helps them learn about giving feedback by observing others do it, and gives the option for the third person to ask coaching questions of the feedback giver and receiver.

You can use these ideas to identify what would strengthen the performance curve culture in your organization. However, if you want to influence a performance curve culture around you, your own role modelling is an important lever, so we turn to that now.

Role modelling a performance curve culture

We have learned that the biggest risk factor for impact in our work with teams is when the team leader is not open to personal growth. If they signal that they do not need or want to change, they are role modelling fixed and victim mindsets, and it is easy (and perhaps safer) for others to follow suit. We have learned to turn down work when we spot this risk factor. But the converse is also true: one of the biggest success indicators is when the team leader is open to personal growth. And, if you are not the team leader, you can also have a significant impact by role modelling what you are seeking to create. Others will, over time, see the benefits to you and them, and be able to copy your methods.

Here are some tips for how to role model the culture you seek:

- *Model intent and effort, not perfection.* You do not need to be a perfect model of being on the performance curve. What counts is sharing your struggles and showing how you are seeking to grow. One big-thinking leader we worked with placed a high importance on his daily mindfulness practice. When he was on work trips, he would talk about needing to stick to his disciplines to keep him balanced and manage his stress levels. Over time, many of the team adopted mindfulness or other practices that helped them centre themselves. Sometimes they would start team meetings with mindfulness, especially when they were under pressure;

- *Talk about your development goals and seek feedback.* Many of the participants on our leadership and coaching programmes will decide to share their 360 reports or development goals with their teams. A step further is to ask for group feedback, i.e. ask a few people to give you feedback at the same time. They can learn from each other, and it allows everyone to practise exchanging feedback in a group;

- *Share your failures.* One successful partner at a professional services firm recently told us, 'We only talk about people's successes here. That creates a myth that you either have what it takes, or you do not. But it takes 99 no's to get a yes, so people need to get comfortable with that and cope with it. And that starts with all of us talking much more about how much we failed, and how we dealt with it.' This is a good illustration of how fixed mindsets can be self-perpetuating in a culture. The good news is, it is easy to break: by talking about your failures, how you coped with them and how they shaped your thinking. Luke Bradley-Jones instituted an Edison award in his department at Sky for the best failure[2]. During a recent significant setback, he tried to 'live the mantra: failure is an opportunity to learn' so others could learn from that, too. If you do the same, people will avoid repeating your mistakes. But, importantly for the overall aim of this book, it reinforces mindsets such as accountability and growth, and shows people how to work on their inner operating systems.

Along with your own role modelling, training is also an important lever for nurturing and maintaining a performance curve culture. Let's look at how to do this.

Using training to cultivate a performance curve culture

Training has a specific place in a performance curve culture, because it builds the skills needed for developing our inner operating system, as well as technical or interpersonal skills. There should be an emphasis on developmental trainings to equip people to create, maintain and benefit from a performance curve culture; in other words, tools and techniques to help them learn deeply and daily, individually and collectively. The following questions will help you see how you could do more of this:

- How many of your learning interventions are delivered in a single session (e.g. over one day or a few days)? What could you do to extend the learning period and help people get brilliant at learning every day, in their regular work settings and interactions?
- What percentage of your training budget is spent on helping people work with their inner operating systems (e.g. mindsets), vs. building skills? How could you make developmental learning a part of every programme?

- To what extent do you help new joiners understand about their inner operating systems, strengthen their growth mindset, and know how to participate in a performance curve culture? How could you do this earlier and better?
- How much do you invest in coaching skills (e.g. asking good questions) inside the line organization (not just HR or using external coaching)? How could you build basic coaching skills in everyone, including individual contributors?
- How much do your executive team and your board work on their ability to model a performance curve culture? If you feel they could do more, what would be the courageous move to make that happen?

Moving on the curve together

We have focused in this chapter on how to create teams and organizations that support you and others to move along the performance curve. And, although we have focused primarily on work settings, hopefully you will have ideas that you could also try out with friends, family or community groups.

If you believe that the ideas we outline in *The Performance Curve* are valuable, are there other places you could help encourage individual and collective growth? We wish we had learned these techniques at school and at home, instead of much later in life, with a lot of effort, and often through our own mistakes. We also wish we had had more easily accessible resources for how to bring these techniques into our home life: in how we form 'performance curve' relationships with our life partners, the children in our lives, our siblings, our parents and our friends. Not to mention all the others whom we influence and/ or depend on, such as doctors, educators, neighbours and fellow volunteers. Perhaps there is a role we could all play in helping each other develop our inner operating systems, to boost our effectiveness and well-being, and realize our full potential.

The final chapter of *The Performance Curve* offers, as a summary, a toolkit of questions drawn from the material throughout the book to help you gain insights on your challenges and propel yourself forwards on the performance curve. We also look at wider systemic issues, and how some of the thinking in this book can be a helpful lens for seeing how we might contribute to solving them.

CHAPTER THIRTEEN

Close: using the three catalysts in your daily life

The performance curve represents a way of living and growing ourselves that helps us achieve effectiveness *and* well-being. The wisdom, fuel and connection catalysts help us get the benefits of being on the performance curve and show how to put into action the three principles of this book:

1) Dissolving the trade-off between effectiveness and well-being is the key to unlocking the higher performance levels of a life well lived;

2) Sustained, and even higher, performance is possible through the ongoing, proactive development of our inner operating system;

3) We can interact with each other in ways that develop our inner operating system to reach even higher levels of performance.

Strengthening the three catalysts benefits us and those around us: we become wiser at bringing and growing our best, find the fuel to sustain our development over the long haul, and build developmental connections with those around us. The catalysts transform our inner operating system: we take more ownership of and make better choices in how we interpret and interact with the world. The result is not only maximizing our potential (being able to deal with more complexity and greater change with less effort and to better effect) but also improved well-being (be it in physical or mental health, relationships or general life satisfaction). This enriches our individual lives and those of the families and communities we are part of at home and at work.

Being on the performance curve has another, wider benefit: it builds the capacities – in us and others – that are needed to solve the more systemic challenges we are facing, such as increasing social inequality and isolation, climate change, environmental disasters, and economic or health crises. Whether inherited from past generations, consequences of our own actions, or forces of nature, these systemic challenges will usually impact the performance and well-being of everyone in the system, not just those who are more immediately affected. That makes them more complex and harder to tackle.

In this final chapter, we offer *The Performance Curve* 'in a nutshell': a toolkit of questions you can use to apply the three catalysts to challenges you want to address – be they at the individual, collective or systemic level. We have covered a lot of ground in this book and, hopefully, you will have gained insight into your current challenges as you were reading. This last chapter equips you with an easy way to apply the performance curve catalysts for the future, when the detailed contents might be less fresh in your memory. This catalyst toolkit is a way of getting on the balcony of all the content of *The Performance Curve* and quickly identifying promising new areas of exploration or action for any challenging situation you face.

Why a toolkit of questions? Questions help our brains to let go of default ways and prime us to think differently. It is through thinking differently that new solutions are born, so regularly using such questions will help you and others find better solutions to problems. In the spirit of *The Performance Curve,* it will also support your inner operating system to develop. It will develop the strength of neural pathways that support reflection, emotional regulation and cognitive flexibility, so you are more likely to bring these qualities in the future and will be more skilful at doing so.

The catalyst toolkit for challenging situations

You can use this catalyst toolkit in situations in which you feel challenged, stuck or reluctant to accept an unsatisfying compromise, or simply when you feel like giving yourself a little performance curve boost. The questions will help you uncover how your operating system is currently working and point you to a possible shift in thinking. There are two ways of working with these questions: 1) take 10–15 minutes to write down a few thoughts in response to all the questions, then review and pick an area that seems most promising to pursue further; or 2) scan the topics and questions and let your intuition guide you towards which to focus on straight away. Either way, you can then always go to the relevant chapters to refresh your understanding or get more ideas for how to work with this topic. You can also bring in tools from the performance curve habits (Chapter 7) to gain further insight.

These catalyst questions are intended to launch you into a new line of enquiry, hopefully leading to further interesting questions, or insights to help you make decisions; they are not an exhaustive end-to-end problem-solving process. As such, they lend themselves not just to individual reflection, but also as conversation starters (and shifters) with others. While we have phrased the questions from the perspective of a single individual, they can also be asked from a collective 'we'. Some of them prompt us to also consider 'others', i.e. those who play a role in the situation but are not participating in this enquiry. You may of course want to consider several groups of 'others', for example if you were thinking about your local education system, you might give different responses as you consider students, teachers, school managers, parents, local government or central government.

When you use the catalyst questions and they open up different directions, just follow your instincts about where to go next. However, we do encourage you to keep asking yourself more questions and not to jump to answers or statements too quickly. Questions keep our minds more open and help us stay in explore mode, which makes it much easier to find good solutions. You should discover that just a quarter of an hour of going down new routes of enquiry can lead to new insights and avenues for action.

Have a look at the catalyst toolkit in Table 13.1 now (ideally with one of your challenges in mind) and then read on for examples that illustrate using it.

Table 13.1 Performance curve catalyst toolkit

Topic/chapter	Questions to increase insight	Questions to guide action
Mindsets and emotions (Chapter 2)	• What mindsets am I holding about myself, others and the situation? • What emotions am I feeling and what can I learn from them?	• What might be a more helpful mindset that could lead to different behaviours or results? • If my assumptions were proven wrong, what would I do differently then? • How can I harness the energy of my emotions?
Protect–explore modes and hidden drivers (Chapter 3)	• To what extent do I feel in protect or explore mode? How does that feel, and what am I thinking? • What am I most afraid of? How might this be connected to my hidden drivers? • How might protect–explore modes and hidden drivers be impacting others in this situation?	• What could I do to move more into explore mode? • How might I support others to be more in explore mode? • If I weren't afraid, what would I do?
Vertical development (Chapter 4)	• Who is influencing (directly or indirectly) how I see the situation and what I do? • To what extent am I co-creating with others? • What am I not seeing?	• What would I do, if I felt free from others' views? What is keeping me from doing that? • How could I draw others in, to solve and move forwards together?

Topic/chapter	Questions to increase insight	Questions to guide action
	• What if this situation were not happening to me, but for me – what could I learn or gain?	• If I saw this as an adventure or a learning opportunity, what would I do?
Three performance curve mindsets (Chapter 5)	• To what extent am I feeling accountable for this situation? • To what extent do I believe it is possible to grow and change to solve this issue? • To what extent do I pay attention to the bigger picture (wider, longer-term)? • To what extent are others bringing these mindsets?	• In what ways am I directly or indirectly contributing to this situation? • And therefore, what could I do differently to move it forwards? • What could I do to help myself/others bring more constructive mindsets?
Habits (Chapter 6)	• In what ways are my habits unhelpful? • What have I struggled to change about how we operate? • Why are my habits sticky, what are sources of friction?	• What would it take to build more traction? • How could I build in a greater sense of reward?
Performance curve habits (Chapter 7)	• To what extent am I aware of our thoughts and emotions in this situation? • What tools might help me increase that awareness?	• What tools might help me reset to be at my best and make better choices in this situation?
Purpose (Chapter 8)	• What really matters here to me, and why? And what matters to others? • How clearly aligned is everyone who is implicated in this purpose?	• How could I build a stronger alignment of purpose and action?
Paradoxical thinking (Chapter 9)	• What is the real dilemma at the heart of this challenge?	• How can I unlock the gridlock and generate extra energy?

Topic/chapter	Questions to increase insight	Questions to guide action
Connection (Chapters 10 and 11)	• How do my connections and interactions contribute to this issue? • What kind of relationships do I want to have? • To what extent am I building emotional bond and offering stretch?	• What would it take to strengthen our connection and interactions to support this issue to move forwards? • How can I cultivate the relationship I want to have? • What would make the relationship more developmental and help me evolve my inner operating system?
Performance curve culture (Chapter 12)	• To what extent is everyone able to bring their best and grow when tackling this issue?	• How could we create the conditions for everyone to bring their best and grow as they tackle this issue?

The catalyst questions in action: 'the new boss'

To illustrate how the catalyst questions can be used, let's apply them to a situation that many of our clients encounter and we have also experienced ourselves: a new boss comes in and we just don't click. One of us authors (Vanessa) vividly remembers such a lack of chemistry with a former boss many years ago. Conversations easily got argumentative and she didn't feel they were on the same team. Vanessa believes she didn't handle the situation well, and it soured the quality and enjoyment of their work. Imagine if Vanessa had used the catalyst questions at that moment in time.

Let's travel back in time to Vanessa as she was facing that situation, and see how the catalyst questions could have helped her find better options. As Vanessa reads down the lists of questions, a few of them spark her interest. Here is her inner narrative as she uses some of the catalyst questions to get insight:

'Asking myself *What could I do to move more into explore mode?* might lead me to run a body scan to centre myself. I might then ask myself *What emotions am I feeling? What can I learn from them?* And I discover that I feel angry and am blaming my boss for our dynamics, not taking much accountability myself. I see that my hidden driver of feeling virtuous had come into play, condemning my boss for being a 'bad' boss to avoid me being seen by colleagues (or myself) as faulty.

Given how focused I am on my boss and not on charting my own path, I could ask myself *What if this situation were not happening to me, but for me - what could I learn or gain?* I might remember that I have always admired people who can keep their composure when dealing with difficult people, and would like to be more like that. Or that I could learn to better share my perspective with others, hear theirs, and come up with a better way together.

This idea of bringing different perspectives together might make me wonder about my boss's views on what is important. What matters to him? I have no idea! I have been so entangled in building up the case against him, that I have lost sight of what the value might be in what he was saying. Asking myself *What really matters in those topics, to me and to my boss?* might then be a next question to help me come up with some actions for moving forwards.'

We stop here, as Vanessa already has a few avenues to explore from this brief reflection. Although the insights and actions Vanessa would have taken from this exercise would have just been first small steps, we can already see they would have begun to reorient her towards growth, courage and possibility. As a result, they would have been more likely to lead to a constructive outcome. Note: we have used a retrospective example here simply because it was a nice 'juicy' situation that we felt would resonate with many people. You could also use the catalyst questions to learn from previous situations, but they are primarily designed for use on current challenges.

The performance curve at the systemic level

The primary focus of *The Performance Curve* has been about developing as individuals and with others. Along with this benefit of effectiveness and well-being for individuals and collectives, we believe the approach contained within *The Performance Curve* can also benefit the wider system(s) of which we are all part.

By a system, we mean the layers above individuals and collectives (such as families, communities, networks or organizations of any kind). Some examples of systems might be a country, an economic area and, ultimately, the world at large. Changes in one part of a system may affect other parts or the whole system, like ripples in a pond. Like an individual or a collective, a system also has its version of an inner operating system of spoken or unspoken rules. The inner operating system of an overall system emerges from the inner operating systems of the people and organizations in it. These rules shape how individual and collective interactions take place, for example to determine the allocation of resources and rights within the system.

We can extend the ideas in this book to look at whether a system is moving on the performance curve. *In a performance curve system, our mindsets, habits and interactions maximize the potential and well-being of the system overall.* That means its institutions and practices support people to:

- be on the performance curve individually, i.e.:
  - bring their best and grow their potential (wisdom catalyst);
  - strengthen their sense of purpose and the mindsets and habits that keep them moving forwards (fuel catalyst);
  - nurture relationships that help them and those around them reach their potential and live healthy, fulfilled lives, individually and collectively (connection catalyst)
- and ensure the vitality of the system as a whole.

In contrast, boom-and-bust dynamics prevail at the systemic level when there is a focus on short-term gains over longer-term losses, and individual profits over collective costs. Similar to individual performance suffering when on the boom-and-bust curve, the consequence of boom-and-bust dynamics for a system is that it also doesn't perform at its best and falls short of its potential overall. Systemic factors then hinder the potential of its parts from being realized, which hinders the overall system from flourishing in return. For example, studies suggest that income and wealth inequality is a problem not just for those who struggle to make ends meet, but for everyone[1,2]. While a certain degree of inequality can spur growth, when it reaches higher levels, it limits the size and growth of the pie for everyone as it restrains the participation and contribution of all its population. Other research focuses on how high levels of inequality contribute to social issues, such as low public health, obesity, overspending, crime and violence[3,4].

We observe that the causes of boom-and-bust at the systems level are related to what drives us as individuals to be on the boom-and-bust curve: being more in protect than explore mode; being in the grip of our hidden drivers; short-term or silo thinking; fixed mindset; and binary thinking leading to either-or trade-offs and zero-sum games where your gain is my loss. When these ways of operating become built into how the system functions, it exerts a powerful drag on everyone within it.

But it is not all bleak: what helps us get off the boom-and-bust curve as individuals is also what can help a system. We might not see how we can directly change the systemic inner operating system as individuals, but many of the ideas in this book can also help us gain insight into how we can play our part in lifting the systems in which we operate.

When looking at complex systemic issues, we might feel powerless or worried, which can trigger us to go into protect mode and create a downward spiral that affects our ability to see what we can do to make a difference. And, if our brain is already overloaded from the complexity of our daily lives, then addressing complex systemic issues may feel even further from our reach.

We have found that the catalyst questions in Table 13.1 can help us think about these systemic issues constructively, to get insight into the issues and see what we might do differently as individuals or collectives. The questions can help us get more perspective on how the system is working, our role in it and how to influence it in positive ways by bringing the best of our own inner operating system. Let's use plastic pollution in the environment to illustrate this. We have chosen this topic because it is something most people will relate to, but you can apply the questions to gain insight into other systemic issues that may be more specific to your region or country.

The catalyst questions in action for the system: 'plastic pollution'

In 2017, David Attenborough's *Blue Planet II* stunned millions of us across the world both with the engrossing beauty of marine life as well as the tragic effects plastics were having on these ecosystems. Attenborough's dramatic footage and his call to action for greater sustainability have been widely credited with precipitating system-wide changes, including the European Union's ban on a wide range of single-use plastic, many retailers and food outlets going plastic-free ahead of governmental deadlines, and a wider social movement to reduce personal plastic consumption.

There was a time when everyone seemed to be talking about switching to paper straws or taking their own reusable coffee mugs to their local coffee shop. While the now-called 'Attenborough effect' might have ebbed and been replaced in the headlines by other topics, it is clear that the problem of plastic pollution is not over yet[5]. Most of the 8.3 billion metric tons of plastic produced in the last six decades have ended as trash and still exist in some form, endangering wildlife, spoiling beaches, and entering our food chain[6]. Despite increased awareness of the issue and greater willingness to take action, analysts still expect plastic production to triple by 2050 and account for a fifth of global oil consumption[7]. Let's use the catalyst questions to look at how we can contribute to tackling plastic pollution from our position in the system.

Many of us will already feel accountable for the plastic we bring into our homes and recycle as much as possible. But what if we investigated this further through the question: *How are we directly, or indirectly, contributing to the situation?* We might ask, 'What are the different ways we use plastic – at home, at work, as a by-product of other products (like plastic wrapping of garments from the manufacturer to the retailer which we consumers do not see when buying clothes in store)? And how effective is the recycling we are doing?' We would find out that, in reality, recycling is even less of an answer today than we thought: recycling degrades the quality of plastic, which limits its usability, and is more expensive than making new plastic. Total recycling of plastic to date is low – less than 10 per cent[6].

We might therefore decide to focus our enquiry on tackling plastic pollution further upstream, i.e. by dramatically reducing the amount of plastic we consume. We could consider our direct *habits around plastic, to what extent they are unhelpful and what would help us shift them.* We could start by looking at our plastics waste to see what it is mostly made up of and how we can reduce it. Depending on what we buy or where we live, we might see different things. For example, we might have a lot of plastic waste from pre-prepared food, such as ready meals or delicatessen products. A range of catalyst questions can help us open the enquiry to different areas and generate ideas, for example:

- *What is the real dilemma at the heart of this challenge?* We might discover a trade-off between plastic reduction vs. time, assuming it takes longer to cook more from scratch or buy ingredients that aren't as heavily packaged from farmers' markets or bulk food shops. Or between plastic vs. money, as buying in these places might be more expensive. So how could we reduce plastic in a way that saves time or money? Exploring this paradoxical thinking can lead to some interesting ideas, for example cooking larger portions and freezing them so they are more cost-effective and quicker to prepare when time is tight, or shopping at the farmers' market doubling up as social connection time with family or friends;

- *What really matters here, and why?* Getting clear on our personal motivation for reducing plastic is important, as we can draw fuel from it to help shift our habits around plastic use. Is it because of the impact of plastic on wildlife? Or the health risks it might pose to us when it enters the food chain? Are we more concerned about the state of the world we are leaving to future generations? Or something else?

- *How do my connections and interactions contribute to this issue?* This question could lead us to consider the influence we have on others. In the UK in 2018, supermarket shoppers left the wrapping of their goods behind at the tills in order to protest against excessive plastic packaging. Since then, a number of supermarkets have made pledges to cut plastic packaging. How else could we change our interactions to make progress on this issue – in our neighbourhood, at work, our children's schools, with friends and family? We might notice the plastic in toys and their packaging, and decide to set up a second-hand toy exchange with local families to reduce more plastic being produced.

There are many further avenues we could explore with this approach, for example the type of clothes we buy, the practices of companies we buy from or invest in, and so on. These ideas are not rocket science, you may well have put some of them in place, and others might not work for you. We are simply illustrating how the catalyst questions can provide a structure to challenge our inner operating system and open us up to new thinking about systemic issues and how we can each play our part in unblocking them. Great collective changes can come from the small steps each of us take.

Closing words

Using these catalyst questions and keeping our eyes on moving ourselves up the performance curve can help us maximize our potential and strengthen our well-being. They can also help us transcend what we believe we are capable of, to help us contribute to a world in which humanity and our environment truly thrives.

We sincerely hope that this book has inspired and equipped you to be on your own individual performance curve for a life well lived. By that act alone, and even more by including the teams, families and communities you are part of in your development, you will send impulses for lifting the wider system as well. You will contribute to the capacities we need to effectively tackle systemic issues and create a world we are proud to hand over to future generations.

Acknowledgements

In creating this book, we are grateful above all to our interviewees who stretched our ideas and brought them alive. Thanks also to the team at Bloomsbury, especially Allie Collins, Amy Greaves, Ian Hallsworth and Matt James for their belief in this book, and a warm and professional partnership (and the book cover!). William Smith brought us robustness with his thorough research, always unflappable and good humoured. We are also grateful to everyone who gave us feedback, advice, permissions, and general encouragement, including Rebecca Carter, Stuart Crainer, Janet Dekker, Maria Farrow, Andrea Frischholz, Ian Hardie and colleagues, Lynn Harris, Robert Kegan, Jana Klimecki, Morgan Krone, Chris de Lapuente, Hector MacDonald, Ben Mandelkern, Tom Miller, Donald Novak, Colin Price, Alison Reynolds, Jeremy Sweeney, Sharon Toye, Anna and Rupert Watkins, and The Enneagram Institute.

Laura: my contributions to this book are born out of work with clients and colleagues over the past two decades. With thanks to Shani Ospina, Jana Klimecki and Hugh Watkins for being supportive business partners through all life's adventures – in and far beyond work. And to others with whom we have co-created or tested these ideas, especially Marci Adler, Christina Afoke, Laura Kind, Jane Kinghorn, Talia Litman, Lynn Woods Strang, Deborah Thomas, Lisa Thomas and Howard Ting. Fatima Amzoug, Conceicao De Freitas, Anne Lorgeoux, Debora Mahieu, Miranda Rock and Kara Stenhouse have been enormously supportive behind the scenes. Pierre Gurdjian, Russ Hudson, Neil Janin, Robert Kegan, Lisa Lahey, Trevor Robbins, David Rooke, Anne Rosser and Barbara Sahakian all shaped how I make sense of this thing called being human. My family, particularly

Elizabeth, Olivier, Alicia, Rupert, Hugh, Anna, Victoria, Abigail and Jacob, as well as my new French family – are precious and unfailingly supportive. And, of course, to Vanessa – for making this experience enriching and fun, as well as leading us through the challenging parts.

Vanessa: writing this book felt like a climb up my personal Mount Everest, with exhilarating highs and mind-frying lows. What put the cherry on top of the former and helped me muster courage during the latter, was the support and companionship of some special human beings I feel incredibly lucky to have in my life. My partner not only made me numerous breakfasts and graciously accepted my reduced presence to him, but also supported every step along the way. Ellika Benn, Rose Eilber and Martina Fischer were caring, patiently listening and giving friends who never doubted the value and beauty of this adventure. This book also exists due to my teachers, colleagues and clients in the corporate world and in my breathwork therapy and yoga communities, who I have had the privilege of learning from about growth, potential and common humanity. Deepest gratitude also goes to my climbing buddy Laura, who inspires (and nudges me when needed) to bring my best and share it with the world. What a treat to be adding a book to our joint experiences! And to Chris Tchen – without whom we might not have met.

Notes

Introduction

1   Based on the theory of cognitive reserve to explain individual differences in the effects of brain degeneration on cognitive performance. For an overview, see Tucker, A.M. and Stern, Y. (2011). 'Cognitive Reserve in Aging'. *Current Alzheimer Research*, 8(4), pp.354–360.

Chapter 1

1   Kozlowska, K., Walker, P., McLean, L. and Carrive, P. (2015). 'Fear and the Defense Cascade: Clinical Implications and Management'. *Harvard Review of Psychiatry* 23, pp.263–287.
2   Arnsten, A.F.T. (2009). 'Stress signalling pathways that impair prefrontal cortex structure and function'. *Nature Reviews Neuroscience*, 10(6), pp.410–422.
3   Kawahara, J.I. and Sato, H. (2013). 'The effect of fatigue on the attentional blink'. *Attention, Perception, & Psychophysics*, 75(6), pp.1096–1102.
4   McEwen, B.S., Nasca, C. and Gray, J.D. (2016). 'Stress Effects on Neuronal Structure: Hippocampus, Amygdala, and Prefrontal Cortex'. *Neuropsychopharmacology*, 41, pp.3–23.
5   Bellet, C., De Neve, J.-E. and Ward, G. (2019). 'Does Employee Happiness have an Impact on Productivity?' *Social Science Research Network*, Scholarly Paper ID 3470734.
6   May, A. (2011). 'Experience-dependent structural plasticity in the adult human brain'. *Trends in Cognitive Sciences*, 15(10), pp.475–482.

Chapter 2

1   Herculano-Houzel, S. (2009). 'The human brain in numbers: A linearly scaled-up primate brain'. Frontiers in Human Neuroscience, 3, Article 31.
2   Drachman, D.A. (2005). 'Do we have brain to spare?'. *Neurology*, 64(12), pp.2004–2005.
3   Sakai, J. (2020). 'How synaptic pruning shapes neural wiring during development and, possibly, in disease'. *Proceedings of the National Academy of Sciences of the United States of America*, 117(28), pp.16096–16099.
4   The phrase 'neurons that fire together, wire together' is commonly used to describe this effect of a neural pathway becoming stronger the more we use it.
5   May, A. (2011). 'Experience-dependent structural plasticity in the adult human brain'. *Trends in Cognitive Sciences*, 15(10), pp.475–482

6   Wu, T., Dufford, A.J., Mackie, M.-A., Egan, L.J. and Fan, J. (2016). 'The Capacity of Cognitive Control Estimated from a Perceptual Decision Making Task'. *Scientific Reports*, 6.

7   Lazar, S.W., Kerr, C.E., Wasserman, R.H., Gray, J.R., Greve, D.N., Treadway, M.T., McGarvey, M., Quinn, B.T., Dusek, J.A., Benson, H., Rauch, S.L., Moore, C.I., and Fischl, B. (2005). 'Meditation experience is associated with increased cortical thickness'. *Neuroreport*, 16(17), pp.1893–1897.

8   Mahmood, L., Hopthrow, T. and Randsley de Moura, G. (2016). 'A Moment of Mindfulness: Computer-Mediated Mindfulness Practice Increases State Mindfulness'. *PLOS ONE*, 11(4).

9   Nummenmaa, L., Glerean, E., Hari, R. and Hietanen, J. K. (2014). Bodily maps of emotions. *Proceedings of the National Academy of Sciences of the United States of America*, *111*(2), 646–651.

10 Ekman, P. (2016). 'What Scientists Who Study Emotion Agree About'. *Perspectives on Psychological Science*, 11(1), pp.31–34.

11 A longstanding framework of six universal emotions has been that of psychologist Paul Ekman, who was the father of studying emotions in the lab (he was also was a scientific consultant on Pixar's movie Inside Out, which shows how emotions work inside us and at the same time shape our outer life). More recently, Ekman and his daughter Eve Ekman compiled the 'Atlas of Emotions', based on a survey of 248 scientists who study emotions. The Atlas lists five core emotions as emotional families that contain different states and intensities within them: enjoyment, fear, anger, sadness and disgust. Whilst researchers generally separate out disgust, we have found our clients make effective use of a simpler framework for the workplace, in which we insert disgust into the anger family.

12 Baron-Cohen, S. Mind Reading Emotions Library. Described in Junek, W. (2007). 'Mind Reading: The Interactive Guide to Emotions'. *Journal of the Canadian Academy of Child and Adolescent Psychiatry*, 16(4), pp.182–183.

13 Torre, J.B. and Lieberman, M.D. (2018). 'Putting Feelings Into Words: Affect Labeling as Implicit Emotion Regulation'. *Emotion Review*, 10(2), pp.116–124.

14 Burklund, L.J., Creswell, J.D., Irwin, M.R. and Lieberman, M.D. (2014). 'The common and distinct neural bases of affect labeling and reappraisal in healthy adults'. *Frontiers in Psychology*, 5, Article 221.

15 Tugade, M.M., Fredrickson, B.L. and Barrett, L.F. (2004). 'Psychological Resilience and Positive Emotional Granularity: Examining the Benefits of Positive Emotions on Coping and Health'. *Journal of Personality*, 72(6), pp.1161–1190.
    In addition, the following is a useful and accessible read:
    www.psychologytoday.com/us/blog/the-mindful-self-express/201906/master-your-feelings-new-tools-inspired-neuroscience

16 Cutuli, D. (2014). 'Cognitive reappraisal and expressive suppression strategies role in the emotion regulation: An overview on their modulatory effects and neural correlates'. *Frontiers in Systems Neuroscience*, 8, Article 175.

17 Moore, S.A., Zoellner, L.A. and Mollenholt, N. (2008). 'Are Expressive Suppression and Cognitive Reappraisal Associated with Stress-Related Symptoms?' *Behaviour Research and Therapy*, 46(9), pp.993–1000.

18   An overview of these mechanisms is in Wood, W. (2019). *Good Habits, Bad Habits: The Science of Making Positive Changes That Stick*. Pan Macmillan.

19   Wood, W., Quinn, J.M. and Kashy, D.A. (2002). 'Habits in Everyday Life: Thought, Emotion, and Action'. *Journal of Personality and Social Psychology*, 83(6), pp.1281–1297.

20   Hofmann, S.G., Heering, S., Sawyer, A.T. and Asnaani, A. (2009). 'How to Handle Anxiety: The Effects of Reappraisal, Acceptance, and Suppression Strategies on Anxious Arousal'. *Behaviour Research and Therapy*, 47(5), pp.389–394.

Chapter 3

1   These brain modes have also been described by other names. A discover-defend axis is one of the core principles of Caroline Webb's book How to Have a Good Day (Macmillan, 2016). The same idea is built into the towards-away response in David Rock's SCARF framework, Dan Siegel and Tina Bryson's The Yes Brain (Simon & Schuster, 2017), and the reactive-creative dichotomy of The Leadership Circle tool.

2   Kozlowska, K., Walker, P., McLean, L. and Carrive, P. (2015). 'Fear and the Defense Cascade: Clinical Implications and Management'. *Harvard Review of Psychiatry*, 23(4), pp.263–287.

3   Steimer, T. (2002). 'The biology of fear- and anxiety-related behaviors'. *Dialogues in Clinical Neuroscience*, 4(3), pp.231–249.

4   Janak, P.H. and Tye, K.M. (2015). 'From circuits to behaviour in the amygdala'. *Nature*, 517(7534), pp.284–292.

5   Shields, G.S., Sazma, M.A. and Yonelinas, A.P. (2016). 'The Effects of Acute Stress on Core Executive Functions: A Meta-Analysis and Comparison with Cortisol'. *Neuroscience & Biobehavioral Reviews*, 68, pp.651–668.

6   Arnsten, A.F.T. (2009). 'Stress signalling pathways that impair prefrontal cortex structure and function'. *Nature Reviews Neuroscience*, 10(6), pp.410–422.

7   Baumeister, R. F., Bratslavsky, E., Finkenauer, C. and Vohs, K. D. (2001). Bad is Stronger than Good. *Review of General Psychology*, 5(4), pp.323–370.

8   DeYoung, C.G. (2013). 'The neuromodulator of exploration: A unifying theory of the role of dopamine in personality'. *Frontiers in Human Neuroscience*, 7, Article 762.
     Further overview in Dixon, M. L., Thiruchselvam, R., Todd, R. and Christoff, K. (2017). 'Emotion and the Prefrontal Cortex: An Integrative Review'. *Psychological Bulletin*, 143(10), pp.1033–1081.

9   Cicero, D.C., Hicks, J.A., and King, L.A. (2015). 'The Role of Positive Affect and Individual Differences in Intuition in the Accuracy of Pattern Recognition'. *Imagination, Cognition and Personality*, 34(4), pp.398–414.

10   Mazzucchelli, T.G., Kane, R. T. and Rees, C.S. (2010). 'Behavioral activation interventions for well-being: A meta-analysis'. *The Journal of Positive Psychology*, 5(2), pp.105–121.

11   Godoy, L.D., Rossignoli, M.T., Delfino-Pereira, P., Garcia-Cairasco, N. and de Lima Umeoka, E.H. (2018). 'A Comprehensive Overview on Stress Neurobiology: Basic Concepts and Clinical Implications'. *Frontiers in Behavioral Neuroscience*, 12, Article 127.

12   Leuner, B. and Shors, T.J. (2013). 'Stress, anxiety, and dendritic spines: What are the connections?' *Neuroscience*, 251, pp.108–119

13   Dimsdale, J.E. (2008). 'Psychological Stress and Cardiovascular Disease'. *Journal of the American College of Cardiology*, 51(13), pp.1237–1246.

14   Cutuli, D. (2014). 'Cognitive reappraisal and expressive suppression strategies role in the emotion regulation: an overview on their modulatory effects and neural correlates'. *Frontiers in Systems Neuroscience*, 8, Article 175.

15   The evidence for the benefits of crying is mixed, and its effects will depend on individual and contextual differences. However, there are theories that rhythmic activities (including sobbing and other repetitive movements) can settle us physiologically, and expressing our emotions may also help us acknowledge them, as the first step to cognitive processing such as reappraisal. See Gračanin, A., Bylsma, L.M. and Vingerhoets, A.J.J.M. (2014). 'Is crying a self-soothing behavior?'. *Frontiers in Psychology*, 5, Article 502.

Chapter 4

1   Petrie, N. (2013). 'Vertical Leadership Development – Part 1'. *Center for Creative Leadership*. White Paper.

2   Anderson, R.J. and Adams, W.A. (2015). *Mastering Leadership*. Wiley.

3   Joiner, B. and Josephs, S. (2006). *Leadership Agility*. Jossey-Bass.

4   Kegan, R. and Lahey, L.L.; with Miller, M.L., Fleming, A., and Helsing, D. (2016). *An Everyone Culture*. Harvard Business Review Press.

5   Early stage theories include Carl Jung and Erik Erickson.
      Modern maps of inner operating system development in the workplace are described in:
           Anderson, R.J. and Adams, W.A. (2016). *Mastering Leadership*. Wiley.
           Joiner, B. and Josephs, S. (2007). *Leadership Agility*. Jossey-Bass.
           Kegan, R. and Lahey, L.L.; with Miller, M.L., Fleming, A. and Helsing, D. (2016). *An Everyone Culture*. Harvard Business Review Press.
           Rooke, D. and Torbert, W. (2005). *Seven Transformations of Leadership*. Harvard Business Review.
      For a more personal and spiritual treatment, linked to hidden drivers: Riso, D.R. and Hudson, R. (1999). *The Wisdom of the Enneagram*. Bantam.

6   Kegan, R. (1982). *The Evolving Self*. Harvard University Press.

7   Kegan, R. (1994). *In Over Our Heads*. Harvard University Press.

8   The exact percentages found at different stages vary somewhat between studies, likely due to differences in populations and assessment methodology. Further detail in *In Over Our Heads* and *Leadership Agility* books (references above).

9   Kegan, R. and Lahey, L.L. (2009). *Immunity to Change*. Harvard Business Press.

10   We recommend:
      The RHETI (The Enneagram Institute)
      The Leadership Development Framework (Harthill)
      The Leadership Circle Profile (Leadership Circle)

Chapter 5

1   Notes: unpublished survey. Top mindset they attributed to their success: growth mindset (and associated qualities of being adaptable and persistent). Second place mindset: taking accountability. Third place mindset: big picture mindset (and associated quality of being collaborative).

2   Hofmann, S.G., Heering, S., Sawyer, A.T. and Asnaani, A. (2009). 'How to Handle Anxiety: The Effects of Reappraisal, Acceptance, and Suppression Strategies on Anxious Arousal'. *Behaviour Research and Therapy*, 47(5), pp.389–394.

3   The first champagne Joseph Krug and team produced in this way was known as Champagne No. 1, and today's equivalent is Krug Grande Cuvée.

4   If you are curious about this you can find out more at www.krug.com or download the app

5   Chen, J. and Silverthorne, C. (2008). 'The impact of locus of control on job stress, job performance and job satisfaction in Taiwan'. *Leadership & Organization Development Journal*, 29(7), pp.572–582.

6   Maier, S.F. and Seligman, M.E.P. (2016). 'Learned Helplessness at Fifty: Insights from Neuroscience'. *Psychological Review*, 123(4), pp.349–367.

7   Samuel, M. and Chiche, S. (2004). *The Power of Personal Accountability*. Xephor Press.

8   The Arbinger Institute. (2000). *Leadership and Self-deception*. Berrett Koehler.

9   Jain, V.K., McLaughlin, D.G., Lall, R. and Johnson, W.B. (1996). 'Effects of locus of control, occupational stress, and psychological distress on job satisfaction among nurses'. *Psychological Reports,* 78(3), pp.1256–1258.

10 Bollini, A.M., Walker, E.F., Hamann, S., and Kestler, L. (2004). 'The influence of perceived control and locus of control on the cortisol and subjective responses to stress'. *Biological Psychology,* 67(3), pp.245–260.

11 McEwen, B.S., Nasca, C. and Gray, J.D. (2016). 'Stress Effects on Neuronal Structure: Hippocampus, Amygdala, and Prefrontal Cortex'. *Neuropsychopharmacology*, 41, pp.3–23.

12 Dweck, C. (2006). *Mindset*. Robinson.

13 Grant, H. and Dweck.C.S. (2003). 'Clarifying Achievement Goals and Their Impact'. *Journal of Personality and Social Psychology,* 85(3), pp.541–553.

14 Mangels, J. A., Butterfield, B., Lamb, J., Good, C. & Dweck, C. S. (2006). Why do beliefs about intelligence influence learning success? A social cognitive neuroscience model. *Social Cognitive and Affective Neuroscience*, 1(2), pp.75–86.

15 Electrical encephalogram studies have shown that the more someone has a growth mindset, the more that spikes associated with improvement after errors are evident, and this leads to better performance next time. By contrast, a fixed mindset seems to dampen down the activity in the brain and break this chain. And, if people go on to get something correct after making an error, brains of people who have a growth mindset are more active than those with a fixed mindset.

    Moser, J.S., Schroder, H.S., Heeter, C., Moran, T.P. and Lee, Y.H. (2011). 'Mind Your Errors: Evidence for a Neural Mechanism Linking Growth Mind-Set to Adaptive Posterror Adjustments'. *Psychological Science,* 22, pp.1484–1489.

16 Ng, B. (2018). 'The Neuroscience of Growth Mindset and Intrinsic Motivation'. *Brain Sciences,* 8(2), pp.20.

17 Aditomo, A. (2015). 'Students' Response to Academic Setback: "Growth Mindset" 'as a Buffer against Demotivation'. *International Journal of Educational Psychology,* 4(2), pp.198–222.

18 Duckworth, A. (2016). *Grit.* Random House.

19 Cowan, N. (2010). 'The Magical Mystery Four: How is Working Memory Capacity Limited, and Why?' *Current Directions in Psychological Science,* 19(1), pp.51–57.

20 Mischel, W. (2014). *The Marshmallow Test.* Bantam.

21 Luo, S., Ainslie, G., Giragosian, L. and Monterosso, J,L. (2009). 'Behavioral and Neural Evidence of Incentive Bias for Immediate Rewards Relative to Preference-Matched Delayed Rewards'. *Journal of Neuroscience,* 29(47), pp.14820–14827.

22 Kahneman, D. (2012) *Thinking, Fast and Slow.* Penguin.

23 The exercise is thought to have been originally developed by a psychologist and gestalt practitioner, the late John Enright

24 Yeager, D. S., and Dweck, C. S. (2012). Mindsets That Promote Resilience: When Students Believe That Personal Characteristics Can Be Developed. *Educational Psychologist,* 47(4), pp.302–314.

Chapter 6

1 Berkman, E.T. (2018). 'The Neuroscience of Goals and Behavior Change'. *Consulting Psychology Journal,* 70(1), pp.28–44.

2 For example: Norcross, J.C. and Vangarelli, D.J. (1988). 'The resolution solution: Longitudinal examination of New Year's change attempts'. *Journal of Substance Abuse,* 1(2), pp.127–134.

3 Reported at www.sports-insight.co.uk/news/strava-reveals-2020-quitters-day

4 JumpstartX 2020 New Year Resolution experiment, run by Jumpstart Development (www.jumpstart-development.com)

5 Miller, E.K. and Cohen, J.D. (2001). 'An integrative theory of prefrontal cortex function'. *Annual Review of Neuroscience,* 24, pp.167–202.

6 Kurzban, R., Duckworth, A., Kable, J.W. and Myers, J. (2013). 'An opportunity cost model of subjective effort and task performance'. *The Behavioral and Brain Sciences,* 36(6), pp.661–679.
Lorist, M.M., Klein, M., Nieuwenhuis, S., de Jong, R., Mulder, G. and Meijman, T.F. (2000). 'Mental fatigue and task control: Planning and preparation'. *Psychophysiology,* 37(5), pp.614–625.

7 Arnsten, A.F.T. (2009). 'Stress signalling pathways that impair prefrontal cortex structure and function.' *Nature Reviews Neuroscience,* 10(6), pp.410–422.

8 Madore, K P. and Wagner, A.D. (2019). 'Multicosts of Multitasking'. *Cerebrum: The Dana Forum on Brain Science,* 2019.

9 Scientist Wendy Wood's thorough but accessible book describes these phenomena in detail: Wood, W. (2019). *Good Habits, Bad Habits.* Macmillan.

10　Stone, A.L., Becker, L.G., Huber, A.M. and Catalano, R.F. (2012). 'Review of risk and protective factors of substance use and problem use in emerging adulthood'. *Addictive Behaviors*, 37(7), pp.747–775.

11　Lunenburg, F.C. (2011). 'Goal-Setting Theory of Motivation'. *International Journal of Management, Business and Administration*, 15(1).

12　Westbrook, A. and Braver, T.S. (2016). 'Dopamine does double duty in motivating cognitive effort'. *Neuron*, 89(4), pp.695–710.

13　Mischel, W. (2014) *The Marshmallow Test*. Bantam.

14　Luo, S., Ainslie, G., Giragosian, L. and Monterosso, J.R. (2009). 'Behavioral and Neural Evidence of Incentive Bias for Immediate Rewards Relative to Preference-Matched Delayed Rewards'. *Journal of Neuroscience*, 29(47), pp.14820–14827.

15　Critchfield, T.S. and Kollins, S. H. (2001). 'Temporal discounting: Basic research and the analysis of socially important behavior'. *Journal of Applied Behavior Analysis*, 34(1), pp.101–122.

16　Henderlong, J. and Lepper, M.R. (2002). 'The effects of praise on children's intrinsic motivation: A review and synthesis'. *Psychological Bulletin*, 128(5), pp.774–795.
　　This article is also useful: https://www.verywellmind.com/differences-between-extrinsic-and-intrinsic-motivation-2795384

17　Warneken, F. and Tomasello, M. (2014). 'Extrinsic rewards undermine altruistic tendencies in 20-month-olds'. *Motivation Science*, 1(S), pp.43–48.

18　Tobler, P.N., Fiorillo, C.D. and Schultz, W. (2005). 'Adaptive coding of reward value by dopamine neurons'. *Science* 307(5715), pp.1642–1645.

19　Berns, G.S., McClure, S.M., Pagnoni, G. and Montague, P.R. (2001). 'Predictability Modulates Human Brain Response to Reward'. *The Journal of Neuroscience*, 21(8), pp.2793–2798.

Chapter 7

1　Mansson, K.N.T., Lueken, U., and Frick, A. (2021). 'Enriching CBT by Neuroscience: Novel Avenues to Achieve Personalized Treatments'. *International Journal of Cognitive Therapy*, 14, pp.182–195.

2　Liu, J.J.W., Ein, N., Gervasio, J. and Vickers, K. (2019). 'The efficacy of stress reappraisal interventions on stress responsivity: A meta-analysis and systematic review of existing evidence'. *PLOS ONE*, 14(2).

3　Goldin, P., Ziv, M., Jazaieri, H., Werner, K., Kraemer, H., Heimberg, R.G. and Gross, J.J. (2012). 'Cognitive Reappraisal Self-Efficacy Mediates the Effects of Individual Cognitive-Behavioral Therapy for Social Anxiety Disorder'. *Journal of Consulting and Clinical Psychology*, 80(6), pp.1034–1040.

4　Winlove, C.I.P., Milton, F., Ranson, J., Fulford, J., MacKisack, M., Macpherson, F. and Zeman, A. (2018). 'The neural correlates of visual imagery: A co-ordinate-based meta-analysis'. *Cortex*, 105, pp.4–25.

5　Finch, K.K., Oakman, J. M., Milovanov, A., Keleher, B. and Capobianco, K. (2019). 'Mental imagery and musical performance: Development of the Musician's Arousal Regulation Imagery Scale'. *Psychology of Music*, pp.1–19.

6   Negd, M., Mallan, K. and Lipp, O. (2011). 'The role of anxiety and perspective-taking strategy on affective empathic responses'. *Behaviour Research and Therapy*, 49(12), pp.852–857.

7   For one example in a high stress occupation (medical surgery), and references to many other studies, see: Lebares, C.C., Guvva, E.V., Olaru, M., Sugrue, L.P., Staffaroni, A.M., Delucchi, K.L., Kramer, J.H., Ascher, N.L. and Harris, H.W. (2019). 'Efficacy of Mindfulness-Based Cognitive Training in Surgery'. *JAMA Network Open*, 2(5).

8   Magalhaes, A.A., Oliveira, L., Pereira, M.G. and Menezes, C.B. (2018). 'Does Meditation Alter Brain Responses to Negative Stimuli? A Systematic Review'. *Frontiers in Human Neuroscience*, 12, Article 448.

9   Mahmood, L., Hopthrow, T. and Randsley de Moura, G. (2016). 'A Moment of Mindfulness: Computer-Mediated Mindfulness Practice Increases State Mindfulness'. *PLOS ONE*, 11(4).

10 Lazar, S.W., Kerr, C.E., Wasserman, R.H., Gray, J.R., Greve, D.N., Treadway, M.T., McGarvey, M., Quinn, B.T., Dusek, J.A., Bensen, H., Rauch, S.L., Moore, C.I., and Fischl, B. (2005). 'Meditation experience is associated with increased cortical thickness'. *Neuroreport*, 16(17), pp.1893–1897.

11 Burklund, L.J., Creswell, J.D., Irwin, M.R. and Lieberman, M.D. (2014). 'The common and distinct neural bases of affect labeling and reappraisal in healthy adults'. *Frontiers in Psychology*, 5, Article 221.

12 Tugade, M.M., Fredrickson, B.L. and Barrett, L.F. (2004). 'Psychological resilience and positive emotional granularity: Examining the benefits of positive emotions on coping and health'. *Journal of Personality*, 72(6), pp.1161–1190.

13 Fox, G.R., Kaplan, J., Damasio, H. and Damasio, A. (2015). 'Neural correlates of gratitude'. *Frontiers in Psychology*, 6, Article 1491.

14 Regev, D. and Cohen-Yatziv, L. (2018). 'Effectiveness of Art Therapy with Adult Clients in 2018 – What Progress Has Been Made?'. *Frontiers in Psychology*, 9, Article 1531.

15 Mastandrea, S., Fagioli, S. and Biasi, V. (2019). 'Art and Psychological Well-Being: Linking the Brain to the Aesthetic Emotion'. *Frontiers in Psychology*, 10, Article 739.

16 Rajendran, N., Mitra, T. P., Shahrestani, S. and Coggins, A. (2020). 'Randomized Controlled Trial of Adult Therapeutic Coloring for the Management of Significant Anxiety in the Emergency Department'. *Academic Emergency Medicine*, 27(2), pp.92–99.

17 Pennebaker, J.W. (1993). 'Putting stress into words: Health, linguistic, and therapeutic implications'. *Behaviour Research and Therapy*, 31(6), pp.539–548.

18 Schroder, H.S., Moran, T. P. and Moser, J.S. (2018). 'The effect of expressive writing on the error-related negativity among individuals with chronic worry'. *Psychophysiology*, 55(2).

19 Marin-Garcia, E., Mattfeld, A.T. and Gabrieli, J.D.E. (2021). 'Neural Correlates of Long-Term Memory Enhancement Following Retrieval Practice'. *Frontiers in Human Neuroscience,* 15, Article 584560.

20 Shah, J.Y. and Kruglanski, A.W. (2003). 'When opportunity knocks: Bottom-up priming of goals by means and its effects on self-regulation'. *Journal of Personality and Social Psychology*, 84(6), pp.1109–1122.

21 Gianaros, P.J. and Wager, T.D. (2015). 'Brain-Body Pathways Linking Psychological Stress and Physical Health'. *Current Directions in Psychological Science*, 24(4), pp.313–321.

22 Mandolesi, L., Polverino, A., Montuori, S., Foti, F., Ferraioli, G., Sorrentino, P. and Sorrentino, G. (2018). 'Effects of Physical Exercise on Cognitive Functioning and Well-being: Biological and Psychological Benefits'. *Frontiers in Psychology*, 9, Article 509.

23 Herrero, J.L., Khuvis, S., Yeagle, E., Cerf, M. and Mehta, A.D. (2018). 'Breathing above the brain stem: Volitional control and attentional modulation in humans'. *Journal of Neurophysiology*, 119(1), pp.145–159.

24 Ulrich, R.S. (1984). 'View through a window may influence recovery from surgery'. *Science*, 224(4647), pp.420–421.

25 Tost, H., Reichert, M., Braun, U., Reinhard, I., Peters, R., Lautenbach, S., Hoell, A., Schwarz, E., Ebner-Priemer, U., Zipf, A. and Meyer-Lindenberg, A. (2019). 'Neural correlates of individual differences in affective benefit of real-life urban green space exposure'. *Nature Neuroscience*, 22(9), pp.1389–1393.

26 Cuddy, A.J.C., Schultz, S. J. and Fosse, N.E. (2018). 'P-Curving a More Comprehensive Body of Research on Postural Feedback Reveals Clear Evidential Value for Power-Posing Effects: Reply to Simmons and Simonsohn (2017)'. *Psychological Science*, 29(4).

27 Davis, M.L., Papini, S., Rosenfield, D., Roelofs, K., Kolb, S., Powers, M.B. and Smits, J.A.J. (2017). 'A randomized controlled study of power posing before public speaking exposure for social anxiety disorder: No evidence for augmentative effects'. *Journal of Anxiety Disorders*, 52, pp.1–7.

28 Kerr, C.E., Sacchet, M.D., Lazar, S.W., Moore, C.I. and Jones, S.R. (2013). 'Mindfulness starts with the body: Somatosensory attention and top-down modulation of cortical alpha rhythms in mindfulness meditation'. *Frontiers in Human Neuroscience*, 7, Article 12.

29 Lucas, A.R., Klepin, H.D., Porges, S.W. and Rejeski, W.J. (2016). 'Mindfulness-Based Movement: A Polyvagal Perspective'. *Integrative Cancer Therapies*, 17(1), pp.5–15.

30 Ma, X., Yue, Z.-Q., Gong, Z.-Q., Zhang, H., Duan, N.-Y., Shi, Y.-T., Wei, G.-X. and Li, Y.-F. (2017). 'The Effect of Diaphragmatic Breathing on Attention, Negative Affect and Stress in Healthy Adults'. *Frontiers in Psychology*, 8, Article 874.

31 Grossman, E., Grossman, A., Schein, M.H., Zimlichman, R. and Gavish, B. (2001). 'Breathing-control lowers blood pressure'. *Journal of Human Hypertension*, 15(4), pp.263–269.

32 Van Diest, I., Verstappen, K., Aubert, A.E., Widjaja, D., Vansteenwegen, D. and Vlemincx, E. (2014). 'Inhalation/Exhalation Ratio Modulates the Effect of Slow Breathing on Heart Rate Variability and Relaxation'. *Applied Psychophysiology and Biofeedback*, 39, pp.171–180.

33 Mark Divine, former US Navy SEALs Commander, quoted in: www.forbes.com/sites/nomanazish/2019/05/30/how-to-de-stress-in-5-minutes-or-less-according-to-a-navy-seal/#6ca98ba63046

34 Fancourt, D., Williamon, A., Carvalho, L.A., Steptoe, A., Dow, R. and Lewis, I. (2016). 'Singing modulates mood, stress, cortisol, cytokine and neuropeptide activity in cancer patients and carers'. *Ecancermedicalscience*, 10.

Chapter 8

1   A useful introduction to organizational purpose: Mayer, C. (2018). *Prosperity*. OUP.
    For the relationship between purpose and motivation: Pink, D. (2009). *Drive*. Canongate.
2   Lunenburg, F.C. (2011). 'Goal-Setting Theory of Motivation'. *International Journal of Management, Business and Administration*, 15(1).
3   Frankl, V. (1959). Man's Search For Meaning. Beacon Press.
4   Mendez, M.F. (2009). 'The Neurobiology of Moral Behavior: Review and Neuropsychiatric Implications'. *CNS Spectrums*, 14(11), pp.608–620.
5   Inagaki, T. K., Byrne Haltom, K. E., Suzuki, S., Jevtic, I., Hornstein, E., Bower, J. E., & Eisenberger, N. I. (2016). The neurobiology of giving versus receiving support: The role of stress-related and social reward-related neural activity. *Psychosomatic Medicine*, 78(4), 443–453.
6   Amabile, T.M. and Kramer, S.J. (2011). 'The Power of Small Wins'. *Harvard Business Review*.
7   Madore, K P. and Wagner, A.D. (2019). 'Multicosts of Multitasking'. *Cerebrum: The Dana Forum on Brain Science*, 2019.
8   Attributed to Dwight Eisenhower, also described in Covey, S.R. (2020 – 30th anniversary edition). *The Seven Habits of Highly Effective People*. Simon and Schuster.

Chapter 9

1   Rothenberg, A. (1996). The Janusian Process in Scientific Creativity. *Creativity and Research Journal*, 9(2-3), pp.207–231. See also for a summary of the history of paradoxical thinking: www.bbc.com/worklife/article/20201109-why-the-paradox-mindset-is-the-key-to-success
2   Liu, Y., Xu, S. and Zhang, B. (2020). 'Thriving at work: how a paradox mindset influences innovative work behavior'. *The Journal of Applied Behavioral Science*, 56(3), pp.347–366.
3   Miron-Spektor, E., Ingram, A., Keller, J., Smith, W.K. and Lewis, M.W. (2017). 'Microfoundations of organizational paradox: the problem is how we think about the problem'. Academy of Management Journal, 61(1).
4   Cognitive dissonance theory argues that the human brain dislikes contradictions, based on the lengths that most of us will go to in order to get rid of these contradictions. Brain scanning studies show elevated activity in parts of the prefrontal and cingulate cortex associated with social pain, alarm and conflict detection and this is associated with resolving these contradictions.
    van Veen, V., Krug, M.K., Schooler, J.W. and Carter, C.S. (2009). 'Neural activity predicts attitude change in cognitive dissonance. *Natural Neuroscience*, 12(11): pp.1469–1474.
    Izuma, K., Matsumoto, M., Murayama, K., Samejima, K., Sadato, N. and Matsumoto, K. (2010) 'Neural correlates of cognitive dissonance and choice-induced preference change'. *Proceedings of the National Academy of Sciences of the USA*, 107(51), pp.22014–22019.

5   Martin, R. (2007). *The Opposable Mind*. Harvard Business School Press.

6   Price, C. and Toye, S. (2017). *Accelerating Performance*. Wiley.

7   Gobet, F., Snyder, A., Bossomaier, T., and Harre, M. (2014). 'Designing a "better" brain: insights from experts and savants'. *Frontiers in Psychology* 5, Article 470.

8   Riel, J. and Martin, R.L. (2017). *Creating Great Choices*. Harvard Business Review Press.

9   Boyatzis, R.E. and Jack, A.I. (2018). 'The neuroscience of coaching'. *Consulting Psychology Journal: Practice and Research*, 70(1), pp.11–27.

10 DeYoung, C.G. (2013). 'The neuromodulator of exploration: A unifying theory of the role of dopamine in personality'. *Frontiers in Human Neuroscience*, 7, Article 762.

11 Kounios, J. and Beeman, M. (2014). 'The Cognitive Neuroscience of Insight'. *Annual Review of Psychology* 65(1), pp. 71–93.

Chapter 10

1   Burklund, L.J., Creswell, J.D., Irwin, M.R. and Lieberman, M.D. (2014). The common and distinct neural bases of affect labeling and reappraisal in healthy adults. *Frontiers in Psychology*, 5, Article 221.

2   Woolley, A.W., Chabris, C.F., Pentland, A., Hashmi, N. and Malone, T.W. (2010). 'Evidence for a collective intelligence factor in the performance of human groups'. *Science*, 330 (6004), pp.686–688.

3   Bergmann, B. and Schaeppi, J. (2016). 'A Data-Driven Approach to Group Creativity'. *Harvard Business Review*.

4   Edmondson, A. (1999). 'Psychological Safety and Learning Behavior in Work Teams'. *Administrative Science Quarterly*, 44(2), pp.350–383.

5   Various studies cited in: Covey, S.M.R. and Merrill, R.R. (2008). *The Speed of Trust*. Simon and Schuster

6   Zak, P.J. (2017). 'The Neuroscience of Trust'. *Harvard Business Review*

7   www.ted.com/talks/robert_waldinger_what_makes_a_good_life_lessons_ from_the_longest_study_on_happiness/transcript

8   Ware, B. (2012). *Top Five Regrets of the Dying*. Hay House.

9   Tabibnia, G. and Lieberman, M.D. (2007). 'Fairness and cooperation are rewarding: evidence from social cognitive neuroscience'. *Annals of the New York Academy of Sciences*, 1118, pp.90–101.

10 Weisz, E. and Zaki, J. (2018). 'Motivated empathy: A social neuroscience perspective'. *Current Opinion in Psychology*, 24, pp.67–71.

11 Bhanji, J.P. and Delgado, M.R. (2014). 'The Social Brain and Reward: Social Information Processing in the Human Striatum'. *Wiley Interdisciplinary Reviews: Cognitive Science* 5(1), pp.61–73.

12 Tomova, L., Tye, K., and Saxe, R. (2019). 'The neuroscience of unmet social needs'. *Social Neuroscience*, pp.1–11.

13 With 25% of participants of a survey in the US in 2004 reporting having no confidants. McPherson, M., Smith-Lovin, L. and Brashears, M.E. (2006). 'Social Isolation in America: Changes in Core Discussion Networks over Two Decades'. *American Sociological Review*, 71, pp.353–375.

14 PwC (2016). 'Redefining business success in a changing world'. 19th Annual Global CEO Survey. Available at: https://www.pwc.com/gx/en/ceo-survey/2016/landing-page/pwc-19th-annual-global-ceo-survey.pdf

15 Gallup, (2021). Engage Your Employees to See High Performance and Innovation. Data cited in April 2021, available at: https://www.gallup.com/workplace/229424/employee-engagement.aspx

16 Zaki, J. and Oschner, K.N. (2012). 'The neuroscience of empathy: progress, pitfalls and promise'. *Nature Neuroscience*, 15(5), pp.675–680.

17 Kosfeld, M., Heinrichs, M., Zak, P.J., Fischbacher, U. and Fehr, E. (2005). 'Oxytocin increases trust in humans'. *Nature*, 435(7042), pp.673–676.

18 Barraza, J.A. and Zak, P.J. (2009). 'Empathy toward Strangers Triggers Oxytocin Release and Subsequent Generosity'. *Annals of the New York Academy of Sciences*, 1167, pp.182–189.

19 Boyatzis, R.E., Rochford, K. and Jack, A.I. (2014). 'Antagonistic neural networks underlying differentiated leadership roles'. Frontiers in Human Neuroscience, 8, Article 114.

20 Fan, Y., Duncan, N.W., de Greck, M. and Northoff, G. (2011). 'Is there a core neural network in empathy? An fMRI based quantitative meta-analysis'. *Neuroscience and Biobehavioral Reviews*, 35, pp.903–911.

21 Harmsen, I.E. (2019) 'Empathy in Autism Spectrum Disorder'. *Journal of Autism and Developmental Disorders*, pp.3939–3955.

22 Fox, M.D., Snyder, A.Z., Vincent, J.L., Corbetta, M., Van Essen, D.C. and Raichle, M.E. (2005). 'The human brain is intrinsically organized into dynamic, anticorrelated functional networks'. *Proceedings of the National Academy of Sciences*, 102(27), pp.9673–9678.

23 Schilbach, L., Eickhoff, S.B., Rotarska-Jagiela, A., Fink, G.R. and Vogeley, K. (2008). 'Minds at rest? Social cognition as the default mode of cognizing and its putative relationship to the "default system" of the brain'. *Consciousness and Cognition*, 17(2), pp.457–467.

24 Eichele, T., Debener, S., Calhoun, V.D., Specht, K., Engel, A.K., Hugdahl, K., von Cramon, D.Y. and Ullsperger, M. (2008). 'Prediction of human errors by maladaptive changes in event-related brain networks'. *Proceedings of the National Academy of Sciences*, 105(16), pp.6173–6178.

25 Using a trust equation such as those from:
Maister, D., Green, C.H., and Galford, R.M. (2002). *The Trusted Advisor*. Simon and Schuster. Or Covey, S.M.R. and Merrill, R.R. (2008). *The Speed of Trust*. Simon and Schuster

26 Dimberg, U., Thunberg, M. and Elmehed, K. (2000). 'Unconscious Facial Reactions to Emotional Facial Expressions'. *Psychological Science*, 11(1), pp.86–89.

27 Neal, D.T. and Chartrand, T.L. (2011). 'Embodied Emotion Perception: Amplifying and Dampening Facial Feedback Modulates Emotion Perception Accuracy'. *Social Psychological and Personality Science*, 2(6), pp.673–678.

28 For more on this theory: Barrett, L.F. (2006). 'Solving the emotion paradox: categorization and the experience of emotion'. *Personality and Social Psychology Review*, 10(1), pp.20–46.

Chapter 11

1   Scott, K. (2019). *Radical Candour*. Pan.

Chapter 12

1   Kegan, R. and Lahey, L.L.; with Miller, M.L., Fleming, A., and Helsing, D. (2016). *An Everyone Culture*. Harvard Business Review Press.
2   After Thomas Edison famously said that he had not failed 10,000 times before inventing the lightbulb, rather he had found 10,000 ways that did not work.

Chapter 13

1   Cingano, F. (2014), 'Trends in Income Inequality and its Impact on Economic Growth', *OECD Social, Employment and Migration Working Papers*, No. 163.
2   Brueckner, M. and Lederman, D. (2015). 'Effects of income inequality on aggregate output', *World Bank*, Policy Research Working Paper 7317.
3   Fajnzylber, P., Lederman, D., & Loayza, N. (2002). Inequality and Violent Crime. *The Journal of Law and Economics*, 45(1), 1–39.
4   For an investigation of various social effects of inequality, see Wilkinson, R. and Pickett, K. (2010). *The Spirit Level: Why Equality is Better for Everyone*; as well as responses to their work.
5   GlobalWebIndex (2019). 'Sustainable Packaging Unwrapped'. Accessible at: www.globalwebindex.com/hubfs/Downloads/Sustainable-Packaging-Unwrapped.pdf.
6   Geyer, R., Jambeck, J.R. and Law, K.L. (2017). 'Production, use, and fate of all plastics ever made'. *Science Advances*, 3(7).
7   Tiseo, I. (2021). '*Global plastics industry—Statistics & Facts*'. Accessible at: www.statista.com/topics/5266/plastics-industry/

Index

Note: page numbers followed by *f* and *t* indicate figures and tables.